POLITICAL HALLEY'S COMET
THE DEATH PENALTY IN GLOBAL COMPARATIVE PERSPECTIVES

CASE STUDIES

of

Canada, India, Apartheid South Africa
Nigeria, Jamaica, Grenada, Uganda
Nazi War Crimes and International Law.

DR. MUNYONZWE HAMALENGWA

POLITICAL HALLEY'S COMET
THE DEATH PENALTY IN GLOBAL COMPARATIVE PERSPECTIVES

CASE STUDIES OF

Canada, India, Apartheid South Africa

Nigeria, Jamaica, Grenada, Uganda

Nazi War Crimes and International Law

Dr. Munyonzwe Hamalengwa

Dr. Hamalengwa is the Dean of the School of Law at ZAOU
(Zambian Open University School of Law).

DIAMOND™ BOOKS

www.diamondbooks.ca

TORONTO, CANADA – 2017

Political Halley's Comet - The Death Penalty In Global Comparative Perspectives

DIAMOND BOOKS™
Toronto, ON, CANADA
http://www.diamondbooks.ca

PUBLISHED IN CANADA

Published in Canada by DIAMOND BOOKS ™, an imprint
of
DIAMOND PUBLISHERS CANADA
http://www.diamondpublishers.com

PAPERBACK EDITION : ISBN: 978-1-988357-46-1

PRINTED IN CANADA

DEDICATION

This book is dedicated to Muhammad Ali, a true champion in the very best tradition. MHRIP.

ACKNOWLEDGEMENT

The last two decades or so have seen so many exonerations of convicted prisoners who could have been executed had the death penalty been carried out. Even though the death penalty is occurring in fewer and fewer countries, the debate as contained in this book, old as it is, is still worthy having. One execution based on a wrongful conviction is one too many.

I wish to thank most profusely, **Diamond Books - Canada** for typesetting the manuscript in perfect form that is pleasing to the eye. I wish to thank **Diamond Publishers** for bringing out this book in record time after getting the manuscript.

Dr. Munyonzwe Hamalengwa
Lusaka, Zambia.
March 25, 2017

PREFACE

The manuscript of this book lay unattended to for years because it appeared that once the Bill to re-introduce the death penalty was defeated in 1987, interest in the subject had waned. However, two major unrelated developments reignited interest in the death penalty in Canada in the 1990's.

The first one was that of the high profile trials and convictions of Paul Bernardo for killing two teenagers and Clinton Gayle for killing a police officer. The application for parole by child killer Clifford Olson also fueled the debate on the re-introduction of the death penalty. These cases and others brought about tough talk on law and order, particularly from the newly formed Reform Party. This party eventually became the official opposition party in the Canadian House of Commons. It became the government of Canada in 2006. Its leader, Preston Manning talked about calling for a referendum on the death penalty. The Prime Minister is Stephen Harper. The sentiment for the dealth penalty as of 2012 is reported to be very high in Canada and the U.S.A.

The second development was the very public exoneration of individuals who had been wrongfully convicted and may well have been executed if the death penalty had existed; or may have led to the execution of those individuals if the death penalty had been imposed and carried out at the time of their convictions. The most well known cases in Canada, include Guy Paul Morin, David Milgaard and Donald Marshall. The exoneration of Steve Truscott was momentous. The kid could have been executed.

Over the last several years all over the world, individuals have been exonerated who otherwise might have been executed for offences which it later turned out, they never committed. Examples include but are not limited to: Rubin "Hurricane" Carter who spent 19 years in prison and Geronimo Pratt who spent 27 years in prison in the U.S.; the Guildford 4 and Birmingham 6 in the U.K.; the Sharpeville 6 in South Africa and many others around the world. The U.S. brings forth on a regular basis numerous examples of people who were at the brink of execution before exoneration. A number of people have been executed in the U.K.; U.S.A.; South Africa under apartheid and elsewhere for crimes it later turned out, they never committed.

Thus the topic of the death penalty will be with us for the foreseeable future. It is like the Halley's Comet. It keeps coming back after a disappearance. This book is a small contribution to that debate.

These essays are of uneven quality. Some are academic, some are commentaries on actual cases and thus practical, some are moralistic, while others are hard edged and condemnatory. They are all relevant and important to the debate in issue. Some essays have been edited to reflect new developments while others have remained reflective of the state of affairs at the time they were written in 1987.

Munyonzwe Hamalengwa
Toronto, CANADA

Friday, November 29, 2013

TABLE OF CONTENTS

CHAPTERS

PART - I
THEORIES OF PUNISHMENT AND THE DEATH PENALTY

PART - II
CANADIAN PERSPECTIVES

3

PART - III
THIRD WORLD PERSPECTIVES

7

8

9

PART - IV
WAR CRIMES AND CRIMES AGAINST HUMANITY

PART - V
THE DEATH PENALTY IN INTERNATIONAL LAW

CHAPTER 1

THEORIES OF PUNISHMENT AND THE DEATH PENALTY

Dr. Munyonzwe Hamalengwa*

The death sentence when it is carried out, is the ultimate punishment. A person is obliterated for ever by an act of state. Of the two major justifications for punishment: retribution and revenge and utilitarianism, (and the various strands of deterrence, rehabilitation, etc.) the death penalty seems to accomplish more the retributive aspect of punishment. The State inflicts the ultimate revenge against the culprit - death. If the death penalty is justified under the deterrence aspect of utilitarianism, it achieves the final specific deterrence against the individual. Because the person is killed, he is therefore 'deterred' for eternity.

It is something else if general deterrence is the one sought after. Are others deterred by the death penalty?

The following papers discuss various theories both justifying and disqualifying the death penalty as a form of punishment. The thread that runs through some of the papers is that general deterrence under which the death penalty is justified has not been achieved. In those societies where the death penalty exists, for example in some U.S. States, murder, which is the major crime that commonly attracts the death penalty, continues to be committed. In some cases the murder rate dropped after the abolishment of the death penalty. In Canada, for example, the murder rate fell from 3.09 per 100,000 in 1975 (the year before abolition) to 2.74 in 1983.

1. The death penalty thus does not affect the rate of murders. In the U.S., the murder rate in death penalty states has differed little from that in other states without the death penalty but with similar populations and social and economic conditions.

2. Others have argued that even if the death penalty has no special effect in deterring others, the execution of the worst offenders is needed to protect society from the risk of their repeating their crimes. The evidence however is that among

offenders released on parole, convicted murderers present one of the lowest risks of recidivism.

3. Most murderers are first time offenders. The implication is that the death penalty is not the answer.

What is the answer? No answer seems to come out clearly in these papers except the suggestion of alternative sentences. This means prison terms are preferred rather than persons being put to death. There may be a possibility of rehabilitation. A life sentence may be the ultimate punishment since an individual is reminded every second, minute and hour of his/her life, why he/she is in prison. The person is given the opportunity to commiserate over the crime every day. The constant realization of the wrong done may be more painful than the death sentence itself whereby the person is gone forever. There can also be minimum sentences e.g. 25 years without parole. This would be enough punishment.

It could, however, be urged that a life sentence is not the ultimate sanction since the person could escape from prison; may be paroled or forgiven; the person may turn into a sadist and not care at all about why he/she is in prison, etc. One person could kill again.

The question seems to be, should there be need for ultimate sanctions in modem society?

There are many reasons for opposing the death penalty. Perhaps the most important one is that it is a very unusual, painful and inhuman form of punishment. It inflicts irreparable damage to the victim more than the victim is likely to have meted out to the person he/she killed, if revenge was the reason for the death sentence. Amnesty International in the report cited above describes how the person sentenced to death has a long painful struggle through various appeals to the day he/she is told that he/she will die on a certain day. The person is then segregated from the other death-row inmates, he/she is shaved and so on. The final day then comes. There are usually last minute appeals, which sometimes lead nowhere.

The pain through the years, months, weeks, days, hours and minutes leading up to the carrying out of the death sentence cannot be fathomed of course by anybody who has not been through the death-row process and reprieved at the last minute. Many death-row inmates experience mental derangement in their last days. That is cruel unusual and inhuman treatment and punishment. It is even more unusual in the sense that it is a deliberate and conscious legal policy by a government to take away a life. The death penalty is in a class by itself. It is intended to inflict painful death by the state.

There is also the question of the execution of the innocent. In a U.S. study, it was discovered that between 1900 and 1985, 349 people were wrongly convicted of offences punishable by death.

4. Twenty-three of these were executed. These are lives that cannot be brought back. In Canada, Wilbert Coffin was hanged on February 10, 1956 for three murders somebody committed in 1953. Coffin maintained his innocence to the bitter end. Many lawyers believed at the time that Coffin was innocent. Also in Canada, Donald Marshall, recently released, spent eleven years behind bars for a murder he did not commit.

5. Convicting and occasionally hanging wrong people is one of the strongest reasons for opposing the death penalty. David Milgaard of Canada was exonerated in 1997.[6]

If the death penalty existed in Canada, Guy Paul Morin who was convicted at his second trial in 1992, but exonerated in 1995, may have been hanged.[7] It goes the same for the Guildford Four and the Birmingham Six in England as well as the Sharpeville Six in South Africa. All these were exonerated after spending years in prison.[8]

Studies on the death penalty in the US demonstrates that blacks receive the death penalty which is disproportionate to their population or the rate at which they commit offences that attract the death penalty.[9] In December 1994, for example, 40% of the men on death-row across the U S were black even though blacks constitute only 11% of the U S population. In Pennsylvania, blacks on death-row now constitute 60% of those on death-row , even though the black population there is merely 9% of the total population. The following facts have further emerged:[10]

(1) defendants charged with killing white victims in Georgia are 4.3 times as likely to be sentenced to death as defendants charged with killing blacks;

(2) race [of the victim] determines whether a death penalty is returned;

(3) nearly six of every eleven defendants convicted of killing whites would not have gotten the death penalty had their victims been black;

(4) twenty of every thirty-four black defendants would not have received the death penalty had their victims been black; and

(5) cases involving black defendants and white

victims are more likely to result in a death sentence than cases featuring any other racial combination of defendant and victim.

Class also plays an important role in the imposition of the death penalty. Poor defendants are more likely to receive the death penalty than rich defendants. The rich can afford to hire experienced and good lawyers while the poor retain court appointed duty counsel on a $2,500.00 U. S. fee! In the meantime, the state unleashes unlimited resources.[11]

In societies where the judicial system is tainted by racial prejudices, for example Apartheid South Africa and the U.S., many people have been convicted and sentenced to death, on flimsy evidence or to satisfy public opinion. If the death penalty is abolished, the racial incidence in biased death sentences will also disappear thereby ensuring equality between races within the criminal justice system. The death penalty is also imposed like a lottery, others get it while others don't. In the U.S. it also depends on where the murder is committed, retentionist state or non-retentionist state.

Lastly, maintaining the death penalty is costly both to the convict and to the State. Millions of dollars are spent to process the appeals and to ensure the existence of facilities for those on the death row. Why should resources be used in such a manner to ensure the killing of a person by the State?

NOTES

* Dr. Munyonzwe Hamalengwa practices law in Toronto, Ontario, Canada

1. See Study Cited in Amnesty International, United States of America:

The Death Penalty (1988) p. 162.

2. Ibid.

3. Ibid at p. 168.

4. Ibid at p. 172.

5. See Marshall Commission Inquiry (1989)

6. Milgaard was vindicated after DNA tests done in England

7. See Kirk Makin Redrum the Innocent, (Toronto, 1994)

8. There are many others around the world

9. See Jesse Jackson, Legal Lynching , (New York, 1996)

10. See Mumia Abu-Jamal, Live from Death Row, (Reading et al, 1995) PP XIX and 35

11. See Mumia Abu-Jamal, Death Blossoms (Farmington, 1997) P.141

CHAPTER

2

THE DEATH PENALTY IN COMPARATIVE PERSPECTIVE

David McRobert

This volume of essays represents an attempt to come to grips with the issue of state killing, a process usually couched in the more neutral terminology of "the death penalty" or "capital punishment." For reasons that need not be recited here, the question of state killing has become very controversial over the past decade and seems likely to remain topical well into the next century. At the beginning of the 1970s few North Americans and Europeans were aware of violent repression in the Third World and the role of their governments in perpetuating conflict in nations such as Chile and El Salvador. Fewer still thought these issues deserved serious attention. Today that situation has altered dramatically, and many people are aware of the repressive governments in Apartheid South Africa and other countries in Central and South America.

In Canada the problem of state repression and the killing and torture of citizens is qualitatively different from that evident in the Third World. However, the increasing discrepancies between sentences handed out to the rich and the poor for similar offences and other issues such as the abuse of powers by officers in the Canadian Security Intelligence Service (CISS) suggest that there are intense structural conflicts and power struggles simmering in the murky brew called the Canadian justice system. Under the calm exterior that is presented to the Canadian public by our political leaders and most of the media, some of these structural conflicts are evidenced as peculiar contradictions that rear their ugly head every decade or so.

One of these contradictions is the push by some neo-conservative agents to reinstate the death penalty in many advanced capitalist nations. Pro-noose advocates argue that it is more economical to destroy people deemed to be "rotten" by the State and the courts than attempt to rehabilitate them. They point to the rising cost of prison facilities to support their position. In the United States, the death penalty has never really faded in importance, partly because of enthusiasm for this approach to policy-making.

Canadians have never shared the same degree of enthusiasm for the death penalty that Americans and their counterparts who support military regimes in the Third World to demonstrate. There are several myths that purport to explain this discrepancy in attitudes. One myth is that our federal legislators, who are mainly lawyers and cognizant of the fact that small mistakes can result in wrongful convictions, and even a tragic death, feel it is better to err on the side of caution than to wrongfully end a life. Another part of this myth is that the courts are not always as free from bias as they purport to be; this was shown graphically in the testimony presented at the Marshall Inquiry in Nova Scotia in 1987 and 1988. In this case, it has become apparent that the judiciary and the police in the province teamed up to frame a young Micmac Indian named Donald Marshall as the killer of another young man. Marshall was later shown to be innocent and released, a result that would have been prevented if he had been wrongfully killed by the State for a crime he did not commit.

Others would invoke the myth that Canadians are a more tolerant peoples as the explanation for our unwillingness to apply the death penalty; thus our justice system reflects an attempt to draw on the best aspects of both British and American legal culture. As a result, most Canadians have less reverence for the system of rough justice that often seems to prevail in the United States.

Whatever the basis of the different attitudes held by Canadians and many other European societies on the matter of state killing, the issue of reinstatement of the death penalty has resurfaced periodically in various nations over the past fifty years. In Canada, the issue took on considerable significance in early 1987 because many people suspected the federal government would be launching a process to revamp laws and reinstate the death penalty. In the 1984 federal election campaign, Brian Mulroney, leader of the Progressive Conservatives, had promised there would be free vote on the issue in the House of Commons if his party formed the government. In stunning fashion, the Progressive Conservatives were swept to power with the largest majority in Canadian history, and pro-noose advocates were quick to claim that Mulroney's support for a vote on reopening the death penalty issue in the House was one reason.

Only days after the election, the campaign for reinstatement of the death penalty began to gain momentum under the leadership of certain Tory backbenchers such as Bill Domm, MP for Peterborough, Ontario. Death penalty advocates pointed to mass murderers such as Clifford Olson, who had murdered many children in a serial fashion in British Columbia in the early 1980s, to argue that society needed protection from uncontrollable killers who were not salvageable through reform programs. After years of lobbying, death penalty advocates finally were able to get a commitment from Brian Mulroney that a vote on whether the issue should be reopened would take place in 1987.

The forces opposed to reinstatement began to regroup and establish their own lobby to ensure that their view was not overlooked once the time frame for the parliamentary debate became clear. Prominent among opponents to reinstatement were Toronto lawyer Eddie Greenspan and the mother of a young girl who had been killed in the Toronto area in 1986. In anticipation of the debate in the House, national magazines such as Maclean's and many newspapers and other media began to feature articles on the issue. At the same time, students at Osgoode Hall Law School who had recently formed a group called the Nelson Mandela Law Society, in honour of the currently imprisoned leader of the African National Congress jailed in South Africa for the past 25 years, began to plan their first conference, tentatively titled "The Death Penalty: A Political Halley's Comet." Their intent was to provide a stimulating forum for discussion of the death penalty, and perhaps even influence the outcome of the parliamentary debate that they anticipated would take place in the Fall of 1987.

As it turned out, Parliament rejected the attempt to reinstate the death penalty in June 1987, following a passionate debate in the House of Commons.

Although some might have viewed this as a major setback, organizers decided to proceed with the conference because the issue remains topical in the international context and, like Halley's Comet, returns to haunt civil rights activists every decade or two.

The conference was held over two days and featured many excellent speakers. Their presentations provided a framework for informal discussion and participation. While it has not been possible to include all of the papers presented at the conference in this volume, all of the presentations merit at least some commentary. However, most of the analysis will focus on the papers contained in this volume.

What was so striking about the conference and the range of papers presented was their international scope. The application of state killing in countries as diverse as Jamaica, India, Chile, Apartheid South Africa, Canada, Britain and Uganda was considered by presenters and participants. While the majority of papers were presented by Canadians the ethnic mix of people who attended the conference was remarkable and added considerable life to the event and depth to this volume.

The event began with an address by Earl Levy of the Ontario Criminal Lawyers' Association. Levy summarized the paper included in this volume prepared by the Association as a brief to the House of Commons during the debate over reinstatement of the death penalty. In summarizing the report Levy reviewed various statistics on the crime rates and the death penalty, concluding that deterrence argument is misleading. "If the death penalty does have a (deterrent) value", he asked rhetorically, "why were 18,500 people killed in the United States in 1985?" In response to his question, Levy cited well-known evidence that most pre-meditated killings are committed by people who do not expect to get caught and many other murders are acts of passion. The only people who might deserve capital punishment, he contends, are terrorists. However, Levy expressed reluctance about this approach to state killing because "using the noose" might make terrorists into martyrs.

Levy then went on to criticize the media for its role in portraying people who kill. He pleaded that "people who kill are three dimensional ... their lives went on before the crime and could go on after it." Moreover, “ if Canadians believe in rehabilitation, then we must not engage in State killing.” In the discussion that followed, Levy was also critical of Victim Impact Statements. Although he acknowledged that the victims of crime have long been the orphans of the criminal justice systems, he feels that their needs are better addressed through counseling.

The next speaker, Kenneth Avio, presented one of the most scholarly papers of the conference. Avio, a professor at the University of Victoria, approached the problem capital punishment in terms of both moral philosophy and economic theory. According to Avio, these two theories suggest that an idealized legislature should reject capital punishment.

In terms of moral philosophy, rights-based theories hold that, as a matter of respect, we should allow an individual to live and repent his or her crime to the community rather than engage in state killing. Avio said that it would be difficult to take the view that state execution could enhance the human dignity of a community and thus, the argument made by some Americans to support the death penalty because it enhances community morality fails to convince.

Avio further argued that state killing is not supported by thorough economic analysis. Avio outlined a form of constrained cost-benefit analysis (CBA) that could be applied to assess the validity of the capital punishment as a deterrence mechanism. Among the key benefits of capital punishment that would factor into such an analysis would be a reduced prison population and the element of deterrence. The costs of capital punishment would include the destroyed "human capital", the cost of the judicial/legislative machinery required for death sentence appeals and the costs of "brutalization effects" of the death penalty.

This last cost is one that Avio has been unable to quantify because little empirical research has been undertaken to date. However, Avio thinks that the CBA for the death penalty hinges on the cost of the judicial / legislative machinery required for death sentence appeals. Avio doubts that the current system can be made cost effective, primarily because it is rife with racism. According to Avio, there is considerable historical evidence that race is the pre-eminent factor in decision on capital punishment cases. He cited statistics showing native Canadians were six times less likely to have their sentences commuted compared to whites who had committed similar crimes based on data for 462 death sentences handed out between 1920 to 1967.

While this does not confirm that the justice system would continue to function in this way if the death penalty was reinstated in Canada, it could be argued that based on this research, Avio believes that a "constrained" CBA would reveal that the arguments made in favour of capital punishment on economic grounds are unconvincing and illogical. Following his presentation, several commentators praised his work as particularly elegant and persuasive.

One of the most stimulating talks was presented by Professor Douglas Hay, a legal historian who teaches at both Osgoode Hall Law School and York University. Over the past decade, Hay has undertaken detailed research on the political significance of capital punishment in England in the 18th and 19th centuries and how the social meaning of the death penalty meshes with ideology. His research shows that in the early

18th century, approximately 90 state executions were carried out in England each year. Of this number, most were executed for property crimes such as theft, and only 20% were killed for committing murder. This pattern continued until the end of the 18th century with the support of the ruling elite as a mechanism for shaping public opinion, disciplining unruly workers, and instilling fear of punishment into the masses.

At the beginning of the 19th century, capital punishment was increasingly challenged by reformers who associated it with "aristocratic oligarchies" wielding power in tyrannous ways. Despite these challenges, the reformers were not successful for more than thirty years. Tories argued that if capital statutes were abolished, criminals would be more bold since policing was inadequate. Thus, an omnibus bill abolishing most capital statutes in England was only passed in 1837.

Other social forces also contributed to the erosion of the popularity of the death penalty. Many Tories believed that public executions were becoming popular, and in the United States hanging was seen as a waste of time because it led to drunkenness and attracted immigrants to congregate in a central area. This could be threatening to the State and no doubt certain critics felt pressure must be brought to eliminate state killing for minor offenses because growing awareness of the contradictions in the justice system might rile the masses who attended these events.

Hay went on to draw out the implications of his analysis for more modern attitudes towards state killing. In the result, Hay maintains that those who support capital punishment do so because it meshes with their world view. Accordingly, instrumental arguments are probably not important to most Americans who support the death penalty. A combination of socialization forces that promote authoritarianism and maintain the popularity of capital punishment are likely most important. Thus, in spite of the convincing arguments against deterrence as a rationale for capital punishment, the popularity of state killing continues to grow in the United States and certain regions of Canada.

In the session that followed, Professor Harry Glasbeek, who teaches a course titled "The Corporation as Criminal" at Osgoode Hall Law School, and has done research on corporations for more than a decade, provided an entertaining commentary on the paradox of debates on reinstatement of the death penalty. Glasbeek observed that those who make the argument for capital punishment often rely on the notion of vengeance based on the biblical adage of an "eye for an eye." At the same time, these individuals also usually advocate the minimal state and challenge state intervention in "normal" market processes such as the vicious killing of workers on the job through exposure to workplace hazards, environmental pollution or white collar crime.

In Glasbeek's view, herein lies one of the intriguing contradictions of capitalism. Somehow an arbitrary distinction between good greed, the premeditated crimes committed by corporations and their leaders, and bad greed, the crimes of thieves or drug pushers, is upheld. This distinction allows corporate executives and other white collar criminals to steal billions and violate occupational health and safety standards without facing serious penalties. Instead, relatively minor crimes such as theft or even crimes of passion are used to justify tougher criminal laws.

Glasbeek went on to observe that this distinction allows certain corporate interests to poison workers and improperly bury PCBs for profit. In an ironic manner, he suggested, with his tongue firmly in his cheek, that perhaps Canadians should welcome the return of the death penalty, particularly if Bill Domm and other pro-noose advocates can be convinced that there are some great candidates from the corporate world who should be all lined up to deal with first. Unfortunately, the papers by Glasbeek and Hay were not available for inclusion in this volume.

The fourth part of the volume contains two of the papers presented in this session. The first paper, presented by Jossi Schwartz, a lawyer at Roach and Smith in Toronto, advocates the death penalty for those criminals guilty of gross crimes against humanity. He begins with a stark inventory of the millions of people killed by the Nazis during World War II. In his view there are no more appropriate candidates for the death penalty, and Schwartz goes on to note that it is despicable that thousands of Nazis escaped to North America, South America and Australia, often with the help of western nations, after the War.

To bolster his case, Schwartz provided numerous examples of war criminals who should have been prosecuted. Specifically, Schwartz identified Nazi criminals such as Josef Mengele, Klaus Barbi and Alfred Boetcher as prime candidates. He suggested that the U.S. government has been reluctant to prosecute potential war criminals because it supports neo-Nazi groups, and it would be hypocritical to do so in view of the U.S. record in Vietnam. Similarly, Schwartz was also critical of the record of Israel in Lebanon, where it is estimated thirty thousand Palestinians and Lebanese were killed when Israel invaded on several occasions in the early 1980s.

In the last presentation on the first day of the conference, Munyonzwe Hamalengwa presented an overview of his argument for the prosecution of people accused of War Crimes and Crimes against Humanity. While Hamalengwa did not go as far as Schwartz in his analysis of the application of sanctions against war criminals in Canada, he agreed with Schwartz that it is deplorable that many despots and tyrants end up escaping to North America.

Hamalengwa went on to argue the new legislation proposed to deal with war criminals and those guilty of crimes against humanity should be used to prosecute Apartheid criminals. In the alternative, he feels it is possible that Botha and some of his cohorts will eventually seek refuge in Canada. Hamalengwa's paper is also included in the fourth part of this volume, but severely edited and limited to the issue of the death penalty under apartheid in South Africa.

On Sunday morning, the Conference recommenced with a fascinating account of the human rights problems in Grenada since the 1983 American invasion. The account was presented by Charles

Roach, a prominent Toronto lawyer hired by the family of one of those charged in an alleged coup attempt which resulted in the death of 11 people, including Maurice Bishop, on October 19th, 1983. Roach summarized a paper written by Tony Gifford, titled "The Grenada Murder Trial: No Case for Hanging."

The background to this series of events was summarized as follows. In October 1983 a conflict emerged between Bishop, the Prime Minister of Grenada from March 1979 to his death on 19th October, 1983, and members of the Central Committee of the New Jewel Movement (NJM). In the eyes of many observers, Bishop's leadership had become "a beacon of progress" in the Caribbean. However, the latter group, led by Bernard Coard, Deputy Prime Minister and Minister of Finance, challenged the moderate policies of Bishop. After a power struggle, Bishop was captured by the Central Committee of the NJM. A brief period of confinement ensued and after a public demonstration, Bishop was killed. Later that month Reagan invaded Grenada under the pretense of regional de-stabilization.

Predictably, the trial of those who were viewed as responsible for the death of Bishop was extremely political. Roach contends that the court which was eventually established did not have competent jurisdiction. In addition, he asserts that millions of dollars were funneled to the Caribbean Judiciary in anticipation of the trial and the jury selection process was extremely irregular. Roach also pointed out that the jury deliberated only three hours on over 190 murder counts which were spread among the 19 people, charged.

In view of these circumstances the trial results were also predictable. Guilty verdicts against 13 men and one woman were returned on 4th December 1986 and these fourteen people were sentenced to the mandatory sentence of death applicable in such cases. Roach does not dispute that some sort of murder trial should have taken place. However, he thinks that in this case the trial was a sham and a violation of Grenadian sovereignty. In his view, a new trial should be held and other investigations should be undertaken regarding the deaths of other people at the hands of the military. If this does not take place, the American government will have effectively used these trials to teach Grenadians that they should not dabble in socialist politics.

Following Roach's presentation, Yola Grant presented a paper on the death penalty in Jamaica. Her analysis relied primarily on a report from Amnesty International prepared in

1984, which is extracted in this volume, and on her personal knowledge of life, having grown up in the country prior to coming to Canada in the 1970s.

As background, Grant noted that prior to 1976 the Jamaican State took the lives of about 5 people a year. Between 1976 and 1980, no executions took place while a series of commissions investigated the "purpose" of the death penalty. According to Grant, a "weak-kneed" report against the death penalty was released and in January 1979, a Bill to abolish it was defeated. As a result, the hangings commenced again in 1980. Since then, the rate of state-killing has accelerated; in one month, over 18 people were killed. Grant believes that this is only part of the problem. She commented that the conditions on death row are appalling - hot and dark with no opportunity for exercise.

Grant went on to comment that there is a class basis for this pattern of execution. According to the Amnesty Report, 80% of those people executed in Jamaica were from the lower economic group. Moreover, two-thirds of those sentenced were first time offenders and many of the murders were committed in emotionally-charged situations.

Another aspect of the problem in Jamaica relates to the fact that many killings take place in the context of political fights during election campaigns. While these killings attract media attention, often the gunmen responsible are not caught and, if they are, police shoot them on the spot. Meanwhile, the widespread problem of "wife murder," which Grant contends accounts for up to 30% of the murders committed in the nation, is ignored by the media. Grant was also critical of the amount of discretion invoked by police in murder cases. She noted that police clear-up rates have declined dramatically recently and that prosecution rates have also dropped to 32% from 71% in the 1970s.

The final session of the conference continued with a presentation by Mariela Morales. Morales, a former lawyer in Chile and currently an advisor with the Ontario Ministry of Labour, surveyed the meaning of the death penalty in context of political repression in Chile. She noted that although the death penalty was part of Chile's criminal code prior to 1973, it was rarely used. Although debates on the death penalty had sometimes taken place, reformers had failed to have the provisions removed. When the military came to power in 1973 in Chile, these provisions became a powerful tool for the government.

However, Morales contends that the decision to apply the provisions again was largely overshadowed by the severe violations of human rights and killings that took place over the next decade. It estimated that over 23,000 people disappeared in Chile during this period. While military officers invoke the defense that they were dealing with terrorists, others have suggested that these disappearances were merely brutal killings. In view of this pattern, the death penalty pales in comparison with the specter of state-sanctioned military killings. Morales' paper is not available in this collection.

Papers that followed surveyed application of the death penalty in India and Uganda. The first by F.S. Nariman on the Indian experience reviews attempts to reform British laws that stipulate the death penalty is an acceptable punishment for many crimes. Nariman was critical of these laws because they allow judges to exercise an enormous amount of discretion in the application of the death penalty, and consequently provides judges with enormous amounts of political power.

Akena Adoko considered the history of the death penalty in Uganda. He concludes that many Ugandans support the death penalty for irrational and emotional reasons. For example, Adoko points out that people fear that exposure to imprisoned murderers may influence the attitudes of other prisoners and prison staff. In this respect, both Nariman and Adoko show that efforts to bring about reform have been frustrated by historical patterns and cultural values infused by Europeans into their cultures over the past few centuries.

The concluding paper was presented by Simon Daniels, an activist from South Africa who has been involved with the African National Congress (ANC) and opposed Apartheid. He provided an update on the crisis in South Africa, noting that the hanging of political prisoners in the nation had increased markedly as criticism of the Botha regime from inside and outside South Africa had mounted in the past few years. He contrasted the behavior of the Botha government with the policies of the ANC, who had signed the Geneva Conventions relating to treatment of prisoners of war. Accordingly, the ANC demanded that Pretoria should treat ANC fighters captured by the South African army as prisoners of war rather than murderers. Since this appeared unlikely to happen, the ANC suggested that crimes of apartheid would be dealt with in an aggressive manner. For example, it was proposed that when the Botha regime was defeated ANC leaders will appoint a special tribunal to mete out appropriate sentences to apartheid criminals.** Daniels's paper was not available for inclusion in this collection.

In conclusion, it is apparent that the papers presented at the conference offered important insights into the nature of state killing in the twentieth century. Those included below are among the best presented at the event, and reflect the sentiments and concerns that motivated the conference organizers.

NOTES

* David McRobert, at the time was with the Ministry of the Attorney General, Constitutional Law and Policy branch.

** After the death of Apartheid, the ANC government set up a Truth and Reconciliation Commission to vet those who would be granted immunity from prosecution for crimes committed during the apartheid era.

PART – II

CANADIAN PERSPECTIVES

CHAPTER

3

THE DEATH PENALTY: CANADIAN PERSPECTIVES

The Ontario
Criminal Lawyers' Association *

3.1. HISTORY:

a). Capital Punishment in Canada

Prior to 1960, our Criminal Code defined murder as a "culpable killing" directly or indirectly, by any means. The only other category of culpable killing was manslaughter. The penalty for murder was capital punishment and was always carried out by hanging. The sentence of death prior to 1955 was almost always carried out. While the Executive Council of the Parliament of Canada exercises a Royal Prerogative of mercy, carried out by the Governor General, the exercising of such a power was extremely rare.

The first attempt to block the death penalty in Canada was a Private Member's Bill in 1914, which failed, and such attempts were repeated in each of the next three years, with the same result. In the mid-1950's, a joint Committee of the Senate and the House of Commons was set up to study the death penalty and corporal punishment. Its Report, issued in 1956, favoured the retention of capital punishment for murder, piracy and treason.

In 1960 the Criminal Code was amended, and among other changes murder was divided into "murder" and "capital Murder", the former punishable by life imprisonment, the latter by death. Capital murder was defined as ordinary murder that was planned and deliberate.

In 1966, the first major debate in the House on abolition took place, and a motion for abolition was tabled but was defeated 143-112. In 1967, the unlawful killing of police officers or prison employees was deemed capital murder, whether planned and deliberate or not. Under the Pearson government, a Bill aimed at abolishing the death penalty for a five year "trial" period, except in cases of capital murder (murder of police officer, prison guard, member of prison staff acting in the course of their duties by the accused, counseling of such an offence, or procuring a third person to commit such an act and military offences was passed), and the five year moratorium began on December 29, 1967.

Upon expiry of the Bill, the law-reverted to its pre-moratorium status, but one week later a five year extension to the Bill was enacted. Before this extension could expire, in the 1975-76 House, Bill C-84, proposing the permanent abolition of the death penalty for criminal offences was debated, and became law on July 26, 1976.[1]

The debate of Bill C-84 was a long and impassioned one. Throughout the 98 hour debate, the numerous controversies relating to capital punishment were examined and re-examined by members of the House of Commons until members voted not along party lines, but according to their informed consciences. In the end, Parliament voted 130 to 124 to retire the hangman in Canada.

The last executions in Canada occurred on December 11, 1962, shortly after midnight, when Arthur Lucas and Ronald Turpin were hanged in Toronto's Don Jail.[2]

3.2. POPULAR OPINION:

This Section deals with the proposition that capital punishment is "too important an issue to be left to lawyers, judges, and politicians". Proponents of capital punishment are often reported as proclaiming: "Let the people decide ". Because opinion polls in recent years have consistently demonstrated that a majority of Canadians are in favour of returning the death penalty "Let the people decide" becomes synonymous with the proposition that capital punishment should be reinstated.

The reliance upon popular opinion manifests itself primarily as a call for a national referendum on capital punishment. For very sound reasons, outlined below, a national referendum would not actually lead to an informed, intelligent, or appropriate policy regarding the death penalty in Canada.

This section also deals with calls for a new "free vote" in parliament on the issue and with the opinions of some fairly popular, and well-respected, Canadians.

a). The Question of a National Referendum

Perhaps it was best said by the late Arthur Maloney, Q.C. an advocate for human rights and the abolition of capital punishment throughout his career as a lawyer, parliamentarian and Ontario's first ombudsman. Commenting on the apparent increasing demand for a referendum on restoring the death penalty in the early 1980s, Mr. Maloney said he felt that such a referendum would be a particularly unsatisfactory way of dealing with this issue because the outcome would depend so greatly on the public mood at the time the referendum was held; hardly an appropriate contingency upon which to decide matters of life and death.[3]

A prime example of this problem was demonstrated shortly after, the second killing of a York Region policeman in less than 2 months in October of 1984. A group of policemen's wives launched a petition demanding a return of the death penalty. No doubt, the event was a terrible tragedy. But that very fact led to emotional and unsubstantiated claims such as the one by Barb McDonald: "The only way to curb violent crime, which includes the killing of six Canadian police officers in the past seven weeks, is to bring back capital punishment."[4] This statement, borne out of the frustration and outrage of the indicated tragic events, has no basis in fact and is not supported by any evidence whatsoever. But it is just the kind of belief which could lead to a pro-capital punishment result in a referendum (see Crime section, below).

It is also interesting to note that in the United States, a polled majority favoured the death penalty "even if new evidence showed conclusively that it did not defer criminals". There are other factors then, apart from public knowledge which could influence a referendum. In fact, the top reason stated for supporting the death penalty was revenge.[5]

In Manitoba, in December of 1984, a survey showed that 86% of Manitobans favoured the death penalty for those committing pre-meditated murder, 82.5% favoured the death penalty for killers of police officers and prison guards. Noting the extent to which recent events may influence public opinion, Gregory Mason, head of the University of Manitoba's Institute for Social and Economic Research said the latter figure is probably the result of the many current murders of Canadian policemen and the then recent killings of two Manitoban prison guards.[6]

In its January 24, 1983 issue, TIME Magazine proclaimed: "Fear, pure and simple, is behind the new advocacy of the death penalty". It hardly needs stating that the decision to institute the state sanctioned taking of human life requires a more reasoned and considered process than one based on fear. At the very least, the decision should be an informed one.

And yet the evidence shows that the Canadian public, who the referendum advocates wish to decide this issue, are quite misinformed. For example, a recent study by the University of Toronto's criminology Center found that those Canadians surveyed thought Canada's homicide rate was about seven times higher than it really is. The truth is that since the abolition of capital Punishment in 1976, the murder rate has never been higher than 2.78 per 100,000 people as opposed to 3.09 per 100,000 people the year before the death penalty was abolished.

8. Criminologists A.N. Doob and J.V. Roberts pointed out in 1984 that Canadians "vastly overestimate" the level of crime and violence in this country, and confuse the information they receive from American television with Canadian events. The U.S. homicide rate is three and one-half times the homicide rate in Canada.

In fact, Ontario Criminology researchers Neil Vidmar and Tony Ditenhoffer have come to the conclusion that if Canadians were informed about the facts of the death penalty, the polls would show the majority of people opposed-to it. Other surveys demonstrate that Canadians tend to believe that more than half of all crime is violent, when in fact 6 to 8 per cent is. Similarly, two thirds of Canadians believe the murder rate has increased since 1976, when in fact it has declined.[9]

Such erroneous public perception tend to increase greatly after a particularly heinous crime makes headlines. But headlines tend to create impressions that relatively rare events are commonplace and that capital punishment is necessary to "stem the tide". But as Toronto lawyer Leo Adler stated: "Those who call for the return of capital punishment based on the apparent dramatic increase in murders should consider the statistics rather than the headlines." Unfortunately, the public often do not get access to statistics; but politicians do.

Of course, the most basic, and common misperception prevalent among Canadians is that capital punishment will deter murderers. As was stated in the English Methodist Recorder:

"It must be said forcibly that this simple reaction, almost wholly emotional, is mistaken. In the first place most murders are not the end products of the sort of calculated planning that provides the puzzle in detective stories. They are domestic tragedies when reason snaps under stress, or are the squalid result of drunken brawls."

It was therefore appropriate for the Inter-church Task Force for the Continued Abolition of the

Death Penalty to state the following in 1980:

The Prime Minister of Canada in the Autumn of 1979 stated, apropos of another matter, that there will not be government by Gallup Poll. Nor should there be. Certainly, Parliament should, of course, show a decent respect for the opinions of mankind, but remember too, that it owes the country its own judgment. It might also be remarked that there is nothing which invests the most recent public opinion poll with the character of the immutable moral law of the universe.

Few issues have been as thoroughly ventilated by Parliament as has the death penalty. No other issue has on four occasions within a decade been the subject of full Parliamentary debate, followed on each occasion by a free vote. Those free votes show a national recognition that the difficult matter is one of conscience, and thus supremely, one for the judgement of the Members and not for a vote based on any impression of public opinion.

The Task Force asserts that the difficult question of the death penalty is a moral one, a matter of conscience which cannot be evaded by putting the burden of decision on any supposed public opinion."[12]

In fact, it is undeniable that Parliamentarians are

better informed, and better equipped, to deal with this kind of issue than the average member of the public. In Canada, capital punishment, abortion, euthanasia and other sensitive subjects are traditionally decided by Parliament, rather than public referendum, in the basic belief of democracy that elected politicians represent the people and have the power of informed choice.[13]

As Criminal Lawyers' Association President Earl J. Levy, Q.C. has stated: "In our Parliamentary system the people choose those who will decide what our laws should be, based on knowledge gained from input by interested groups from various segments of the public including police and lawyers. To seek a public referendum goes against one of the hallmarks of our Parliamentary system. Any decision on capital punishment should be based on informed opinion - not gut reactions and emotionalism.[14]

Indeed, in our Parliamentary system, our elected representatives have a duty to exercise their informed judgment. On November 3, 1774, English parliamentarian Edmund Burke made this now famous statement: "Your representative owes you, not his industry only, but his judgment; and he betrays instead of serving you if he sacrifices it to your opinion."15 This sentiment was echoed by Prime Minister Brian Mulroney on

September 25, 1984: "Yes, I do rule out the idea of a referendum. If you believe in the British parliamentary traditions and system, and I do, that calls upon members of Parliament to assume their responsibilities."[16]

b). The Alleged Need for a new "free vote" in Parliament

When they are not calling for a national referendum on the issue, advocates of capital punishment are almost invariably demanding a "free vote" in the House of Commons on the death penalty.

It is submitted that this suggestion is inappropriate for two reasons.

In the first place, the vote would be somewhat less than "free" in the context of the present government because of the overwhelming majority of the Progressive Conservative Party. Traditionally, Tory back-benchers have tended to support hanging and polls of the present Honourable members suggest nothing has changed in this regard - and the Tories hold 211 of the 282 seats. Most commentators believe a bill to restore the death penalty would pass.[17]

In the second place it must be recalled that a

lengthy and informed debate was already undergone in the House in 1976 which resulted in the decision of Parliament to abolish the death penalty. Certainly, nothing has occurred in the intervening period which would justify a change in that decision. The 1976 decision to abolish capital punishment was reached by means of a free vote and it was arrived at only after exhaustive discussion of the issue.[18]

c). Popular Opinion Favours Capital Punishment

While it may be true that a simple majority of Canadians favour the death penalty, it is also true that one should have regard to just whose opinion is being expressed. A more careful survey reveals that the list of abolitionists includes many names of Canada's most informed and respected men and women as well as groups which are so sensitive to the value of human life - such groups as the Salvation Army, the John Howard Society, the Elizabeth Fry Society and Amnesty International. The list would also include virtually all major churches in this country as well as the United Nations.

3.3. MORALITY AND RELIGION:

This section deals with propositions that it is morally correct to kill murderers. One usually finds that such a position is usually derived from either a perceived moral imperative imbuing the state with a right to kill, in order to fulfill its obligation to protect its citizens, or from the oft-quoted biblical precept “an eye for an eye, a tooth for a tooth".

a). The Moral Right of the State to Kill

It has been said that capital punishment merely represents society's most profound way of demonstrating that murder is wrong. By taking the life of one who engages in the most immoral of acts - the intentional taking of the life of another ¬society indicates its revulsion of murder and clearly indicates that right prevails over wrong. Transgressing the ultimate wrong may morally lead to the ultimate loss for the immoral transgressor.

Apart from the logical fallacy of proposing that it is morally right to kill someone in order to demonstrate that killing someone is wrong, there is the question of whether or not the death penalty actually does what its proponents tell us it does.

Do executions help convince society that violence and murder are morally wrong? Commentators suggest that executions lead society to the completely opposite conclusion - and in the completely 'wrong' direction: i.e. toward more murder and violence.

This question is important because even if we concede that the state has a moral right to take the life of the condemned man, the late Arthur Maloney pointed out to Parliament in 1960 that "there are many things which we are morally entitled to do but which we are not morally obliged to do." 19 The effect of capital punishment on the moral fibre of society is, accordingly, something we must have regard to.

Henry Schwarzschild, of the American Civil Liberties Union, put it this way: "A society that believes that the killing of a human being is a solution to any problem is deeply uncivilized. ... The marginally demented guy sees an execution as a prescription, not a threat. He thinks, 'if the state has a quarrel with Gary Gilmore, it kills him. Then if I have a quarrel with someone, I'll kill him.' We say we think human life is sacred. And then to prove that, we kill somebody, that's wrong".[20]

In reality, the principle laid down by Jeremy Bentham still holds true: the state affects the conduct and actions of its citizens more by the standards of its own behaviour than by the penalty it inflicts on others. [21]

There is a danger in forgetting this point and charging on with a destructive course of action vindicated only by our own declaration that it is morally correct. As Thomas Carey, a Brampton lawyer once wrote:

"Killing another person for his crime is not "the ultimate penalty" - it is the ultimate folly. If it is motivated by a sense of outraged self-righteousness, it can reach the extremes of the regime of the Ayatollah Khomeini in Iran.

The people of Iran do not see themselves as mad, nor do they see themselves as brutal or uncivilized. Rather, in carrying out thousands of executions of people accused of everything from theft to prostitution to treason, they rely on a moral imperative based on their religion and claim that they are ridding society of useless and evil people whose death will ensure they will sin no more. Are those motives so different than those who today urge the return of the noose to Canada.[22]

Indeed to reinstate the death penalty in Canada would be to place this country in the same dubious league as such 'moral' regimes as Iran, Apartheid South Africa, Saudi Arabia and the Soviet Union.23 It is important to note that apart from the United States, Ireland and Liechtenstein, all Western industrialized countries have abolished the death penalty.[24] When one considers the kinds of oppressive and repressive regimes which practise capital punishment on a regular basis - they also tend to be the same regimes that regularly practise torture - it becomes clear that there are some means which no government can morally use to protect society, because in using such means, one destroys the very values that make that society worth protecting.[25]

Execution is an act of violence. As such, it can never be moral in a society which abhors violence. This is particularly so because it has been demonstrated repeatedly that violence tends to provoke further violence.

If there is any moral duty of the state, it is to protect the life of all persons within its jurisdiction without exception.[26]

b). The Bible ... says "An eye for an eye"

It is true that the Old Testament makes reference to certain Punishments which audited the formula of "an eye for an eye, tooth for tooth", and so on. But the Bible says many other things which death Penalty advocates seem to conveniently exclude. For example, the Bible also says "thou shalt not kill." It does not say "Thou shalt not kill, unless you are a publicly financed executioner".

Indeed, Salvation Army chaplain Cyril Everitt, who was present during the last executions in Canada, in 1962, said recently: "The Bible says: "thou shalt not kill", and if it is wrong for a person to kill - and I say it is - then it's wrong for the state to kill".[27]

But the advocates of capital punishment prefer to say that the sixth commandment is meant to be selective in its application, and they recite certain isolated Bible passages - such as "an eye for an eye" - to prove their point.

There is however, a fundamental theological problem, in selecting isolated passages from the scripture, to prove a religious point. Theologians point out that, "in seeking to discern God's will related to any complex social issue, more than reference to specific isolated passages is necessary. This is especially obvious in the controversy over capital punishment since one cannot use one passage as right and ignore a conflicting passage".[28]

This point is expressed well by Robert McAfee Brown in The Bible Speaks to You:

The Bible does not give us a blueprint for a "Christian political order." Whenever you find someone quoting isolated bits of Scripture to "prove" a point with regard to some specific piece of legislation, you are entitled to be suspicious. During the Civil War, preachers quoted the Bible to support slavery and to repudiate slavery. What usually happens in such cases is that a person believes something and then goes hunting the "proof texts" in the Bible to back it up. During war-time, militarists, produce verses showing God's support of blood-thirsty Israelite wars, while non-militants isolate sayings like "Love your enemies." Anyone can find what he (or she) wants in the Bible by stressing the things that agree with his (or her) position and ignoring the things that do not. It is particularly easy to lift statements out of context in playing this fruitless game.[29]

It is clear then, that proper Biblical interpretation involves reading the scripture passages within context. This means examining both the Bible's internal context and the historical context within which it was written/issued.

In his famous John Howard Anniversary sermon preached at the Church of St. Martins-in-Fields in 1930, Archbishop William Temple said:

The most obvious contradiction is provided by the words, "Ye have heard that it hath been said, Love your friends and hate your enemies, but I say unto you, Love your enemies." What did the old law of retaliation really mean when it was written? It was not a licence to exact vengeance; there was no need for such a licence in the early world; vengeance took place of itself provided that men were strong enough. What was needed was a limitation of vengeance, and what the law of retaliation, "An eye for an eye and a tooth for a tooth," meant, was not, "You are at liberty to take an eye for an eye and a tooth for a tooth," but, "You must not take more than one eye for an eye, nor more than one tooth for a tooth." The whole purpose of the old law was to set a limit to the nature of the vengeance which might be exacted. But our Lord carries the principle of limitation further. Retaliation for the sake of retaliation must not be exercised at all. [30]

To simply quote "an eye for an eye" then, does not necessarily demonstrate God' s will as much as it reflects the personal opinion and preference of the person quoting. Many people quote the passage "an eye for an eye" as a prescription for how justice ought to be done; but these same people rarely cite other passages where the Bible calls for death penalty; such as the case where one rebels against one's parents.

In fact, the Old Testament Mosaic Code Prescribes the death penalty for eighteen crimes, only one of which is murder. Ask anyone who says "an eye for an eye" if he or she believes we should follow the bible literally and prescribe death for all of these crimes:

(1) Murders - Exod. 21:12-14,20; 22:2-3; Lev.20:2; 24:17,21; Num. 35:11-21,30; Deut. 19:11-13.

(2) Accidentally causing the death of a pregnant woman or her baby if injured in the course of a fight - Exod. 21:22-25.

(3) Killing of a person by a dangerous animal that had killed before, yet was not kept caged (both the animal and the owner to be killed) -- Exod. 21: 28-30

(4) Kidnaping - Exod. 21:16; Deut. 24:7.

(5) Rape of a married woman (but not rape of a virgin) Deut. 22: 25-29

(6) Fornication - Deut. 22:13-21; Lev. 21:9; exception, Lev. 19: 20-22

(7) Adultery - Lev. 20:10; Deut 22:22-24; Num 5:12-30.

(8) Incest - Lev. 20:11-12, 14

(9) Homosexuality - Lev. 20:13

(10) Sexual intercourse with an animal - Lev 20:15-16; Exod. 22-19.

(11) Striking a parent - Exod. 21:15.

(12) Cursing a parent - Exod. 21:17; Lev. 20:9

(13) Rebelling against parents - Deut. 21:18-21

(14) Sorcery, witchcraft - Exod. 22:18 Lev. 20:27.

(15) Cursing God - Lev. 24:10-16.

(16) Attempting to lead people to worship other Gods- ¬Deut. 13:1-16; 18:2b; Exod. 22:20.

(17) Avenging a death despite acquittal by the law- Deut. 17:12.

(18) Intentionally testifying falsely against someone in jeopardy of the death penalty - Deut. 19:16-19.

It becomes obvious that there is a very real danger in attempting to apply words found in the Bible literally to today's society. For Christians, such selective Old Testament text citation is particularly illegitimate because, as Canada's Roman Catholic bishops pointed out to Parliament in 1973:

"We consider it an illegitimate use of the Bible, especially the Old Testament, to quote texts in order to argue, in our time, for the retention of the death penalty. Each such Old Testament text must be weighted against any passages in the New Testament where Jesus constantly rejects the normal human tendency to redress injury by injury and calls instead for generosity. He establishes a norm that violence and hostility are not correct by counter-measures of violence and hostility."[31]

Even within the confines of the old Testament, passages calling for the death penalty must be placed in proper context:

In seeking to understand what light these passages throw upon capital punishment today, it is essential to see the function these laws played in their time. In that historical period, violent attitudes and acts of revenge were common (see Psalm 137). Even a slight offense could result in the death of the offender (see Genesis 4:1-8,23). Consequently, laws which linked the death penalty with particular offences provided a way to control and limit vindictive killings. The penalty was more nearly related to the offence committed. Laws of retributive punishment were actually reform measures seeking to limit violence"[32]

To follow the logic of the Old Testament today, seems to call for even more reform; i.e., further limiting violence in our own time, including the violence of the state. It must also be recalled that although the Mosaic code apparently called for the death penalty, the Mosaic laws relating to evidence, judgment and sentencing were much more restrictive than the Canadian judicial system. The standard of proof amounted to thorough certainty, and not our "proof beyond a reasonable doubt."

In addition, conviction required the testimony of more than one witness. No one could be convicted on the evidence of one witness or by circumstantial evidence. Clearly, if the Mosaic code of law were adopted there would not be nearly as many convictions for murder as there are now. Those who lobby to restore the death penalty for biblical reasons ought to understand the full implications of adopting Old Testament law, including its more stringent safeguards.

The other major distinction between the modern approach to capital punishment and that of Bible times is the issue of responsibility. The sentence of death in the Bible was to be carried out by stoning. The common stoning of the victim made it impossible to conceal responsibility (Deuteronomy 21:21).

John H. Leith of the Union Theological Seminary in Virginia has made the following observation in this regard:

Today the responsibility for an execution is so diffused that neither the police, nor the prosecutor, nor the jury, nor the judge, nor the governor has to take full responsibility. Citizens in general are far less aware of their personal responsibility for the execution. The common stoning, when each member of the community had to cast a stone, had the advantage of clarifying the issue. Personal responsibility does not prejudge the rightness or wrongness of the death penalty; it does mean that all Christians and citizens ought to hold themselves accountable for public policy on this issue. [33]

For Christians, the issue of responsibility must b+e addressed for it impacts upon the Christian's right to participate in the death penalty. "Let one who is without sin cast the first stone" said Jesus (John 8:53-8:11).

Iindeed, the Bible has much more to say than "an eye for an eye". The Bible also says that "violence begets violence"34 . The scriptures preach mercy as well as retribution. In numerous biblical passages Jesus makes it clear that we are to "repay no one evil for evil" so as to compound and multiply the very evils we are seeking to minimize (Cf. Romans 12:17-21, 1 Peter 3:8-9). Christ said on the cross: "Father, forgive them, for they know not what they do."

c). The View of the Churches

It is indeed curious that many advocates of capital punishment defend the death penalty by characterizing it as the triumph of moral Christian values over the pagan evil personified in the person of the condemned criminal. This is curious because, as we shall see below, virtually all leaders of Canada's mainstream Churches have spoken in opposition to the death penalty. Men and women who consider themselves to be very religious, and "good Christians", continue to agitate for the return of the noose notwithstanding the strong opposition to capital punishment on religious grounds, of the very churches to which they belong.

It is often said, for example, that capital punishment is needed to protect the righteous and the moral from the depraved and the dangerous. This is said despite evidence of rehabilitation through programs of personal contact with inmates. It has led the Committee on Outreach and Corporate Witness of the Presbyterian Church in Canada to ask the following questions:

"When can a Christian give up on an individual? What responsibility do we as a Church and as individuals have for the rehabilitation and redemption of offenders? Is it possible that the reinstatement of the death penalty would be an easy way out for us, removing our res-possibility to care for those whom we might label as 'enemies'?" [35]

One of the important reasons for church opposition to capital Punishment is its complete denial of the possibility of reform; there remains no question of repentance or rehabilitation. "And yet", wrote Jack Costello S.J., "this 'hope for conversion' is the pivot of Judeo-Christian-faith. Without the constant hope that every heart can turn to God and ask for forgiveness, we act out of something less than, and other than, the gospel. Jesus asked His followers to show mercy as He showed mercy." [36]

This thought was echoed in 1983 by the Bishop of St. Germans of the Church of England, the Right Rev. Brother Michael, SSF, who, at the General Synod's debate on capital punishment, said that there had to be room for forgiveness to be offered to a murderer, time for him to appropriate it, repent and bring forth fruits of repentance. This, he said, would also allow room for society to correct errors. [37]

It should come as no surprise then, to read the reflections of Rev. Thomas Dailey of St. Augustine's Seminary in Toronto who writes that: "leading Catholic theologians are now saying that the death penalty is incompatible with Christian teaching on reverence for life."38 Indeed, in January of 1983 Pope John Paul II sweepingly recommended "clemency, or pardon, for those condemned to death. [39]

The concrete manifestation of this principle in Canada is the fact that the Canadian Council of Churches in Toronto, which represents 13 Protestant denominations, and the Canadian Conference of Catholic Bishops are both "implacably opposed" to the death penalty. [40]

Indeed, on April 19, 1986, Toronto Star Religion editor Michael McAteer wrote:

"In the face of frequent loud public calls for the restoration of the death penalty, Canada's mainline Christian denominations have preserved an unwavering solid front in opposition to capital punishment.

In statement after statement, the churches have voiced their opposition to the death penalty, calling it a barbaric, vengeful, violent act that brutalizes society and breeds more violence.

The churches have argued that there is no evidence that capital punishment is a deterrence and have also called for a whole re-examination of Canada's penal system.

Canada's Roman Catholic bishops have persistently opposed the death penalty and have said they consider the use of scripture, especially the Old Testament, to support the death penalty as "an illegitimate use of the Bible." The spirit of the Gospel, the bishops say, directs Christians towards forgiveness, clemency and reconciliation and not towards vengeance. [41]

It should be noted that Jewish rabbis have also been largely opposed to the death penalty. When the State of Israel came into being in 1948, the rabbinate objected to provision in the law for the death penalty. Formal abolition was enacted in 1954, except for offences under the Crime of Genocide Law of 1950. [42]

If anything, more and more Churches and religious organizations are making statements opposed to the death penalty.- In July, 1983, the British Methodist Conference, for example, affirmed its opposition to the death penalty 43 as did the General Synod of the Church of England. 44 As recently as June, 1986, the Baptist Convention of Ontario and Quebec went on record as opposing capital punishment.[45]

3.4. DETERRENCE:

In this section we deal with the general question: "Does capital punishment deter would-be murderers?" Deterrence of police killings is dealt with in the section dealing with "PROTECTING THE POLICE".

a). Are there alternative deterrents?

In subsection (ii) we shall deal with the question of whether or not capital punishment serves as a deterrent to murder. Suffice it to say, the overwhelming majority of studies on the subject indicates that it does not. But let us assume for a moment that it does. Or let us assume that we do not know. An important question remains: whether or not capital punishment deters murders, are there other deterrents which could serve equally well without our having to resort to the grisly business of legalized state murder?

As early as 1960, respected lawyer and parliamentarian Arthur Maloney was able to point to a "wealth of incontrovertible evidence" which "demonstrates to the point of moral sureness and certainty that the penalty of death is not the only effective deterrent to the crime of murder and that a sentence of imprisonment for life has proven, where these experiments have been made, to be equally effective."

"This evidence is to be found in some 40 jurisdictions, countries and states that are spread across the world... This embraces all different types of countries. It embraces a complete cross section of people of all races and of all religious creeds. The inescapable conclusion is that the incidence of homicide, the number of homicidal killings in any jurisdiction, bears no relationship whatever to the presence or absence of the penalty of death but is related instead to other factors altogether including cultural, sociological, geographical and other factors."

Maloney added that if death were not the only effective deterrent then this horrible certainty would be quite needless. "The point I am endeavoring to make," he told Parliament "is that the alternative sentence of imprisonment for life has proved itself to be equally effective as a deterrent and therefore, having regard to the horrible character of the death penalty, a much more satisfactory sentence for the law to impose.[46]

By concentrating only on the penalty of death, capital punishment advocates neglect other alternatives, and possibly more effective, means to deter killing. New York University Law Professor Anthony Amsterdam has noted that: "The degree of punishment is not necessarily a deterrent even to someone who thinks rationally. What deters people from crime is the likelihood of getting caught and undergoing punishment."[47] This conclusion has been borne out by Canadian studies.

In a Law Reform Commission of Canada study completed in 1976, a survey of all studies available comparing the effects of certainty of punishment to the effects of severity of punishment was published.

The studies encompassed not only Canada but Europe and the United States as well. The study states that no support was found for severity of sentence alone as a deterrent to crime, but a consistent moderate effect was found for certainty of punishment. The introduction of more severe penalties usually results in a temporary decrease in the incidence of the proscribed behavior. At the same time, as punishment is increased, the attitude towards marginal cases becomes more permissive.

Certainly, this indicates that our best efforts in deterring crime are being misdirected. As Thomas Reppetto, of the Citizens Crime Commission of New York City, has observed; "I always favour something that will get tough with a lot of offenders instead of setting very tough with just a handful." [48]

But instead of taking concrete steps to actualize such a goal, we waste time and money attempting to resolve just how severely we will punish those murderers we have already caught. one would hope our best efforts should be aimed at saving lives.

In this regard, the comments of Jim Manly, M.P. during the 1984 debates on the Execution of Mass Murderers Act is instructive:

It was revealing that when the news of the Olson murders first broke several years ago,, a psychologist pointed out that there were five or six young people, children, in British Columbia at that time who, he believed, had the potential to act in the same manner as Clifford Olson. He was saying this at the same time that British Columbia was shutting down facilities to help such children.

Why are we not demanding diagnostic or treatment facilities for children in crisis so that they have some possibility of growing up and living normal and decent lives? We have to attack this kind of problem at its roots instead of waiting until we have a crisis, saying that we will take the life of a person we all find objectionable and feeling that somehow we are dealing with the problem. [49]

b). The Fear of Execution Will Deter Criminals

It may be appropriate to begin with this quote from the January 24, 1983 edition of TIME Magazine: "To work at all, deterrence requires murderers to reckon at least roughly the probable costs of their actions. But if a killer is drunk or high on drugs, that kind of rational assessment might be impossible. Passions are often at play that make a cost-benefit analysis unlikely ... Says New York University Law Professor Anthony Amsterdam: 'People who ask themselves those questions - 'Am I scared of the death penalty? Would I not be deterred? - and think rationally, do not commit murder for many, many reasons other than the death penalty."[50]

This point was expressed equally well by M.P. Terence Nugent during the commons abolition debate in 1966: "The only excuse society has for taking the life of any person is if it is proven necessary to do so for the protection of society and our way of life ... I have not yet found a criminal who ever plotted a crime and guided his conduct on the basis of the length of the punishment which would be awarded for such an offence."[51]

The point that the death penalty will never act as a deterrent to murder has been stated most eloquently by Anthony Genovese: a man who has himself been incarcerated for some 20 years. He has known the kinds of perpetrators of the vast majority of killers: the professional thief, the amateur, and the domestic killer. None are deterred by the thought of their ultimate punishment.

The professional criminal never intentionally kills. His experience tells him to avoid confrontation because it greatly increases the risk of detection. Deaths occur as a result of unexpected events: a sudden move from the victim, the sudden appearance of a policeman, the interference of a would-be hero: "The choice is then and there. He has but one split second, life or death. Capital punishment is not among his thoughts. The hero lunges, the gun fires, and he is now a killer ... There was no intent; there was no premeditation."[52]

The amateur is uncertain, he is nervous and he is fearful. "He is unpredictable and often dangerous ... Life has no meaning to this criminal. He fears imprisonment yet will not fear the ultimate fate of death ... He finds it difficult to spell capital punishment let alone comprehend its meaning. He will kill at the slightest provocation and without thought. Without thought, there is no pre-meditation."

The domestic killer can be anyone. This killer is a neighbour, a friend, a doctor, a janitor. He acts out of passion, he acts spontaneously without thought and without care. "That lack of thought, that blind rage that took the life of a loved one would not have been deterred by the consequences of his own ultimate death at the hands of the state. There was no premeditation."

Despite these insights, advocates of capital punishment insist that the possibility of execution may hold back some people from killing. But the facts show that this is unlikely. In Canada, about 40 per cent of murders are within domestic relationships, and about 33 per cent among acquaintances or business colleagues. [53]

Josh Zambrowsky, executive director of the Canadian Criminal Justice Association has observed: "Experience from years of working with people convicted of violent crimes makes it clear that the consequences of the act are virtually never in the mind of the perpetrator."

"In Britain, a study by the Home Office statistical division found that "Murders of women and children were mainly due to rage or jealousy. Sexual motives and motives of gain accounted for most of the remainder. Murders of men were also largely emotional. Rage, quarrels, jealously and revenge accounted for about half the known motives. Theft or other gain was next ... Feuds or murders while escaping or resisting arrest were only a small proportion of the total."[54]

In a sense, it is curious that we attribute to the criminal a quality of reason and rational foresight absent even in ourselves. The point has been ably made by Jack Costello SJ:

to be relatively incapable of comprehending our own destruction. Ernest Becker called this the denial of death. And we do it every day.

No one expects personally to die in a car or plane crash, in a war, from cancer - or even of old age. We fly, we settle in areas of high risk from storm or earthquake, we smoke, we drive cars. As Martha Wylie notes, “almost all our decisions are a denial of death, not just as a certainty, but even as a possibility."

So too, the 'rational' killer denies that he will be caught, convicted and executed ¬just as a petty thief denies apprehension; just as we all did when we raided the cookie jar as kids, and as we still do with our grownup crimes, peccadillos and risk-taking. So we must ask ourselves - if this killer is as 'rational' as any of us, then is it not likely that the death penalty is the least of his worries when he makes his decision?"55

Even the graphic proximate reminder of public execution has been shown to have little or no deterrent effect on actual criminals because they believe they won't get caught. As Camus noted in his 1957 essay on capital punishment: "When pickpockets were punished by hanging in England, other thieves exercised their talents in the crowds surrounding the scaffold where their fellow was being hanged."[56]

Montreal psychologist Paul Williams, executive director of the John Howard Society of Quebec, has spent years dealing with offenders in and out of prison. He says: "In 20 years I never encountered a single convicted murderer for whom capital punishment would have worked as a deterrent. Almost always, murders are committed in a moment of uncontrollable emotion. The concern about capital punishment comes later."57 Certainly no one whose mind is clouded by alcohol or drugs will weigh the consequences of his or her actions.

This is particularly true of the mentally unbalanced, insane and deranged persons who commit a significant proportion of murders. Indeed, as Brampton lawyer Thomas J.P. Carey has pointed out:

"If a psychopathic killer thinks at all about the consequences, the prospect of execution probably is seen as sort of a glorious martyrdom in his distorted mind. Most shoplifting offences involve a higher degree of planning and forethought than the average mur-der, which is classically an act of momentary rage, drunken violence or secondary to an escape from another crime." [58]

One must consider the conclusion of Stanford Psychiatry Professor Donald Lunde:

"For every person for whom the death penalty is a deterrent, there's at least one for whom it is an incentive."[59] Even Charles Dickens had wondered whether it was a "craving for notoriety which produced the incentive and impulse to commit murder" citing the statistics of 167 persons who were under the sentence of death at the time, 164 of whom had witnessed a public execution.[60]

The truth is that there is no evidence to show that violent criminals are deterred by the death penalty. In fact the lowest murder rates are found in those countries and states where the death penalty has been abolished for a long time - in the United Kingdom, Sweden, Austria, Italy, Minnesota, Wisconsin, Maine. [61]

What the evidence shows is that most of the popular arguments about deterrence reflect the response of society to murder and not of murderers to criminal sanctions.[62]

c). Statistics: Abolition and the Murder Rate

Any notion that the Canadian murder rate would decrease if capital punishment were reinstated should be completely dispelled by the indisputable fact that the Canadian murder rate actually decreased only after the abolition of capital punishment in 1976.

According to Statistics Canada the homicide rate in 1975, the year before the death penalty was abolished, was 3.09 per 100,000 people. That rate has never been reached since the abolition of the death penalty. In 1985, the last year for which figures are available, the homicide rate was 2.78.

The following are the Canadian Crime Statistics breakdown of the average annual homicide rates per 100,000 people from 1979 to 1985 in Canada: Newfoundland 1.2; Prince Edward Island - 0.4; Nova Scotia - 1.7; New Brunswick - 1.9; Quebec - 3.0; Ontario ¬2.0; Manitoba - 3.4; Saskatchewan - 3.3; Alberta - 2.9; British Columbia - 3.9; Yukon - 11.3; Northwest Territories - 12.4.

The newest study by Statistics Canada 63 shows some interesting trends which run contrary to public opinion: less than 1% of all violent crimes committed over the past 25 years in this country were murders the percentage of homicides throughout this period has been consistent; serial killing is rare in this country; and 77% of all homicide offences involve relationships where the suspect and the victim knew each other beforehand.

This same study shows that there has been an increase in first degree murder charges from 202 per 100,000 people in 1977 to 338 per 100,000 people in 1985, an increase of some 65%. However this statistic should not be viewed as having anything to do with the fact there is no death penalty. They are charges only, not convictions. It is this Association's feeling that, particularly with the emergence of many vocal victims' rights groups, some police forces and / or Crown Attorneys are more prone than before to charge first degree murder rather than second degree murder in borderline cases in order to escape public outcries. In addition, by charging first degree murder the prosecution has more plea bargaining strength than if second degree murder was charged. Our view is confirmed in part by the fact that during the period of this rise in first degree murder charges, second degree murder charges dropped from 1.83 to 1.23 per 100,000 people.

It cannot go unnoticed that the most recent statistics from Statistics Canada show that in

1986 first degree murder charges dropped 23% from 1985.

Evidence from the United States is no less persuasive. TIME Magazine reported the following results from studies of homicide rates of states that did and did not prescribe the death penalty:

The most persuasive research compared the homicide rates of states that did and did not prescribe the death penalty. For instance, Michigan, which abolished capital punishment in 1847, was found to have had a homicide rate identical to adjacent states, Ohio and Indiana, that were executing. Similarly, Minnesota and Rhode Island, states with no death penalty, had proportionately as many killings as their respective neighbors, Iowa and Massachusetts, which had capital punishment. In 1939 South Dakota adopted and used the death penalty, and its homicide rate fell 20% over the next decade; North Dakota got along without capital punishment for the same ten years, and homicides dropped 40%.

Similar before-and-after studies in Canada, England and other countries likewise found nothing to suggest that capital punishment had deterred murderers any better than the prospect of long prison terms. And in Britain during the 1950s, a typical "lifer" actually served only about seven years, compared with a much tougher average U.S. "life" term today of 20 years. A comprehensive study in the U.S., by the National Academy of Sciences in 1978, also found that the death penalty had not proved its worth as a deterrent.[64]

In another study, "U.S. Professor Thorsten Sellin studied 15 states over a 43 year span (1920-1963) and found that homicide death rates in all the states had followed the same trends, with no discernable differences among the states with capital punishment and those without. The rise and fall of the homicide rate in all the states was parallel over the period.[65]

The state of Florida has had 16 executions since the Supreme Court's 1976 ruling that the death penalty was not "cruel or unusual punishment". These executions are exceeded in number only by the state of Texas which has had a total of 20. Florida's death row houses approximately 260 convicts, which is more than any other state. Yet Amnesty International has noted that Florida's murder rate is higher at the present time than it was during the period between 1964 and 1979, when the electric chair was not used.

The only logical conclusion which can be drawn from such studies is that there is no demonstrable evidence that capital punishment has ever actually had a significant deterrent effect on the rate of homicide, including murder. These results "dove-tail" with findings concerning the actual perpetration of murders. Statistics Canada reports that most victims continue to be single males who are usually killed in their own homes by someone they know, most likely a relative. Alcohol or drugs often contribute to the murder.66 In such instances, deterrence - that is foresight on the part of the killer - is highly unlikely to play a factor because murders in such circumstances are thoughtless explosions of violence, usually associated with highly agitated passionate scenarios.

In the same report, Statistics Canada also re-iterated just how rare homicides are in Canada. Between 1975 and 1984, there was an annual average of 2.78 homicides for every 100,000 Canadians, compared with 14 suicides and 20 motor-vehicle deaths for every 100,000 people.67 If our interest is truly in saving lives, then our best efforts should clearly be directed in pursuits other than the re-introduction of capital punishment.

Despite the overwhelming statistical evidence that capital punishment will not lead to a reduction in the murder rate, death penalty advocates continue to claim that death is at least necessary to ensure that the specific convicted murderer is permanently deterred from killing again. Statistics show that this claim is false. Of 384 paroled murderers between 1970 and 1984, not one murdered again. The most recent study by the National Parole Board shows that between 1975 and 1986, 473 convicted persons were released on parole. Two murderers murdered a second time, both of these murderers had originally been convicted of non-capital murder.68 No murderers have been convicted of manslaughter, attempted murder or even wounding. While it is true that certain paroled persons convicted of manslaughter killed again upon their release, these people would not have faced the death penalty anyway.[70]

The simple truth is that death Penalty retentionists have no statistical evidence to support their contention that capital punishment is a deterrent to murder.71 Indeed, as Brian Cameron of Amnesty International, Ottawa, has observed: "States with the worst murder rates tend to have death penalties."[72]

Even The Canadian Association of Chiefs of Police, a long time capital punishment advocate, has recently conceded that it is useless to argue for capital punishment on the basis of deterrence. "The association concludes the deterrence value of capital punishment is selective and marginal. It is quite likely we will never know with certainty if capital punishment deters one who is contemplating murder" it says.[73]

d). The Isaac Erlich Study

Despite its numerous flaws, the work of economist Isaac Erlich is still cited by capital punishment advocates as a kind of proof of death penalty deterrence. Using econometrics modeling techniques to build a "supply-and-demand" theory of murder, Erlich argued in 1975 that capital punishment prevents more murders than do prison sentences. Because of the 3,411 executions carried out in the United States between 1933 and 1967, says Erlich, enough potential murderers were discouraged so that some 27,000 victims' lives were saved.[74]

Erlich's work was extremely theoretical and highly dependent upon complex mathematical modeling techniques and regression analysis. Erlich's work is replete with assumptions, any of which are subject to argument.

Suffice it to say that econometrics critics of Erlich have pointed out that his estimated coefficients may reflect "the response of society to murder behaviour, not to murder behaviour to criminal sanctions."[75]

Other critics have pointed out that Erlich did not compare the effectiveness of the death penalty with that of particular prison terms. Also, his formula does not work if the years between 1965 and 1969 are omitted; and in accounting for the increase in homicides during the 1960's, he neglects the possible influences of racial unrest, the Viet Nam War, a loosening of moral standards and increased handgun ownership.

3.5. JUSTICE:

This section deals with the notion that the law has become weakened with the abolition of capital punishment and that its re-introduction is required to bring back real "justice" for murderers. In fact, as will be seen below, the death penalty defeats the cause of justice in many ways.

a). People Are Getting Away With Murder

It seems as though some people believe that without capital punishment, murderers are not punished for their misdeeds. It must be remembered that a murder conviction results in a mandatory sentence of life imprisonment. A first degree murder conviction results in no eligibility for parole for 25 years. The minimum eligibility period for persons convicted of second degree murder is 10 years. This is hardly "getting away with murder". It should also be recalled that release is not automatic after 25 years - in the case of a first degree murder conviction. The decision lies within the discretion of the National Parole Board. The sentence for murder is life. There is no eligibility for parole for 25 years. The significance of this sentence should not be underestimated.

As criminologist Bernard Henheffer stated in 1984: "Imagine the hopelessness of someone confined to prison until 2009." Of course, the year 2009 may very well pass without any change. Jaime Llambias, a Montreal sociologist who visited the maximum security penitentiary at Dorchester, N.B., told Maclean's magazine in 1983 that at least three lifer's declared: "This is worse than death. It is not worth living under these circumstances."[76]

Of course, not all "lifers" opinions are so extreme. But the comments reveal that the murderer certainly has not "gotten away with it".

Some proponents of the death penalty complain that the 25 year parole eligibility for first degree murder is illusory because an application can be made after 13 years for release. The application however must be made before a jury. It is a jury who will decide on the applicant's release; not a judge and not the parole board. If a jury of the applicant's peers feel that he or she should be released before the 25 year eligibility date, what stronger comment could be made by the representatives of the public against the death penalty?

b). We Need Capital Punishment to Bring More Murderers to Justice

If it has any effect at all in this regard, the death penalty results in less murderers being brought to justice. This is because juries are more likely to acquit if they think there is any possibility of sending an innocent person to his or her death. Sociology professor Jim Hackler has observed the following:

"When we punish more severely we risk making

greater mistakes, juries are more hesitant to make such mistakes; thus they convict less easily. When the stakes are high a larger percentage of guilty offenders are acquitted. This pattern does not seem to be a recent one, according to a Ph.D. thesis at the University of Montreal by Pierre Tremblay in 1984.

Looking at Canada, the United States, and Norway, a pattern that persists for 100 years shows that when we punish often, we punish less severely. When punishment is severe, it is used less.

My argument is that we get better mileage out of our imperfect system if we use less severe punishments and use them more frequently. We are more likely to maintain the delicate balance be-tween hurting the innocent and being sure that guilty people get some punishment." [77]

Professor Hackler goes on to conclude:

"If punishments become more severe, we will reduce the certainty that criminals will be punished. The certainty factor is one of the most important variables for effective deterrence. Similarly, justice suffers when the penalties are severe.

We may give high-status people traffic tickets, but if the death penalty is involved, the powerful can muster such an effective defence that it is unlikely that they will ever be executed.

The mistakes made executing the losers would probably remain hidden."

The truth seems to be that technicalities which, in any other case, would receive short shrift, in a capital case receive anxious consideration as the judges strain to avoid invoking the extreme penalty. The views of Lord Denning, one of the most eminent of British judges, were expressed similarly to the British Royal Commission on Capital Punishment in 1950: " ... in many cases which are plainly murder," he said, "juries return verdicts of manslaughter, because they do not think the death penalty is appropriate."[78]

This conclusion is borne out by the evidence. A federal study in Canada shows that during the capital punishment years the conviction rate for manslaughter climbed dramatically, but murder convictions declined from 37.8% in 1941 to 33% in 1960.

"Nobody wants to be burdened with sending an innocent man to his death," says Dahn Bachelor, a Toronto criminologist who has presented briefs on capital punishment in the United Nations.

"Convictions are more difficult to get. And even after a death sentence there are numerous appeals and most of the people condemned don't die. It's becoming an expensive way of ensuring that very dangerous criminals have to stay behind bars for the rest of their lives."[79]

One more example, presented in the position paper of the Inter-church Task Force on Responsible Alternatives to the Death Penalty:

"Students of social history will be reminded how, in 1830, when England still had over 200 capital offences, the bankers petitioned Parliament to abolish the death penalty for the offence of forgery. The Petition recited that even the possibility of the infliction of the death penalty prevented the punishment of criminals and then prayed for "that protection to their property which they would derive from a more lenient law." Under that new, more lenient, law, convictions for forgery rose![80]

c). Murderers Commit More Violent Crimes Once Paroled

From 1977 to 1981, there were 1,344 murder and manslaughter offences across Canada. Although convicts serving their sentence on parole were responsible for less than 2% of those crimes, the public has come to believe - wrongly - that repeat offenders are common.

In fact, many of the much publicized horror stories about convicts engaging in violent crime "on parole" are really about convicts who have been released by penitentiary officials or on mandatory supervision programs, both of which are beyond the control of the Parole Board.

"We're very tough in enforcement," said Mickey Stapleton, a parole officer in Toronto. "If someone is caught drinking who has a requirement to abstain, their parole is suspended."[81]

As far as paroled murderers - to whom capital punishment might have applied - are concerned, not one of the 384 released between 1970 and 1984 murdered again.82 Between 1975 and 1986 473 convicted murderers were released on parole. Two murderers murdered a second time, both of these murderers had originally been convicted of non-capital murder.83 No murderers have been convicted of manslaughter, attempted murder or even wounding.[84]

d). Are Death Sentences Just or Arbitrary and Discriminatory

As South Carolina lawyer David Bruck notes in his article "Decisions of Death" it must be remembered that even where the death penalty exists, only a fraction of convicted murderers end up on death row: "It falls to the judicial system of each of the ... states that retain capital punishment to call the few who are to die from the many who are convicted of murder.,, What does experience tell us about the selection criteria? Bruck's extensive study shows that in the United States people are convicted because they committed murder, but they are executed "because of race, or bad luck, or both."

Capital punishment in the United States is administered chaotically or arbitrarily, and the statistics show that death sentences do tend to be meted out according to criteria that are certainly less than just. Bruck cites a 1980 study by two Northwestern University criminologists:

"What they found was that in cases where white victims had been killed, black defendants in all three states were from four to six times more likely to be sentenced to death than were white defendants. Both whites and blacks, moreover, faced a much greater danger of being executed where the murder victims were white than where the victims were black. A black defendant in Florida was thirty-seven times more likely to be sentenced to death if his victim was white than if his victim was black; in Georgia, black-on-white killings were punished by death thirty-three times more often than were black-on-black killings; and in Texas, the ratio climbed to an astounding 84 to 1. Even when Bowers and Pierce examined only those cases which the police had reported as "felony-circumstance" murders (i.e., cases involving kidnaping or rape, and thus excluding mere domestic and barroom homicides), they found that both the race of the defendant and the race of the victim appeared to produce enormous disparities in death sentences in each state." [85]

Much of the race bias is the result of prosecutorial discretion. In 1984, TIME

Magazine reported the following:

" ... clear bias remains, much attributable to prosecutorial choices. A recent study of homicide cases in Houston's Harris County is troubling. In cases where a black or Chicano had killed a white, 65% of defendants were tried for capital murder; only 25% of whites who killed a black or Chicano faced the death penalty. "I don't think it's overt racism," says University of Texas

Law Professor Ed Sherman. But prosecutors want to win, and they "perceive that a Texan jury is more likely to give the death penalty to a black who killed a white." A similar South Carolina study found an almost identical pattern..."[86]

Discrimination in the application of the death sentence is not limited to grounds of race. In the United States, as in any case in Canada, the result is very often dependent upon the quality of lawyer arguing the case:

A serious problem is the quality of legal help for murder defendants. The Texas study, conducted by the Governor's judicial council, found that three-quarters of murderers with court appointed lawyers were sentenced to death, against about a third of those represented by private attorneys.

Amsterdam, who has argued eight capital cases before the Supreme Court, contends that lawyering at the right time would save virtually everybody who is going to be executed." Scharlette Holdman, director of Florida's Clearinghouse on Criminal Justice, persuades volunteer lawyers to represent death-row inmates. "Every person sentenced to die comes from a case fraught with errors," she says. "If you're adequately represented you don't get death. It's that simple."87

The sad result of this state of affairs has been expressed well by John H. Leith of the Union Theological Seminary in Virginia:

"The persons who are finally given the death penalty are usually financially poor, powerless, sick and confused. They are frequently not the worst criminals in our society, nor are they more destructive of human order than thousands of others who escaped the death penalty.

One solid, pragmatic ground for opposing the death penalty is the arbitrariness, caprice, and human discretion that are always at work in the imposition. The result is a great selectivity that is standardless in the imposition of the death penalty, frequently rendering it upon the more pathetic rather than the more arrogant and powerful criminals. The contemporary practice of the death penalty, apart from more substantive arguments is unfair and unjust."[88]

The same biases are present in Canada and, hence, the same kind of results would likely obtain if the death penalty were re-instituted here. The comments of Arthur Maloney on this subject are worth quoting in full.

"There is another aspect that alarms me. It is the gross inequality of its application. This inequality manifests itself in a number of different ways. There is inequality in the trial judge before whom the accused appears for trial. Trial judges are human beings, different in outlook, temperament, attitude and personality. Some believe the death penalty is a necessary punishment of the law. Others have a feeling of revulsion to this kind of penalty. There can be no doubt that an accused person's chances of being acquitted of murder and convicted only of manslaughter are greater if he appears before one judge rather than before another.

There is a difference, too, in crown prosecutors. They have a difference in attitude and approach to the task they have to perform, some regarding themselves as ministers of justice with a duty to unfold the whole case for and against the accused, and others with utmost sincerity taking a totally different attitude toward their function. There can be no doubt that a man's chances of being acquitted of murder and convicted only of manslaughter can well depend on the differences in the personality of the prosecutor by whom his case is prosecuted. There is a difference, too, in the skill of counsel for the defence. Too often these capital cases are cases which are experiments for budding Blackstones who have just graduated out of law school. There can be no doubt that a man's chances of being acquitted of murder and convicted only of manslaughter or of being acquitted altogether can hinge upon the skill and experience of the counsel who defends him. These are all human variables around which a man's right to spend out the rest of his life in a prison or to die on a gallows should never, in my opinion, be permitted to hinge.

Finally, its selectivity and its discriminatory character is a factor which alarms me. In the great majority of cases the condemned men are both poor and friendless and, in my experience, in many cases they are quite alone. I detest any law or system that discriminates unfairly between the rich and the poor." [89]

As Sociologist Jim Hackler has pointed out:

"Many Canadians like to think that our courts are more just than those in-the United States. We also deceive ourselves into believing that racial prejudice is rare here. In fact, Canada's justice system shows similar biases. It is harsher on low-status members of the society than on high-status members. It is less likely that a Prime Minister's wife will be prosecuted for smoking marijuana than a lower-class juvenile.

This bias is particularly pronounced in the use of the death penalty. People with money, those who can present themselves well in court, and women have rarely been executed. We tend to execute less attractive, ill-mannered losers. In addition, our system does not like to admit that it made a mistake.

Ontario lawyers will probably remember the case of the young man who witnessed an attack on a woman and reported the crime to the police. The dead woman had some hair under her nails. An expert witness testified that these hairs were similar to the hair of the young man who reported the crime. He was convicted of the murder.

A persistent defence lawyer was convinced of the innocence of the young man and found a more qualified expert who testified that there were similarities between the hairs found on the victim and the young man, but there were also differences which made it clear that they were from two different persons. The prosecutor did not wish to reopen the case and, in order to discourage the accused, charged him with first-degree murder instead of second-degree murder when the second trial was heard. Although the young man's innocence was established in the second trial, it demonstrated that justice is not always the primary concern of those working in the system."[90]

In all death penalty cases it must be remembered that the distinction between who is executed and who is not depends not only on the crime but also on a series of recommendations and decisions made by the Prosecutor, by defence counsel, by the trial judge, by appellate judges and by politicians or clemency boards. As Amnesty International notes: "It is impossible to rule cut the possibility that somewhere along this chain of decision, a step will be taken leading to one prisoner being executed while another, having committed a similar crime in similar circumstances, is not."[91]

e). The Consequences of Mistake

There is no monetary compensation, no form of release, no kind of apology which can rectify the execution of an innocent person. Many Canadians are now familiar with the case of Donald Marshall, the Nova Scotia man who spent eleven years in prison for a murder he did not commit. Donald Marshall is testimony to the fact that our justice system is not perfect. Although Marshall was convicted of second degree murder and would not be a candidate for the death penalty under the proposed new legislation which seeks the death penalty for first degree murder, his case strongly points out that someone can be wrongfully convicted of a murder - whether it be first degree or second degree.

It is no defence to say that Marshall's was a rare case. In the first place, any execution of an innocent man is a tragedy unparalled in our society and our revulsion to the crime of murder only validates this point. In the second place, mistakes in the justice system are less rare than one might think. No one knows with certainty how many innocent persons in this country have been convicted whether for homicides or other crimes. Professor Neil Boyd, in his recent study of 120 murder cases states that 4 or 5 of those convicted were made on very little evidence of murder. They hanged. Some seemed to be clear cases of self-defence. In about 20 other cases, the evidence clearly supported a conviction on a lesser offence, such as manslaughter.[92]

In the United States a recent study on wrongful convictions for murder has produced chilling results. In the study by two university professors, Hugo Bedau and Michael Radelet, conservative criteria were used. Those considered wrongfully convicted were not persons who were convicted of murder and after new trials were found not guilty by reason of insanity or guilty of a lesser offence or acquitted because they acted in self-defence.

These were convicted persons who were not legally or physically responsible for the homicide. Lawyer Michael Bolton summed up this study in part as follows:

"In a study by Professor Hugo Adam Bedau of Tufts University in Massachusetts and Michael L. Radelet of the University of Florida, released at a recent meeting of the American Society of Criminology, the authors identify 343 clear cases of persons wrongfully convicted of a capital offence between 1900 and 1985. This amounts to an average of 38 wrongful capital convictions in the United States per decade. Twenty-five innocent people were executed and others came within a short time, even hours, of being executed. Many others spent lengthy terms in prison, some as long as 25 years."[93]

Lawyer Michael Bolton has examined this study and reports the following:

"The conservatively-chosen raw data reveal that one-half of one percent of the total number of executions in the U.S. this century had been erroneous. Comparing the erroneous convictions to the number of actual executions, the authors find that the rate of error is equivalent to one definite erroneous conviction for a potentially capital crime for every 20 executions.

Putting this together with the possibility that defense lawyers, prosecutors, jurors, judges and appeal courts are more demanding of certainly in capital cases, the figures yield a disturbing inference of occasional error in our criminal justice system. The authors' point, of course, is that all this confirms the need to abolish capital punishment."

Bolton also notes that:

"Nineteen of the 343 cases are "close calls", in which execution was nearly carried out but was averted within a day or two, perhaps by a few hours, and in half a dozen cases there was less than an hour to spare."94

3.6. CRIME & CRIMINALS

There appears to be a widespread belief that the rise in the rate of crime, of any kind, is somehow related to the abolition of the death penalty. The resultant pleas for capital punishment are based upon the notion that the existence of the death penalty will somehow send a message to all criminals that their criminal antics will not be tolerated in our society. In some cases, such as with mass murderers or with terrorists, it is felt that certain crimes can only adequately be dealt with by means of capital punishment. As we shall see below, this kind of thinking not only reveals an unfortunate ignorance with regard to the causes of crime but also with regard to the most effective ways of dealing with crime.

a). Crime Occurs Because Criminals Need Not Fear for Their Lives

Arthur Maloney may have said it best when he said this:

"The death penalty is not the answer to the problem of crime and of criminals. Crime has its cause and crime has its cure. Its causes are clear. They can be stated like the litany: they are slums, they are broken homes; they are poverty; they are drunkenness, divorce, lack of opportunity, lack of education. These are the causes of crime. As a lawyer, day after day, I see far too often, and still see far too often, in far too many cases those factors, or some of those factors, or a combination of all those factors. Those factors are the cause of crime; they are the common denominator in a great majority of cases that come before our courts from coast to coast day after day."95

Variations on this statement have been repeated countless numbers of times by sociologists, criminologists, psychologists, psychiatrists and many others who have undertaken to study crime and criminals.

Despite this often heard truth, people continue to waste their best efforts trying to revive capital punishment instead of trying to get at the major causes of crime and work at its actual diminution. The following statement was made by Mr. Jim Manly, a Member of Parliament, during debate of a bill whose sole effective purpose was the execution of mass-killer Clifford Olson:

"It was revealing that when the news of the Olson murders first broke several years ago, a psychologist pointed out that there were five or six young people, children, in British Columbia at that time who, he believed, had the potential to act in the same manner as Clifford Olson. He was saying this at the same time that British Columbia was shutting down facilities to help such children.

Why are we not demanding diagnostic or treatment facilities for children in crisis so that they have some possibility of growing up and living normal and decent lives? We have to attack this kind of problem at its roots instead of waiting until we have a crisis, saying that we will take the life of a person we all find objectionable and feeling that somehow we are dealing with the problem."[96]

Psychiatrists tell us that those who were abused as children are more likely to become child abusers themselves when they become parents. When they were children our hearts went out to them or the trauma they had suffered and for what such abuse must have done to their minds. Yet when they become what we knew they had a good chance of becoming - child abusers, even child killers - we want their death. Would not the time, energy and expense spent on trying to restore the death penalty be better used and more satisfying in trying to identify and cure the mentally disturbed?

By concentrating on capital punishment as a kind of crime cure-all, we tend to neglect less extreme legislation that effectively curtails crime. At a recent meeting of the Canadian Association of Chiefs of Police, Anthony Bouza, chief of the Minneapolis police department, made it clear that one of the major causes of violent death in the United States is the prevalence of handguns. Some 20,000 people will die this year by handguns, notwithstanding the American death penalty. There are 70 million handguns in American homes today: there will be 100 million by the end of the decade. Bouza made it clear where police priorities should lie today.

"Hang on with all your might to your tough handgun restrictions" he said. "Ours is a national disgrace."[97]

b). We Need Capital Punishment to Curb Violent Crime and to Make Canada Safer

The truth is that there is no evidence that shows that the death penalty has any effect on violent crime. In fact, the lowest murder rates are usually found in those countries and states where the death penalty has been abolished for a long time ¬- in the United Kingdom, Sweden, Austria, Italy, Minnesota, Wisconsin and Maine.

Consider the following excerpt from the Statement of the Solicitor General of Canada on the Abolition of Capital Punishment May 3, 1976:

"In a recent article published in the journal Crime and Delinquency, Daniel Glaser and Max S. Zeigler have examined possible explanations for the fact that the American states which have historically used executions most are the same ones which have the highest murder rates. Their concluding paragraph is worthy of very careful consideration by all Honourable Members:

"Demands that capital punishment be restored are raised whenever the public is outraged at a particularly heinous and highly publicized killing, but the geographic facts presented here suggest that this 'gut response' is counter-productive as a means of reducing the prevalence of murder. The evidence shows that where use of the death penalty is most frequent, there is less long-run outrage against killers than prevails in states that forbid any murder, whether by private parties or by the government. The alternatives to violence are, in addition to a respect for the sacredness of life, the many civilized procedures and practices of analyzing, negotiating, legally adjudicating, or simply tolerating disagreements. All of these alternatives are impaired or impeded rather than nurtured when the government resorts to the murderer's methods."

If this conclusion is correct - that the carrying out of executions by the state not only does not prevent murders, but actually may serve to create or maintain a climate where more murders and more violence exist - then the argument that the death penalty is a justifiable and fitting punishment in our society in order to show our outrage against murder must be seen to be empty, and dangerous rhetoric.

If we are to show our disapproval of killing, then we cannot support killing in society's name .....

... The death penalty cannot be shown to be a deterrent to murder any more effective in protecting the public than is a long sentence of incarceration."[98]

If anything then, state sponsored death under the guise of capital punishment is liable to increase, rather than decrease societal violence. Consider the words of Archbishop William Temple from his sermon on "The Ethics of Punishment":

"I believe Jeremy Bentham was perfectly right when he laid it down that the main influence of the State should be exercised always on the side of the limitation of penalties, as any form of excessive punishment defeated its own aim in that it encouraged a callousness in people by the very violence of the suffering inflicted, and thus did more harm by lowering the public impression of the accepted standard of treatment of citizens than it did good by its deterrence. I suggest that the defense of the death penalty has always been based in the main on its deterrent power and I believe that the example of the State taking life even when it only does so in return for a life already taken, does more to lower the value of human life in the minds of its citizens than the deterrent influence of this penalty can do to protect the lives of the citizens. In this way, I believe that the main influence of the retention of the death penalty is rather to increase than diminish the number of murders."[99]

"The real benefit of the death penalty," says Amnesty International's Larry Cox, "which is not a benefit to society but to a few of the people who are in charge of running the society, is that it gives the appearance of doing something about violent crime without having to touch in any way the basic structures and relations in the society which might actually/ have something to do with violent crime."[100]

Anyone who believes that they would feel safer with the death penalty in place should ask themselves if they would feel safer in places where the death penalty actually exists. Is it actually safer in New York, Los Angeles, Iran, South Africa or the U.S.S.R.?

As was stated in the Toronto Star, "there is no country in the world in which a death penalty, unsupported by severe political and military oppression, has proved effective in braking an escalating homicide rate."[101]

For reasons more thoroughly discussed in the section on DETERRENCE, above, the death penalty could not have an appreciable impact on violence because of the situations where violence tends to occur. Murder and violence do not always happen on the "mean streets". In Canada, about one-third of all murders occur within domestic relationships and another roughly third are within social or business relationships.102 Because most murders are obviously committed in emotional circumstances, fear of execution is not a factor in the perpetrator's mind. The other major factor to be considered in this argument is whether Canada has in fact become so violent that our safety might depend on something so extreme as the death penalty. Statistics suggest that much of the fear driving the rush toward the death penalty is either exaggerated or needlessly alarmist.

The first thing to be remembered is that homicides are not actually increasing. Murders may get all the publicity but between 1975 and 1984 there was an annual average of only 2.78 homicides for every 100,000 Canadians. Of course, any homicide is a great tragedy but compare this figure with the 14 suicides and 20 motor vehicle deaths annually for every 100,000 people during the same period.[103]

The public perceives violence as being a major part of crime, but in fact, recent statistics show that violent crimes account for less than 8% of all crimes in Canada.104 Homicides are even rarer, comprising less than 0.5% of violent crimes in Canada.[105]

c). Mass Murderers

It is thought by some that if society were only to bring back capital punishment for some very limited purpose, it would be for the execution of mass murderers.

The problem with such a narrow application of the death penalty is that it cannot possibly adequately address the very concerns such action would hope to address. The execution of a mass murderer could in no way relieve Canadians of their fears in general or lessen the grief or remove the anguish of the families of the victims.

One of the other major problems with such a law is one of definition. When does a murderer become a mass murderer and how do we justify the distinction. In December of 1984 a bill was introduced in Parliament which called for the execution of murderers of ten or more victims. Vince Della Noce M.P., in the course of his criticism, said the following:

"Murderers convicted of killing at least 10 people certainly deserve a particularly severe penalty and unequivocal condemnation of their actions which I would describe as savage. There is no question about the panic caused by a series of murders in a community or of the anguish suffered by the families of victims. However, by what logic would these murderers be condemned to death while others who have committed actions just as monstrous, such as nine murders, would be spared?"[106]

According to a new study by Statistics Canada those who kill more than once is a rarity in this country. Between 1962 and 1985, 93% of all murderers killed only once, 5% killed twice and 11 (0.1%) killed six or more.[107]

d). Terrorists

There are a number of reasons why the death penalty may be a particularly inappropriate method of dealing with terrorism.

The first, of course, is one of definition. It is now trite to say that one man's terrorist is another man's freedom fighter. Similarly, what some consider to be necessary military counterinsurgency actions others see as state terrorism. In many countries yesterday's generals and heads of state are today's terrorists. The confusion goes on and on.

But let us assume that society is capable of agreeing on who ¬at least in this country is a terrorist and who is not. The death penalty is still not the appropriate method for stopping terrorism. Indeed, it is likely to increase it.

This very question was dealt with by the British parliament during the capital punishment re-introduction debate in 1983. The eminent French newspaper Le Monde approved of the approach of the British Commons:

"Terrorism, too, was a prominent issue in the debate on hanging. Some ministers, including Northern Ireland Secretary James Prior, had quite clearly seen the hazards of trying to combat terrorism by applying the death penalty. There was a moral danger should a great democracy resort to the expeditive and barbarous methods used by its enemies? But the political risk was no less. The execution of terrorists would, of course, have provided the IRA, INLA, and other armed organizations in both Northern Irish communities with ready-made martyrs. And martyrs are invaluable for drumming up support.

The terrorists in Northern Ireland realized this full well; just a few hours before the House of Commons was due to re-examine the question of capital punishment, they carried out a terrible act of provocation which cost the lives of four part-time soldiers near Belfast."[108]

Certain Ulstermen could see the folly of attempting to combat terrorism with death:

"The ARCHDEACON OF NOTTINGHAM (the Ven. R.K. Williamson) said that, as an Ulsterman, he would regard the reintroduction of capital punishment as catastrophic. The situation in Northern Ireland would not be helped one iota by the introduction of another form of violence.

So much of the violence in Ulster fed on memories of the past, and it was those memories that needed healing. To reintroduce the death penalty would produce a new crop of martyrs and build up more bitter memories on which future violence would feed."[109]

The comments of Amnesty International's Eric Prokosch also illustrate the wisdom of the British Parliament for not instituting the death penalty for terrorists:

"Opposition fighters would not be deterred by the

death penalty", they said. Ten prisoners belonging to violent opposition groups had fasted to death in 1981, and their deaths had gained publicity and money for their organizations. To execute such men would be to create revolutionary martyrs around whose memory stronger opposition would be rallied. "Ireland would burn the moment the first person died," one former minister said.

Introducing the death penalty for "terrorist" killings would mean conferring political status on something which the British Government had always intentionally treated as a purely criminal act. There would be the difficult legal problem of defining the word "terrorism". There would be the anomaly, as with other attempts to define categories of capital offence, of implying that "terrorist" murders were more atrocious than others. There would be the risk that opposition arouses would have assassinations carried out by children, who would escape execution because of their youth. There would be the risk of hostage-taking in reprisal. And there would be the very real problem of obtaining convictions."[110]

3.7. THE POLICE:

a). We Need Capital Punishment for Police Killers Because the Police Require Special Protection

Actually, a number of police officers, themselves, would disagree. In his "viewpoint" Criminal Lawyers' Association President Earl J. Levy, Q.C. has said the following:

"It is notable that the cry for restoration of the death penalty seems to receive its greatest impetus when police officers are killed. I have talked with a number of police officers who feel that their lives should not be treated as more valuable than, for example, their wives and children. They have taken their job knowing and accepting its risks, they are paid for it (perhaps not enough) and are trained to defend themselves."[111]

Indeed, Chief of Police Robert Lunney of Edmonton has said: "The Canadian police community has never been of the opinion that capital punishment should be an option reserved only for the killing of police officers or correctional guards."112 As Dalhousie law professor Wagner McKay put it: "Police are on the line but do we want to say that a policeman's life is worth more than someone else's?"[113]

In truth, a police officer is statistically safer than a firefighter, a miner, a sailor or virtually any other employment that has an "element of risk in it". [114]

In 1985, professors James Hackler and Christian Jansen published a study on police killings between 1961 and 1981. After presenting their statistical data they concluded as follows:

"Policemen appear to face a higher risk of homicide than the comparable group of males aged 20 to 49 in the population at large. However, studies of public attitudes do not indicate a growing hostility toward the police; on the contrary there is a danger that the police may mis-perceive public opinion and overreact to the killings. While the data presented above does not necessarily sup-port the "contagion" hypothesis, they are consistent with it. Over-dramatization of these events may in fact influence the least stable and most irrational elements in our population and stimulate those behaviors that we hope to avoid." [115]

The general conclusion then was that it is in fact safer to be a policeman in Canada today than it was 20 years ago.[116]

The other significant factor to consider is the non-deterrent value of capital punishment. An examination of the killings of police officers in the last two years reveals that capital punishment would not have saved the policemen's lives.

This was-expressed in a 1984 Toronto Star editorial:

"It's hard to see how the existence of capital punishment would have saved the lives of any of the three officers who died recently.

If the man who engaged in a shoot-out with Constable Dunmore and other officers ¬and who ultimately was fatally shot himself wasn't deterred by the prospect of immediate death at the hands of armed and trained policemen, it seems unlikely he would have been deterred by the more remote prospect of future death by hanging.

The man who stabbed Peel Regional Police Constable Dwayne Piukkala to death last month subsequently used the constable's gun to commit suicide. The threat of capital punishment clearly would have been irrelevant in his case.

And it seems safe to assume that whoever shot York Regional Police Constable Douglas Tribbling while he was investigating a burglary last month was thinking in terms of escape, not the consequences of capture. Indeed various studies have indicated that most killings are committed either by people acting in the heat of passion without regard to the consequences, or by people who expect to evade being caught and paying the consequences."[117]

"Ironically" wrote the Star's Trish Crawford, "it is the civilian present during a crime who is much more likely to be murdered by a criminal. The variety store owner, bank teller, shopper and innocent bystander is 10 times more likely to be killed.

Between 1961 and 1974, crooks in Canada killed 53 police officers while on their crime sprees, but they also murdered 55 citizens."[118]

The archetypal police killer is hardly influenced by the possibility of capital punishment, in part because he tends to be suicidal. "Suicide and murder are both parts of the same destructive violent package, the experts say," Crawford wrote. Dr. Fred Jensen, clinical director of the Metro Toronto Forensic Center operating out of the Queen Street Mental Health Center added that confronting a police officer violently "is an easy way to commit suicide. Its a reasonable idea that the police will respond. The person knows that the police shoot to kill, not to maim." [119]

Death is not a deterrent to such men, it's a positive incentive.

One of the policemen shot in 1984 was killed by a man dressed as Sylvester Stallone in the film First Blood. He was apparently obsessed with the film and viewed it over and over. In the same week as the shooting a U.S. psychologist told a Toronto conference: "Commercial cinema and T.V. violence have the power to teach both children and adults how to commit violence. Repeated violence viewing in films clearly incites some viewers to engage in violent behavior." [120]

If death penalty advocates are really concerned about growing violence, one must aware why they are not agitating for increased research into the effects of media violence. Again, are efforts being made in the wrong place?

b). Police Killings Since Abolition: Statistics

It may surprise some people to know that notwithstanding the rash of police killings in 1984, there were more police killed when the penalty for such was death than after the abolition of capital punishment.

"From 1967 to 1976," wrote Earl Levy, "Canada experimented with a partial ban on hanging, restricting the capital punishment option to judges sentencing persons for killing policemen and prison guards. But in the five years before Parliament's abolition decision there were 19 police killings, compared to 18 in the subsequent five-year period."121 Thus, it could hardly be said that more police died as a result of the decision to abolish the death penalty.

If we compare the number of policemen killed with the total number of officers on Canadian police forces, we find that since 1962 there has actually been a general decline in the number of policemen killed through criminal acts in the line of duty per 1000 of police force. It is also interesting to note that this downtrend in the number of policemen murdered per 1000 of police force has occurred during the same period as an increase in the number of homicides generally. In their analysis of these statistics, James Hackler and Christian Janssen observe: "The findings suggest ... that the police may actually be experiencing falling homicide rates while the population at large is experiencing rising rates."[122]

In an October, 1984 Globe and Mail article, the following information was given:

"The statistics show that 11 Canadian police officers were killed in 1962, and six were slain in both 1974 and 1978. Five officers died in 1968, as well as in 1969, 1973, 1977,and 1981.

The 86 policemen killed in Canada in the 23 years since StatsCan began keeping records of police homicides pales in comparison to the 79 slain in the United States in 1982 alone.

A Canadian policeman's chance of being killed on duty is about six times greater than that of most civilians, but is less than that of a miner, a construction worker, a farmer or someone working for a transportation company or public utility.

About 18 per cent of police slayers subsequently took their own lives, leading criminologists to believe they possess a death wish."[123]

The yearly average for police murders in Canada is 3.5. Despite considerable growth in the number of police, this number has remained very stable over the years. From 1961 to 1970, 36 police officers were wilfully killed. From 1971-1980, the number was 37. The highest number over this period was 11, and occurred in 1962, when the death penalty was still in effect, and executions were still being carried out. This constant figure must also be perceived in light of the growing crime rate over the period.

From statistics available from Statistics Canada, one can compare the number of police officers per 100,000 people to the average rate of 3.3 police murders per year from 1960-1980, and see that while police murders remained fairly constant, the number of officers went from 143.6 per 100,000 in 1960 to 222.4 per 100,000 in 1979. In addition we can compare the number of police murders to the crime rate, which increased from 5,211.9 criminal acts per 100,000 people in 1970 to 8,307.4 in 1980. In comparing these figures, the number of police murders in relation to criminal acts and police officers at risk has decreased.[124]

Statistics Canada reports that 38 police officers were murdered in Canada between 1966 and 1975 compared to 37 in the ten years after the death penalty was abolished. During this period of 20 years the number of police officers almost doubled.[125]

Statistics Canada reports that in 1986, four police officers were slain, consistent with the average over the past decade.

c). The Police Want Capital Punishment and They Know Crime Better

Do they really? Or should we accept that they are human beings like the rest of us and tend to speak out - particularly when some of their brethren are killed - on the basis of emotionalism and-not on the basis of knowledge. In February of 1985 John Gault put it this way:

"What the reborn capital punishers have managed to do is manipulate people's perceptions. Consider, for example, the comments of York Regional Police Chief Bruce Crawford at the funeral of a young officer killed October 9, the sixth policeman to be killed in seven weeks. "Many crosses will have to be borne by those who have sat idle during the past years and watched this beautiful Canada of ours descend into the scandalous state of lawlessness we see today," is what Crawford said. "York Chief rakes lawless Canada"' was the headline for the Sun's story. "Spate of deaths 'national disgrace' mourners told," said the Star."

Citizen Crawford has the right to any opinion he wants to hold, and so does Police Chief Crawford. But it seems to me that Police Chief Crawford has an added responsibility, which is to support his opinion with facts. But he chose not to, and the reason he chose not to, I suggest, is that the facts do not support that opinion. There is simply no evidence whatsoever that Canada has descended into a state of lawlessness, scandalous or otherwise, over the past seventeen years - since capital punishment was officially abolished for all murders save those of police and prison guards. (Abolition became total in 1976). One can only assume that the chief was deliberately rabble-rousing, a questionable pursuit for one in his ;profession, and that the reporters were either too ill-informed or too complicitous to call him out on it."[126]

Shortly after Metro Toronto Police Officer David Dunmore was shot on September 19, 1984, police began their calls for the death penalty. Paul Walter, the president of the Metro Toronto Police Association said the reinstitution of the death penalty was a necessary step to protect society.

He said this notwithstanding the fact that figures from Statistics Canada indicated that the murder rate for police officers had declined since the early 1960s and has shown no increase since the abolition of the death penalty.[127]

Indeed, the police have called for the death penalty at times knowing full well that it would not have prevented the deaths of their comrades.

At the funeral described by John Gault, above, Police Chief Crawford also said that the death penalty may not have prevented recent police killings but it is the "only appropriate punishment. 128 He gave no reasons as to why the death penalty was the "only appropriate punishment".

In fact, it seemed like a particularly inappropriate punishment in the case of the officer at whose funeral Crawford was speaking, because the killer had shot himself with the officer's service revolver after he drove into the officer's cruiser.

Police have had a tendency to automatically assume that the death penalty as a deterrent to murders of policemen even though all evidence points to the contrary conclusion. Referring to the refusal of the federal Progressive Conservative government to reopen the debate on capital punishment, Paul Walter said: "They are procrastinating as police officers are dying. The responsibility for some of the deaths may rest on their shoulders."[129]

Well, it is apparent that not even the Canadian Association of Chiefs of Police believe that any more. At their last conference during the summer of 1986 the association concluded that it could no longer argue for the death penalty on the basis of deterrence. The evidence simply could not support such an argument. Unfortunately, they have not dropped their demand for the death penalty. But not as "a gesture of revenge; it is based upon a moral imperative" said Moncton Chief Greg Cohoon, the association's current President. 5 We must now ask ourselves; on what factual basis is a moral imperative derived? Indeed, in what way can the purposeful killing of a human being ever be characterized as stemming from a moral imperative?

3.8. RETRIBUTION:

Retribution is really a nicer way of saying 'revenge'. This section deals with arguments that capital punishment should be reinstated so that society may properly take revenge upon the murderer for what she/he has done.

a). Retribution is Society's Right

The first question one might ask is: "what kind of a society do we want to live in?" And do we want to live in a society where retribution is considered a right. Consider societies where it is.

Criminal Lawyers' Association President, Earl Levy has put it this way:

"Retribution and vengeance should not be what motivates a civilized society. Retribution and vengeance are the handmaidens of terrorists and the underworld; retribution and vengeance are ever present in the penitentiaries where we continually hear of prisoners killing each other. Has our society become so desensitized to killing that we are prepared to emulate the lowest elements of our society?"[130]

Former Prime Minister Pierre Trudeau asked essentially the same question during the Commons abolition debate in June of 1976:

"Are we, as a society, so lacking in respect for ourselves, so lacking in hope for human betterment, so socially bankrupt that we are ready to accept state vengeance as our penal philosophy? ...To retain (capital punishment) in the Criminal Code of Canada would be to abandon reason in favour of vengeance; to abandon hope and confidence in favor of a despairing acceptance of our inability to cope with violent crime except with violence."[131]

One of the major problems with revenge is that it is a human dead end. "What revenge brings into the world," wrote Jack Costello, "is simply a heaping of injury upon injury with no break in the cycle, without any healing of the basic hurt."

Costello goes on to point out that it is commonly believed that those who really require retribution are the families and close friends. But as Rev. Thomas Daily of St. Augustine's Seminary in Toronto observed: "What they need is friendship and solace and the healing power of time - not the death of another human being." [132]

Some people base their claim on the right to retribution upon the principle of restitution or compensation. But as Albert N. Wells observes, "Clearly, there can never be total compensation for, say, a life that has been taken away by violence. But simply demanding the offender's life in return does nothing to improve the situation. It cannot bring any degree of good out of what clearly was an evil act." [133]

Pastor Wells then went on to say:

"Many of our attitudes and policies only aggravate our common problems. Capital punishment, for example, simply perpetuates violence under the name of what some would call "justice." But it is a poor justice indeed. In fact, capital punishment actually prevents justice being carried in the fuller, more adequate sense we have described. When we carry out the death penalty, we only create another victim, with all the attendant agony and horror that families of "capital" crimes already know. Who will be advocates for the families of the people upon whom we corporately visit the violence? We all shall be responsible. Our hands all will be on the switch."[134]

b). Only Death Will be Appropriate Retribution for Murder

Let us assume for a moment that, notwithstanding any of the foregoing, we still feel justified in exacting at least some retribution from the offender. We must then ask ourselves whether or not capital punishment is appropriate. By its use, are we in fact exacting an amount of revenge equal to the crime the offender committed? Or are we taking more and are thereby exacting more than revenge.

Consider that the condemned convict, unlike his or her original victim, spends every waking moment contemplating his or her impending and certain violent death. The wait may be years. No victim has had to undergo such torment. Speaking about such condemned men, Arthur Maloney said: "These men have died a thousand deaths. They suffer more torment and torture than was ever meted out by any murderer to his victim."[134]

Indeed, the torture may not end with the actual execution. The only form of capital punishment ever used in Canada is hanging.

From Maclean's:

"Since Confederation, there have been more than 700 hangings in Canada - the only method of legal execution ever used in the country - and not all of them were swift and efficient. In some cases hangmen have miscalculated to the point where condemned persons have strangled or, as in the case of Thomasina Sarac, who was 40 lb. heavier than the hangman expected at her 1935 execution in Montreal, were decapitated. Indeed, hanging may be one of the most cruel and drawn-out forms of legal execution used in modern times. [135]

We must also ask whether a life sentence isn't just as harsh for the offender as execution. If it is, then the execution is not required, not even for the purpose of revenge. A moment's thought should reveal that imprisonment for life without parole eligibility for the next 25 years is as harsh a punishment as anyone could imagine having to undergo.

c). Murderers Should Get Their "Just Desserts"

What people who say this kind of thing in relation to the death penalty often mean is that murderers should receive exactly the same treatment they meted out to their victims. Although this may sound logical in theory it soon becomes ridiculous when we attempt to apply such a rule as part of our criminal justice system. Are we to start running over dangerous drivers, assaulting muggers, burning down arsonists' homes and vandalizing the homes of vandals?

An often heard corollary to this argument, however, is that murderers are especially liable to extreme retribution because they simply 'deserve' to die. They deserve to die because they have committed acts which put them outside of the human race. Being something other than a human being, the condemned murderer is not entitled to human rights.

The problem is that history has shown us that we embark on a rather dangerous route when society begins declaring which of its members are people and deserving of basic human rights and which members are deemed to be no longer deserving of such rights.

This kind of distinction is of paramount concern to groups opposing torture and promoting human rights such as Amnesty International:

" ... because governments are always telling us that it is not that they are torturing, or "disappearing" or locking up people; they are torturing, "disappearing" and locking up terrorists, or communists, or counter-revolutionaries or CIA agents, people who because of their acts should no longer be treated as part of the human race. Those governments do not like to be reminded that the very meaning of human rights is that they are inalienable. Human rights are not awards given by governments for good behavior, and they cannot be taken away from people for bad behavior. But it is simply difficult to kill or torture people if you regard them as being human, if you see some shared humanity."136

In North America, we are told that those who ought to be killed by the state are not really people - they are monsters, or they are animals, or they are cancers which have to be cut out of the social body. But should the analysis end there? Again, from Amnesty International's Larry Cox:

"The people on death row in the United States have in fact committed -- many of them, most of them -- terrible acts of cruelty that ought to be condemned. It doesn't do any good -- in fact, I would submit that it does a lot of harm -- to romanticize who those people are, or to somehow cover up the horrible cruelties that they have committed. But it is not an objection to romanticism or sentimentality that explains the outrage which is directed so often against anyone who tries to point out that the people, the lives of the people on death row cannot be summed up in one single act that they have committed; that the people on death row have histories, and that those histories predate what they have done; and that those histories often show that they themselves were the victims of abuse and neglect by society long before they committed the acts for which the society now proposes to kill them. The reason that line of argument is so offensive to people is because it reminds them that these are in fact people. And again, it is very hard to kill someone when you are reminded that he or she is a human being." [137]

3.9. PUNISHMENT:

a). Only Through Severe Punishment Will We Stop Crime

When we are not trying to deter criminals - either specifically or generally - we are trying to punish them. While the merits of punishment as an effective method of dealing with crime has been debated numerous times, it remains fairly clear that our criminal justice system is not exclusively concerned with punishment. Treatment and rehabilitation are certainly important interests within the criminal justice system.

Nonetheless, advocates of capital punishment often concentrate on punishment alone as being the sole goal and raison d'etre of criminal justice. The death penalty thus appears reasonable as being the ultimate punishment for the ultimate crime. But there is a problem with the basic premise of this argument because it is the height of social naivete to believe that punishment in and of itself is effective in dealing with crime and criminals.

Lawyer Arthur Maloney had made this clear in remarks given upon his receiving the John Howard Society's Award for Distinguished Humanitarian Service from the Lieutenant-

Governor, John Aird in 1982. The remarks were reported in the John Howard Society Newsletter:

"Mr. Maloney maintains that the most critical concern in criminal justice continues to be the popular belief that all criminal misconduct must be answered by penalties and punishment without regard to the causes of crime and criminality. He said we must give up the myth that very crime must be punished and work at alleviating the social causes of crime - ¬poverty, lack of education, lack of opportunity. He is convinced that a more sophisticated, more realistic and more common sense approach to the causes of human misbehavior would result in a great advancement in solving the problems of crime." 138

It is said by some, that only through punishment does the offender recognize the evil of his misdeeds and the sanctity of life. But, as Walter MacLean, M.P. now a member of the federal government, once pointed out:

"... capital punishment degrades life and thereby facilitates murder. The abolition of the death penalty lifts life to a higher plane - even the life of a criminal - and gives him and us the incentive to respect ourselves and others; for the person who cannot respect himself will seldom respect others." 139

It is, in this context, instructive to have regard to this statement of Sir Christopher Ewart-Biggs:

"... In my view it should be the responsibility of a civilized society to contain the destructive elements within it without resorting to similar methods. This whilst striving through social reform to eradicate the root causes of crimes and violence. We must judge the criminal, condemn and isolate him, but not emulate him....."[140]

b). Capital Punishment Isn't Murder, It's Punishment

Capital punishment is the intentional killing of a human being and is therefore, by definition, murder. Nonetheless, some people believe that murder by the state is somehow better - is even justified - because it is done to punish one who has already murdered.

Punishment carries with it an aura of moral supremacy. The state punishes the offender to make it clear that the offender has transgressed the state's moral code. It punishes killers to demonstrate that killing is wrong. It is correct in doing so, say the advocates of the death penalty, even if it kills as a punishment and thereby transgresses its own moral code - in the name of which it claims the right to punish.

But capital punishment, observes U.S. lawyer Joel Berger, attempts to vindicate one murder by committing a second murder. And the second murder is more reprehensible because it is officially sanctioned and done with great ceremony in the name of us all." TIME Magazine's Kurt Andersen went on to add:

"Not simply just as bad, but worse: this may be the central emotional truth for those who most passionately disapprove of executions. The cretinous killer or the seething psychopath is a loose cannon. But the well-orchestrated modern execution, careful, and thoroughly considered, is horrible because of its meticulous sanity. Executions are worse, in the abolitionists moral scheme, because the government is always in control: it knows better, but kills anyway."[141]

3.10. COST:

a). It Costs Too Much to Keep Murderers Alive

In the first place, a society which decides who shall live and who shall die on the basis of money considerations is a very inhuman and dehumanized society indeed.

In the second place, capital punishment is not as cheap a process as its advocates would have us believe. The existence of execution as a penalty means that any and all appeal procedures will have to be exhausted. It also means that the initial determination of whether or not the ultimate sanction is to be imposed makes for an exceedingly meticulous, and therefore expensive, trial.

The U.S. experience, as David Brock pointed out, shows us that imprisoning convicts for life may actually be a bargain for the taxpayers when compared with the costs of adding capital punishment to our justice system:

"So far, the power of the death penalty as a social symbol has shielded from scrutiny the huge demands in money and resources which the death sentencing process makes on the criminal justice system as a whole. Whatever the abstract merits of capital punishment, there is no denying that a successful death penalty prosecution costs a fortune. A 1982 ¬study in New York state concluded that just the trial and first stage of appeal in a death penalty case under that state's proposed death penalty bill would cost the taxpayers of New York over $1.8 million - more than twice as much as imprisoning the defendant for life. And even that estimate does not include the social costs of diverting an already overburdened criminal justice system from its job of handling large numbers of criminal cases to a preoccupation with the relative handful of capital ones." [142]

This subject was also analyzed in TIME:

"The careful legal course demanded by the Supreme Court is expensive. Last year the New York State Defenders Association estimated the trial costs for a typical capital punishment case: a defense bill of $176,000, about $845,000 for the prosecution and court costs of $300,000. The total: $1.5 million, and this before any appeal is filed. Getting a writ before the Supreme Court, just one appellate step, might cost $170,000.

It is often argued, with blithe inhumanity, that there are good fiscal reasons for executing murderers: prison is too costly. It is cheaper to send a student to Stanford for a year than it is to keep a con in nearby San Quentin ($10,000 vs. $20,000). But imprisoning one inmate for 50 years would require less than $1 million in New York, not bad compared with the costs of the painstaking appeal process."[143]

NOTES

* This paper was summarised by Earl Levy, President of the Criminal Lawyers' Association

1. Capital Punishment - Handout Fact Sheet.

2. "Hanging", MacLean's, Oct. 8, 1984.

3. John Howard Society of Ontario Newsletter.

4. Toronto Daily Star, Oct. 14, 1984.

5. N.Y. Times, Feb. 3, 1985.

6. Globe & Mail, Dec. 13, 1984.

7. TIME Magazine, Jan. 24, 1983.

8. Maclean's Magazine, March 16, 1987.

9. Toronto Daily Star, Jan. 27, 1985.

10. Globe & Mail, Sept. 27, 1984.

11. Methodist Recorder, July 7, 1983.

12. Task Force Position Paper, Winter, 1980.

13. Op.Cit. (9).

14. President's Viewpoint.

15. Macleans, Oct. 8, 1984.

16. Ibid.

17. Maclean's, Oct. 8, 1984.

18. John Howard Society of Ont. Newsletter.

19. Arthur Maloney, House of Commons debates (Hansard) Feb. 18, 1960.

20. TIME, Jan. 24, 1983.

21. Quoted in "The Death Penalty" (London, The Spectator 154 (Jan. 25, 1935) (111-2).

22. "Viewpoint" Brampton Guardian Oct. 3, 1984.

23. "Decisions of Death" by David Bruck, Dec. 12, 1983.

24. Madean's, Oct. 8, 1984.

25. Amnesty International, Speech, June 23, 1984.

26. Amnesty International, Declaration of Stockholm, 11 Dec., 1977.

27. Toronto Star, April 19, 1986.

28. HANGMAN A Study Resource Kit prepared by The Committee on Outreach and Corporate Witness, The Presbyterian Church in Canada.

29. The Bible Speaks to You, Robert McAfee Brown.

30. Archbishop William Temple, "The Ethics of Punishment", John Howard Anniversary Sermon.

31. Rev. J.A. Davidson, Ottawa Citizen - Jan. 5, 1985.

32. Ibid. Source (2).

33. John Leith, "Theological Reflections on the Death Penalty".

34. Dr. Richard Devor, Catholic New Times, Oct. 22, 1978.

35. HANGMAN Resource Kit, Presbyterian Church in Canada.

36. Costello, "Can a Christian Support Capital Punishment, Catholic New Times, Oct. 22, 1978.

37. Church Times (England), July 15, 1983.

38. Quoted by Costello, in (2) supra.

39. TIME, January 24, 1983.

40. Macleans, Oct. 8, 1984.

41. Toronto Star, April 19, 1986.

42. Inter-church Task Force for the Continued Abolition of the Death Penalty, Position Paper.

43. Methodist Recorder, July 7, 1983 (England).

44. lbid, (3) supra.

45. Toronto Star, June 21, 1986.

46. House of Commons debates, Feb. 18, 1960.

47. TIME, January 24, 1983.

48. Ibid.

49. House of Commons debates, Dec. 13, 1984.

50. TIME Magazine, January 24, 1983.

51. Commons Abolition Debate, March 23, 1966 quoted in Macleans, October 8, 1984.

52. Whig-Standard, Dec. 4, 1984.

53. Toronto Star, Oct. 14, 1984.

54. Ibid.

55. "Can a Christian Support Capital Punishment" Catholic New Times. Oct. 22, 1978.

56. TIME, January 24, 1983.

57. Maclean's, Oct. 8, 1984.

58. Brampton Guardian, Viewpoint, Oct. 3, 1984.

59. TIME, January 24, 1983.

60. The Lesson of the Scaffold by David D. Cooper, p. 79 published by Allen Lane.

61. HANGMAN Study Resource on Capital Punishment, Fact Sheet.

62. Position paper, Inter-church Task Force for the Continued Abolition of the Death Penalty.

63. Historical Homicide Data and Other Data Relevant to Capital Punishment Issue.

64. TIME, January 24, 1983.

65. Rubel, "Notes on the Death Penalty".

66. Maclean's Magazine, March 16, 1987.

67. Globe and Mail, August, 1986.

68. 1987 Study by the National Parole Board.

69. 1987 Study by the National Parole Board.

70. Globe and Mail, April 11, 1986.

71. Toronto Star, October 14, 1984.

72. Ibid.

73. Toronto Sun, August 27, 1986.

74. TIME, January 24, 1983.

75. Canadian Coalition Against the Death Penalty, Position Paper Issued Winter, (1984/85).

76. Maclean's, October 8, 1984.

77. "Executed in Error" Ontario Lawyers Weekly April 12, 1985.

78. Quoted in Position Paper (Winter, 1980) of the Inter-church Task Force for the Continued Abolition of the Death Penalty.

79. Toronto Star, October 14, 1984.

80. a.k.a. The Canadian Coalition Against the Death Penalty Position Paper (working draft).

81. Globe and Mail, June 2, 1984.

82. Globe and Mail, April 11, 1986.

83. 1987 Study by the National Parole Board.

84. 1987 Study by the National Parole Board.

85. All of the foregoing from Bruck's article, published in New Republic Dec. 12, 1983.

86. TIME, January 24, 1983.

87. Ibid.

88. From "Theological Reflections on the Death Penalty" by John H. Leith.

89. House of Commons Debates, Feb. 18, 1960.

90. Ontario Lawyers Weekly, April 12, 1985.

91. Address given to the 9th International Conference on Criminology (Vienna, September 30, 1983) by Eric Prokosch (Amnesty International).

92. Globe and Mail, April 10, 1987.

93. Column: From the Far West by Michael Bolton, Criminal Lawyers' Association Newsletter.

94. Ibid.

95. House of Commons debates, February 18, 1960.

96. House of Commons debates, December 13, 1984.

97. Toronto Sun, August 27, 1986.

98. Quoted in "Hangman" Resource Kit. Committee on Outreach and Corporate Witness.

99. Preached at the Church of St. Martins-in-Fields, 1930.

100. Speech Given at Amnesty International U.S.A.'s Annual General Meeting, June 23, 1984.

101. October 14, 1984.

102. Homicide in Canada, 1982, Statistics Canada, 1984.

103. Globe and Mail, August, 1986.

104. Crime & Traffic Statistics, Statistics Canada.

105. Globe and Mail, April 4, 1985.

106. House of Commons Debates, December 13, 1984.

107. Historical Homicide Data and Other Data Relevant to the Capital Punishment Issue.

108. LeMonde editorial July 14, 1983.

109. Church Times, July 15, 1983 referring to the vote on hanging of the General Synod of the Church of England.

110. Address given to the 9th International Conference on Criminology (Vienna, 30 September, 1983).

111. Reprinted in Ontario Lawyers Weekly, Nov. 2, 1984.

112. Maclean's, October 8, 1964.

113. Ibid.

114. Leo Adler, Globe and Mail, September 27, 1984.

115. "Police Killings in Perspective" Canadian Journal of Criminology, April, 1985.

116. Globe and Mail, April 26, 1985.

117. Toronto Star, September 19, 1984.

118. Toronto Star, October 13, 1984.

119. Ibid.

120. Toronto Star, September 24, 1984.

121. Levy, Ontario Lawyers Weekly, November 2, 1984 adapted from Maclean's, October 8, 1984.

122. Police Killings in Perspective, Canadian Journal of Criminology, April, 1985.

123. Globe and Mail, October 11, 1984.

124. Howard Rubel, "Notes on the Death Penalty".

125. Maclean's Magazine, March 16, 1987.

126. "The Surge to Kill" by John Gault Toronto Life, February, 1985.

127. Globe and Mail, September 10, 1984.

128. Toronto Sun, October 13, 1984.

129. Ibid.

130. Ontario Lawyers Weekly, November 2, 1984.

131. Maclean's, October 8, 1984.

132. "Can a Christian Support Capital Punishment?" Catholic New Times, October 22, 1978.

133. "Toward a More Biblical Understanding of Justice" The Presbyterian Outlook, April 26, 1982.

134. Commons Debates, February 18, 1960.

135. Macleans, October 8, 1984.

136. Speech given by Larry Cox at the Annual General Meeting of Amnesty International, U.S.A. (Chicago, June 23, 1984).

137 Ibid.

138. The John Howard Society of Ontario Newsletter, Summer, 1982.

139. From a sermon by Reverend Walter MacLean, M.P. reprinted in “Hangman” Capital Punishment Resource Kit.

140. Manchester Guardian Weekly, July 15, 1979.

141. TIME, January 24, 1983.

142. "Decisions of Death" The New Republic December 12, 1983.

143. TIME Magazine, January 24, 1983.

CHAPTER 4

CAPITAL PUNISHMENT: A MODIFIED WEALTH MAXIMIZATION APPROACH

Kenneth L. Avio *

1. The 1976 and 1987 debates on capital punishment in Canada differed markedly in character. The earlier debate centered on deterrence. This was the clear focus in both the House of Commons and in the media. Moreover, the Canadian courts took a related consequentialist perspective in the major Canadian case on capital punishment, which just happened to be decided in 1976.1 In marked contrast, the 1987 debate focussed on deontological matters such as rights, justice, desert, and the duty of the state. William Domm, the backbencher who spearheaded the pro-capital punishment cause, claimed that deterrence was

only a peripheral issue.[2]

Here, I'm going to argue that this switch in emphasis is not entirely desirable. I consider the following stylized question: in a regime where the rule of law applies, how should an idealized legislature go about deciding the capital punishment question? That is, what general justifications support the adoption of the death penalty, and are these justifications sufficient to move the idealized legislature to adopt the supreme sanction? The discussion is limited to the crime of murder, and I shall assume that the idealized legislature achieved its authority by legitimate means.

I first consider the reasons for the shift in emphasis noted above. This will lead to a brief consideration of two competing theories of punishment which are fashionable amongst social theorists. Shortcomings in the applications of these theories to capital punishment will be identified, and an alternative basis for reaching a decision proposed. This third approach combines elements of the two competing theories. Recent empirical work will be relied upon to partly implement this approach, and the additional (currently unavailable) information necessary to reach a conclusion will be noted. The paper ends with the speculation that were the full information available, the idealized legislature would reject capital punishment.

2. The radical change in the nature of the capital punishment debate over the past decade or so appears to be a reflection of changes in philosophical thinking on matters of social policy in general, and penal philosophy in particular. Three trends may be noted. First, there has been a revival of interest in rights-based social and political theories. With the possible exception of the Law and Economics literature, consequentialist philosophies have been overshadowed by the resurgence in deontological lines of thought. The contributions of philosophers such as John Rawls, Robert Nozick, and Ronald Dworkin all broadly reject consequentialist philosophical programs. The focus of these philosophers is on the nature of rights, what these rights properly consist of, and the source and authority of these rights. Natural rights theorists, social contractarians, and moralists all reject the notion that social

policy should, broadly speaking, be guided by some forward-looking goal such as the maximization of aggregate or average utility.

Second, with respect to penal philosophy itself, The consequentialist-based emphases on rehabilitation, treatment and 'corrections," which dominated thinking in the 1960's and through the mid-1970's, has given way in the face of a perceived failure of programs based upon such philosophies. The work of Martinson is a case in point.3 In Canada, a forced rehabilitative correctional model was replaced by an "opportunities" or "facilitation" model.4 No longer would the state use its coercive power to attempt to change the behavior of those convicted of crimes. Instead, while the prisoner served out his period of incarceration, the state would simply make available resources that could be enlisted by the prisoner to effect his own transformation into a law-abiding citizen. If the offender refused the opportunity, so be it. The payment of a prisoner's debt to society simply involved putting in one's times and did not require any effort on the part of the offender to learn new skills or to otherwise rehabilitate himself.

Third, there has been an increased emphasis on the once forgotten but now restored actor in the crime-punishment relationship, the victim. Beginning in the late 1960's in the United States, a great deal of academic and practical work has focused on the plight of the victim. While the theme of vengeance has not been particularly prominent in this work, the idea of the offender making rectification of atoning for an act which brought harm to a real person, has been. While one could argue that the ultimate purpose of the victim's movement is to prevent future crime, it is the offender-victim nexus of the criminal act itself that is the focus of victimologists, and not the prevention of harm inflicted by future yet unknown offenders upon future yet unknown victims.[5]

While none of the above-mentioned three factors is directly related to the capital punishment issue, each in the recent past has played a major role in how we think about the state's responsibilities, and how we think about the criminal law. Hence any particular issue pertaining to criminal law and discussed by the legislative body may be at least, indirectly influenced by the deontological theme that underlies these factors. With respect to capital punishment, a sympathetic discussion would focus on the appropriate punishment for murder, where propriety would be judged not in terms of some ulterior and contingent goal of the state such as deterrence, but in terms of an internal justificatory framework for punishment which relates to the just desert of the convicted offender. The question which I address next is whether such an approach yields a reliable and dispositive answer to the capital punishment question.

3. Kantian retributivism anchors the class of recently rehabilitated rights-based theories as applied to crime and punishment. Two principles are the common ground of this diverse set of theories. First, moral guilt and harm are claimed to be jointly necessary and sufficient for punishment to be deserved. Second, the severity of the punishment must be proportional to the wrong-doing. The first of these principles rejects the punishment of the innocent (the necessity of guilt and moral harm) and consequentialism (the sufficiency of moral guilt and harm). The second principle is simply a rendering of the biblical lex talionis. These two principles by themselves are insufficient to guide an idealized legislative body to a definitive answer an the capital punishment question. A brief excursion into Kantian moral philosophy will clarify why.

Kantian moral philosophy is grounded in what is often termed the respect principle. Basically, this principle demands that persons be treated as ends, and never as means to some other goal, even if that goal serves some larger social purpose. Individuals are to be treated as rational beings, capable of autonomous and responsible moral decision-making, and all individuals are to be treated as equals in the Kingdom of Ends.

Perhaps the retributive theory of punishment ' with the greatest currency at the present time is the Reciprocity Theory.6 A crude paraphrase follows: The respect principle is said to require an equal distribution of the burdens and benefits of law. But those who break the law gain an unfair advantage because the law has not constrained their activities whereas it has constrained those of law-abiding citizens. The "balance" is restored by the state imposing proportional suffering onto the law-breaker.

Note that this theory, like all true retributive theories, does not admit vengeance or a desire for revenge or retaliation as rationales for punishment. The guilty law-breaker is punished because he deserves to be punished by virtue of the autonomous act of seeking self-advantage in an unfair manner. Moreover,, it could be argued that, in punishment, offenders are getting what they asked for. This line of thinking relies on the Rawlsian notion of a social contract adopted behind a veil of ignorance, That is, it may be supposed that all individuals would unanimously support the rule of law (including punishment) in a hypothetical choice situation where individual characteristics and endowments are unknown to the choosers. Then it could be said that, ex ante, offenders have willed their own punishment, and that they have a "right" to proportionate suffering.

What conclusion does the Reciprocity Theory yield when applied to capital punishment? On the one hand, the respect principle would seem to suggest, via the Reciprocity Theory, that the "proportional" punishment of state execution would be warranted. On the other hand, the respect principle would seem to be fundamentally inconsistent with certain acts, which may include executioner for example, torture as punishment violates the respect principle even if the crime for which punishment is being exacted is torture.' The capacity for rational thinking is suspended during the torture session; the offender is reduced to little more than an animal. In contrast, legal execution irrevocably destroys this capacity, which leads some philosophers to argue that execution directly violates the respect principle. Others argue that a proper interpretation of the respect principle simply requires that the state foster the capacity of ratiocination in living beings, which would seem to rule out torture but perhaps allow execution. In this view the manner of execution would seem to play an important role, but capital punishment in principle would be permissible. What is required is that the process (of state execution) comports with human dignity (the death of Socrates is taken as the quintessential example).9 Whether a real world penal system could realize this objective is not considered here. However, there exists the conceptual objection that legal execution ends the possibility of innate human growth and development, which is arguably a capacity protected by the respect principle.10 In sum, reciprocity-style retributive theories based on the categorical demand that all individuals be treated as autonomous moral agents are not dispositive on the capital punishment issue; "reasonable" legislators starting from the same set of premises may disagree.

A second class of models based on Kantian principles stresses the expressive function of the criminal law and legal punishment. The recent important book by Duff is illustrative.11 Duff argues that the state, in punishing offenders, expresses the moral outrage of the community. Moreover, punishment provides the opportunity for, and indeed invites, the repentance of the offender and encourages his reconciliation with the community. This approach is inherently retributive because offenders are treated as autonomous moral agents who, via the process of punishment, are led to see the moral harm they have inflicted and to realize the nature and impact of their actions. This awareness may have the fortuitous consequence of stimulating offenders to their own reformation. However, this reformation is never enforced, even if the attempt is doomed to failure. The acknowledgment of the offender's status as a person requires that the offender be allowed to make his own choice, but the state, via the punishment process, invites, assists, and exhorts the offender to realize his own reformation.

Unfortunately, when Duff applies this approach to capital punishment, he finds that the result is not dispositive. On the one hand, he notes that capital punishment may be a rightful expression of society's outrage at crimes which by their heinousness are destructive of the community itself. The purpose of the punishment is to reconcile the offender, by his death, to the community. In Duff's words: "In consenting (as we hope and intend that he will consent) to his execution, he expresses his understanding of the implications of his crime, and his renewed commitment to the community and its values; in and by his death he is reconciled to those with whom he can no longer live."12 On the other hand, Duff points out that one could argue, in a vein similar to the objection presented above (i.e., that no punishment should destroy the capacity of a human being to continue to flourish and develop) that "every offender must be given the chance to repent his crime and to restore himself, in life and not just in death, to the community..." [emphasis added].13 Thus, as with the reciprocity variety of retributivism, Duff's expressive and reformative Kantian-based theory does not lead to firm conclusions on the capital punishment issue. Our idealized legislature will have to look elsewhere for a reliable philosophical account yielding an unambiguous solution.

4. Before turning to alternative accounts, a potentially -important oversight in the retributive models discussed above should be noted: third party effects are largely ignored. Does the respect principle require that such effects be considered, or do retributivist principles require that such ulterior consequences be ignored?

The conflict can be clarified with reference to the capital punishment issue. Suppose that the idealized legislature follows a retributivist approach and in the first instance, is somehow convinced of the impropriety of the capital sanction in all circumstances. Now let us suppose that the legislature obtains new and irrefutable information that the execution of rightfully condemned murderers would prevent, via a deterrence mechanism, a number of future murders, an impact that could not be obtained by any alternative punishment. Would the idealized legislature, under the given assumptions, be swayed to reconsider its position?

Alternatively, suppose that the idealized legislature, again acting on retributivist (but obviously different) grounds, supports capital punishment but then receives irrefutable information that executions have a "brutalizing" effect, and no off-setting deterrent effect. That is, suppose executions induce murders in excess of those induced by any alternative punishment, perhaps because of the impact of the news of executions upon the minds of unstable individuals, or upon murderers when their capture appears imminent. Again, would the new information change the position of the legislature?

Retributivists typically deny the relevance of deterrence in punishment, and the relevance of ulterior consequences in hard cases in general.14 In the scenarios sketched above, the truly retributivist legislature would be bound to ignore the empirical information. But how could ignoring the information be consistent with the respect principle as applied to the (ex ante unidentifiable) additional victims? Have these victims been treated as equals in the Kingdom of Ends?

It appears that third party effects may render the retributivist position precarious or even internally incoherent. It will not do to claim that an increased risk of victimization is consistent with equal treatment on the grounds that all citizens ex ante face the same risk (assumed). The inequality of treatment is based upon a comparison of prospective victims' situations in the alternative punishments scenario. Prospective victims are treated differently depending upon which punishment (imprisonment or death) is adopted by our idealized legislature. Moreover, in the brutalization scenario one could argue (along Dufiian lines) that it would be unfair to the convicted offender to impose the lighter sentence which it may be supposed is not sufficient to arouse his reformation. But it would be bizarre for the idealized legislature to compare these two harms and decide in favor of convicted offenders and against the innocent prospective victims.

In summary, two points have been made. First, Kantian moral principles, notoriously ambiguous as they may be, are not dispositive on the capital punishment issue. Kant himself insisted upon capital punishment for murderers, whereas many Kantians reject this position based upon Kant's own respect principle. It is unlikely that an idealized legislature adopting a generalized retributivist approach would be unanimously and unalterably convinced of one view or the other. Indeed, acceptance of a retributive approach will practically guarantee periodic flip-flops in policy (the "political Halley's Comet' title of this symposium). Second, even if policy reversals could be avoided, hard choices may arise for the idealized legislature following Kantian principles. Treating one group in accordance with the respect principle may result in treating a second group in a manner violative of the same principle. One could argue that the legislature does not will the violation to the prospective victims, but if the legislature knows the effect of its action (even in a probabilistic sense) then the notion of distinguishing effects on the basis of volition breaks down.15 On a less theoretical plane, it would seem odd that an idealized legislature would and should ignore evidence or information such as the deterrent effectiveness of capital punishment if indeed that information were reliable. Yet, making use of such information suggests either that retributive accounts must be extended to include third party effects, or else that retributivism must be replaced by an alternative theory. A consequentialist approach which in its general form has recently enjoyed considerable but controversial discussion is considered next.

5. The "economic theory of punishment" may be treated as a part of the Law and Economics literature.16 It posits that the level of crime is determined in part by the amount of resources society devotes to the police, the courts and penal institutions. Society may also choose between different forms of punishment: fines, loss of liberty, corporal punishment - each of which entails different social costs. All these choices are made with reference to the overarching goal of maximizing social wealth, or alternatively, minimizing the social cost of crime. This suggests an important difference between this particular consequentialist theory and purely retributive accounts. ¬Resource allocation plays a central role here whereas it is largely ignored in traditional deontological approaches.[17]

As an example of this difference, consider Kant's demand that a society even in the process of dissolution has the moral duty to seek out and execute all murderers within its jurisdiction. This account fails to acknowledge that the demanded executions require the use of social resources, however small in amount. Thus Kant's approach would result in the reduced wealth of society (relative to simply ignoring the offenders), and hence the potential reduced well-being of every individual (other than perhaps the offenders themselves) in that society. On this interpretation, the coherence of Kant's paradigm therefore depends upon interpreting "dissolution" to mean that the society is in a situation where the present discounted value of the resources to be used for the executions is zero. Or to put it another way, the "opportunity cost" of these resources is zero. But even a society in the process of dissolution would value productive resources positively as long as they could be the source of utility, however brief the span of enjoyment. Thus Kant's scenario and the implications he draws have little relevance for actual social policy. One criticism, then, of the purely retributivist account of punishment is that it fails to perceive that punishment is resource-using and that this use of resources by itself potentially reduces the well-¬being of the citizenry.

This failure can be seen in a second aspect of retributive models of punishment. These accounts largely ignore the matter of the selectivity of punishment. That is, only those who are caught and convicted are subjected to punishment. What do retributive accounts tell us about those who are not caught? Is the apprehension and punishment of only a portion of those who have committed crime consistent with retributive doctrine?

Retributive principles fail to present a complete account of the criminal system, which would require an informed view as to how many of society's resources should be devoted to the apprehension of law-breakers. It will not be sufficient to say that retributivism simply requires that each law-breaker be at equal risk of capture, regardless of the social resources devoted to punishment. Some offenders are easier to apprehend than others, so equating the risk for a given expenditure of resources will result in fewer offenders captured. In the limit, it may take “all" of society's resources to impose a positive risk on the one criminal poised to commit the "perfect" murder.[18]

In contrast, the economic model of punishment appears to provide a consistent argument for punishing as well as for determining how many of society's resources should be devoted to the task. Is this approach entirely empty of Kantian notions, which possess an undeniable, intuitive appeal? The emphasis on the scarcity of resources directs attention to the foregone cost of any activity. If the Kantian ideal of humans developing as rational, autonomous and responsible moral agents requires the use of scarce resources (time, effort, human capital), then any social policy which is sub-optimal, by definition results in a reduction of opportunities by at least one individual to participate to the fullest extent in the quest to develop and flourish as moral agents.19 In this sense then, the economic model, which appears anti- or a least a-Kantian, can be interpreted as embodying Kantian principles; its precepts allow for the fullest possible potential moral development. Obviously this account would have to include some notions of distributive principles and rights, which. are typically lacking in standard law and economic treatments.

6. At this point one familiar and powerful objection to consequentialist accounts of punishment must be considered: these models allegedly invite the punishment of the innocent, which directly violates Kantian principles. That is, in furthering the consequentialist goal, the punishment of the innocent may be required. Is this the case with the economic model?[20]

In the economic model of punishment, marginal deterrence is achieved through increasing the risk of punishment of offenders, as well as through increasing punishment severity. Now suppose that the idealized legislature has chosen optimal values for these variables and that the system is in equilibrium. The retributivist attack posits the existence of a third variable, the probability of punishing the innocent, and assumes that the consequentialist program yields a positive equilibrium value for this variable.[21]

Before proceeding, it is helpful to distinguish two forms of punishing the innocent: by design and by mistake. Punishing the innocent by design would involve intentionally setting (by the appropriate allocation of social resources) the probability of punishing the innocent at some positive level. Agents now have two probabilities to consider in deciding whether to commit crime: the probability of punishment if guilty, and the probability of punishment if innocent. Setting the latter figure above zero by design would have no independent deterrent effect, and in fact may induce individuals on the margin to commit crime. That is, if one is to be punished whether one commits a crime or not, one might just as well commit a crime.22 In economic terms, the opportunity cost of crime falls when the risk of punishing the innocent increases, other things being equal. Thus it would be inefficient for the idealized legislature to invest social resources to raise the expected cost of punishing the innocent above zero unless there were some compensating benefit.

Such compensating benefit may accrue if it were possible to punish the innocent in such a way that only the authorities knew that the person being punished was innocent - a kind of secretive scapegoat policy. The authorities could then consider such a possibility with the purpose of increasing, at least cost, the subjective expected cost of punishment for the guilty.23 If punishing the innocent can be justified on these grounds within the economic model, then it must fail the retributivist moral challenge.

But could such a policy be sustained? The true (unapprehended) offender would recognize the falsity of the government's claim, and a corrective adjustment would emerge. This mechanism works as follows: the true offender recognizes the true accounting of his crime, and this information is of more or less value to all decision-makers in the community. Since the production of the true information to the true offender is costless, but is of value, it would be available for "sale" in a hypothetical information market.24 Thus a policy of raising the subjective expected price of punishment for the guilty by convicting individuals that the state knows are innocent could not be successfully sustained as an equilibrium wealth-maximizing solution.

The above Account of punishing the innocent assumes that such a policy is by design of the legislature. But suppose the punishment of the innocent is due to mistake, and that such mistakes can only be prevented or rectified by the expenditure of social resources. In these circumstances is it possible that wealth maximization dictates an equilibrium where the expected value of punishment for the innocent is non-zero? I see no reason why not. While the higher the risk of punishing the innocent the lower the opportunity cost of crime, there is an offset; it may take increasingly more of society's resources to reduce this risk by an additional unit. The arithmetic may come out that some non-zero value of this variable is required.[25]

The inadvertent punishment of the innocent suggests a violation of basic retributive principles. This defect is particularly odious in situations where ex post compensability is impossible, as with wrongly executed offenders. In these cases at least, the economic account must be rejected as it stands; a powerful side-constraint protecting the innocent from mistaken punishment must be incorporated into the model.

7. A second short-coming of the economic approach concerns the application of unprincipled factors such as race, wealth or gender. A policy of setting differential punishments for different groups in society may be wealth maximizing.26 Suppose, for example, that individuals born with green hair have higher demand elasticities for

murder. Then it may be efficient for the authorities to adopt higher penalties (say executing a higher proportion) for people with green hair. Such a policy would seem to be inherently unjust and violative of Kantian principles. Thus a second side-constraint forbidding the application of unprincipled factors is required.

8. We are now in position to suggest to the idealized legislature an approach to the capital punishment issue that embodies both consequentialist and retributivist notions of punishment and that in principle is dispositive.

As noted above, given the special nature of the capital sanction, retributivist concerns suggest that, in principle no one be wrongly subjected to legal execution. The retributive imperatives then (side-constraints) are that social resources be invested to the point where (1)the probability of executing an offender who did not commit murder approaches zero, and (2)the probability of "unprincipled factors" affecting the decision approaches zero.

Within these constraints, the authorities simultaneously choose values for the social control variables as well as the optimal forms of punishment. In recognition of the decentralization of the criminal justice system, we posit for our idealized legislature the problem of choosing the optimal form of punishment - imprisonment or state execution -- for the crime of murder, assuming that all control variables are set at their efficient levels in each of the two alternative regimes. Solving the wealth maximization problem is equivalent to a cost-benefit analysis of the restoration of capital punishment. Here such a calculus will be sketched, but the analysis is speculative, and awaits a more formal and extended treatment.

Counted as the social benefits of capital punishment would be a monetized measure of the deterrent effect,27 if any, plus the saved costs of imprisoning convicted murderers, all properly discounted. The social costs of capital punishment include a monetized measure of the brutalizing effect, if any, plus the costs of the destroyed human capital. Also included as a cost are the judicial and legislative resources necessary to support the retributivist side-constraints. In the discussion that follows, the costs of these constraints are briefly noted. First however, comes a cursory attempt to summarize where we stand on the deterrence-brutalization issue.

9. What kind of evidence on deterrence should the idealized legislature rely upon? In the 1987

debates in Canada, much was made of the fact that the homicide rate had fallen since Parliament's 1976 vote. This information was stressed in media accounts, and was widely touted by opponents of capital punishment in the House of Commons. But in isolation such information is worthless in evaluating the deterrent effectiveness of capital punishment. The reason is straightforward -- no attention is paid to changes in the actual risk of execution (conditional upon conviction). It likely did not change over the period 1976-1987. Hence simply observing in these circumstances that the homicide rate changed, allows our idealized legislature no inference other than there are factors other than the risk of execution which influence the homicide rate. More generally, since there are many variables which could affect the homicide rate, the simple observation of a change in the homicide rate does not allow attribution of this change to any single potentially causative factor. No conclusion can be drawn unless changes in all the relevant variables are simultaneously examined. Econometrics models utilizing time-series data over periods when risks vary may satisfy this requirement.

Studies of this sort for Canada, the United States and the U.K. all display the same pattern: if the series is truncated in the early 1960's, there is little or no evidence of a unique deterrent effect attributable to the conditional risk of execution. Extending the time-series beyond these years seems to reverse the finding.[28] However, there is compelling (although controversial) evidence that this reversal is an artifact of the data. In the U.S., for example, Passell and Taylor, and others, have found that (1) Ehrlich's time-series is unstable, and (2) truncating Ehrlich's time-series in the early 1960's results in a finding of no deterrent effect.[29] Similar results hold for Canada. For example, I have found that, consistent with some speculations by James Q. Wilson,[30] there is an unstable relationship between the homicide rate and the proportion of the population that is in high-crime age groups. Statistically accounting for this instability removes any evidence of a deterrent effect attributable to the conditional risk of execution.[31]

In summary, my reading of the empirical evidence on capital punishment favors a finding of "no deterrent effect," but further research is needed and the matter is not closed. Data problems and model-specification problems loom large in this literature, and at this time only a tentative conclusion can be given. At the same time there is little evidence of a brutalization effect, although tests here are less conclusive because the theoretical structure of such a model have not yet been satisfactorily spelled out.32 It appears that the latter thesis involves implications for the change in the number of legal executions, whereas the deterrence hypothesis, properly specified, relies on allegations about the impact of risks, which are interpreted as frequency ratios.

10. I turn now to an examination of the social cost of ensuring that unprincipled factors and mistakes do not play a role in the punishment process. With respect to the former issue, empirical evidence in both the United States and Canada suggests that unprincipled factors have infected the decision process in capital cases, and that attempts to eradicate the bias will be socially costly. Here I briefly review the Baldus, et. al., study,33 which was the focus of the recent McCleskey decision in the United States Supreme Court,34 and my own study of the Canadian Cabinet's exercise of clemency in capital cases.35

Baldus and his co-authors, in examining post-Furman Georgia data at all stages of the capital case process, found that, after standardizing for a large number of variables, the race of victim had independent significance. Murderers of whites have an odds ratio of receiving the death sentence approximately 4.3 times higher than murderers of blacks.

My research on decisions made by the Canadian Federal Cabinet in capital cases over the years 1926-1957 also found statistically significant evidence on unprincipled factors affecting the clemency decision. Again after standardizing for a large number of legitimate aggravating and mitigating circumstances, I found that Native persons, Eastern Europeans and French Canadians had odds-ratios respectively 6.1, 3.8 and 2.4 times higher than those for Anglo Canadians. That is, convicted non-Anglos were found to have substantially higher risks of being executed than Anglos in similar circumstances. Moreover, non-¬whites murdering whites had an odds-ratio 14.4 times higher than that for any other racial configuration. Occupational circumstances and gender of the offender also appear to have played a role.

Regardless of the U.S. Supreme Court's decision in McCleskey,36 our idealized legislature would not permit the kind of disparate effects found in these American and Canadian studies. The side-constraint of unprincipled factors affecting the decision is violated, whether or not purposive.37 Hence procedures must be implemented to meet the side-constraint. Are these procedures likely to be expensive?

Consider the state of Georgia. Georgia has a bifurcated trial system (separate trials for guilt and penalty), as well as an automatic proportionality review by the state Supreme Court (to guard against excessiveness in individual cases). But as Baldus and his co-authors demonstrate, these safeguards are insufficient to meet the retributive side-constraint.

Moreover, any regime which adopts capital punishment must face a large array of complex and costly legal challenges. The specific nature of the challenges will depend upon the laws themselves but a brief look at the recent judicial history in the U.S. is instructive. Below is an incomplete list of challenges:[38]

1) Does the sentencing authority have unlimited discretion in setting penalty? (Furman v. Georgia, 1972)

2) Is capital punishment cruel and unusual per se? (Gregg v. Georgia, 1976)

3) Is a mandatory death sentence constitutional? (Woodson v. Georgia, 1976)

4) Is there a limit on the range of mitigating factors that must be considered by the sentencing authority? (Lockett v. Ohio, 1978)

5) Are death sentences for non-active accomplices in felony ¬murders constitutional? (Emmund v. Florida, 1982)

6) Is it permissable to exclude opponents of the death penalty from juries? (Witherspoon v. Illinois, 1968: Wainwright v. Witt, 1985: Lockhart v. McCree, 1986)

7) May the trial judge overrule a jury's recommendation for a life sentence? (Spazino v. Florida, 1984)

8) May the death sentence be administered when the defense counsel is incompetent? (Strickland v. Washington, 1984)

9) Is a proportionality review required? (Pulley v. Harris, 1984)

10) Must the state provide free psychiatric assistance for defenders pleading an insanity defense? (Ake v. Oklahoma, 1985)

11) May the death penalty be carried out if the prisoner is insane? (Batson v. Kentucky, 1986)

12) Is unevenness in application of the death penalty permissible? (McCleskey v. Kemp, 1987)

13) Is it constitutional to impose the death penalty on minors?

The list of possible challenges is limited only by the ingenuity of defense counsel. Certainly the adequacy of due process in clemency decisions would be raised.

With respect to our cost-benefit analysis, one could argue that challenges such as these need only be adjudicated once.

Each case may be regarded as an instance of investment in capital which depreciates very slowly, if at all. However, since the, capital itself is regime-specific, any new jurisdiction considering adopting capital punishment would have to consider these issues from the perspective of its own legal system. Moreover, the investment cost of this accumulation of capital is largely "up-front". It is incurred prior to the receipt of offsetting benefits, if any. Thus the time-discounting of costs and benefits, which is required in any wealth maximizing framework, weights these particular costs of capital punishment more than the benefits. One other up-front cost largely overlooked is the opportunity cost of legislative time. In Canada, if the capital punishment vote had passed, a committee was to have been formed to debate and recommend the appropriate form of the law. The hours of Parliamentary discussion and reports are all prior to any tangible benefits, and hence count more heavily in any cost-benefit calculation.

Other costs could be discussed, such as Cabinet time in reviewing each capital case, special facilities and procedures for death-row convicts, additional appeals in capital cases, special assistance for insanity defenses, etc. Some representative discussions of these costs are included for reference,39 but in my opinion no definitive study has yet been undertaken. However, the overall impression is that the discounted costs far outweigh the discounted benefits, which are small indeed if deterrent effects are non-existent. Moreover, even if the deterrent effects were relatively large, society may not value the reduction in the risk of victimization very highly. Also, it may be cheaper to reduce these risks by reducing the unemployment rate or by other social policies such as hand-gun control than by introducing capital punishment.

11. Final Comments. The reference to Halley's Comet in the title of this symposium echos an implicit assumption of this paper: that virtue resides in an approach to capital punishment that is dispositive, and dispositive in two senses. First, the adoption of some particular framework ideally yields a unanimous solution. Second, over time the unanimous vote does not swing from one position to the other.

The nature of the rights-constrained wealth-maximizing approach in principle dictates a unanimous vote in our idealized legislature and hence is dispositive in the first sense, whereas retributive approaches are not. The second and more important question is which approach is less likely to lead to reversals in policy over time. I think one could argue that reversals in capital punishment policy violate basic retributive principles. An illustration related to a lower level of policy may be helpful. I demonstrated in my study of Cabinet commutation policies that Cabinet was less willing to commute, other things equal, when the homicide rate was increasing. That is, the risk of execution for convicted murderers varied from year to year as the homicide rate itself changed. Cabinet's implicit rationale may have been to induce a heightened deterrent effect. What principle of justice can support such a policy when: (1) there was no evidence of a deterrent effect, and (2) even if there were such evidence, offenders alike in all respects except the dates of their crimes were treated differently? In the mundane world of state activity at large, policy reversals may be tolerated and even desirable, but it is unlikely that reversals of this sort could be defended in the capital punishment context.40

The remaining question then, is not whether the rights constrained wealth-maximization approach could ever yield policy reversals, but whether it is less likely to lead to reversals than retributive approaches. Relative prices, including the opportunity cost of lawyerly and judicial effort, may change, as might knowledge of deterrence effects. However, I doubt that such considerations could upset what I perceive to be an inefficient proposition. Moreover, it is more likely that retributive-based policies will result in policy reversals simply because they are not based on empirical information. There may be arguments over data and the intricacies of statistical tests, but at least there is common-ground; in principle, these problems could be largely settled. As I have shown, this is not the case for purely retributive approaches to capital punishment, which depend upon contentious ethical judgments.

I acknowledge that many people will be repelled by the framework for decision-making that I have sketched in this paper. It will be said that state execution is simply wrong, and that empirical information is beside the point. However, if capital punishment is wrong, the reason must be articulated. What I have indicated in this paper is that standard retributive arguments are unequal to the task.

For policies involving the allocation of scarce resources, some principles of decision-making seem more reliable than others. Society does not devote all the resources necessary to eliminate disease and other physical and mental afflictions. We do not buy automobiles and (through our votes) highways that are accident-proof. We do not invest in safety equipment to the maximum extent possible. The requisite expenditures for these endeavors would mean drastic reductions in aggregate social wealth. To yield rational solutions to such problems, which are arguably moral in tone and involve life and death issues, cost-¬benefit calculations are implicitly, if not explicitly, undertaken. Capital punishment has related moral content in that lives (or the risks of death) are at stake. Consistency alone suggests that a social cost-benefit analysis bounded by retributive constraints is an appropriate way to address the capital punishment issue.

NOTES

* Kenneth Avio is a Professor of Economics at the University of Victoria, Victoria, B.C.

1. R.V. Miller and Cockriell, 63 D.L.R. (3d) 193 (1975); 70 D.L.R. (3d) 324 (1976).

2. Quoted in the Toronto Globe and Mail, April 19 1987. Also see "Revenge Argument Favored in Debate," Toronto Globe and Mail, March 3, 1987.

3. "What works? --questions and answers about prison reform," Robert Martinson, The Public Interest, Spring 1974.

4. See The Role of Federal Correction in Canada, Task Force of the Creation of an Integrated Canadian Corrections Service (Ottawa: Supply & Services Canada) 1977. Also see Report to Parliament by the Sub-Committee on the Penal System in Canada [The MacGuighen Report], (Ottawa: Supply & Services Canada) 1977 which uses language which is strikingly Kantian in tone (p. 37).

5. For an account of the growth of the victim's movement around the world and in Canada, see Paul Rock, A View From the Shadow: The

Ministry of the Solicitor General of Canada and the Justice for Victims of Crime Initiative, (Oxford: Clarendon Press, Center for Socio-Legal Studies).

6. Development of the theory is attributed to Herbert Morris, "Persons and Punishment", The Monist vol. 52 (1968) and Jeffrie Murphy, Retribution, Justice, and Therapy (Boston: D. Reidel Publishing Co., 1978). Also see John Finnis, Natural Law and Natural Rights, (Clarendon Press: Oxford) 1980, Chap X.

7. This conflict between the respect principle and proportionality is explicated in M. Margaret Falls, "Retribution, Reciprocity and Respect for Persons," Law and Philosophy, 6 (1987) 25-51. Falls' own retributive account relies upon the notion that the offender does not benefit by committing crime, but indeed harms himself (morally). Such a view renders the Reciprocity Theory incoherent, unless one distinguishes an individual's well-being from his preference satisfaction.

8. See, for example, Jeffrie Murphy, p. 147, "Crime and Punishment", in The Philosophy of Law: An Introduction to Jurisprudence (1984).

9. Murphy, op. cit., p. 150.

10. Murphy, op. cit., p. 156.

11. R.A. Duff, Trials and Punishments, Cambridge University Press, (1986). Also see Joel Feinberg, "The Expressive Function of Punishment," reprinted from The Monist, (July 1965) in Doing and Deserving: Essays in the Theory of Responsibility, (Princeton University Press: Princeton) 1970.

12. Duff, op. cit., p. 281.

13. Duff, op. cit., p. 282.

14. However, see J. B. Cederblam and Gonzalo Munevar, "The Death Penalty: The

Relevance of Deterrence," Criminal Justice Review,, Vol 7, No I (Spring 1982) 63-66.

15. On this controversial matter see, for example, Philippa Foot, "Abortion and the Doctrine of the Double Effect," Oxford Review 5 (1967) and Judith Jarvis Thomson, "Killing, Letting Die, and the Trolley Problem," in Rights, Restitution & Risk: Essays in Moral Theory, (Cambridge Mass: Harvard University Press) 1986.

16. Richard A. Posner, Law and Economics, (Boston: Little, Brown) 3rd edition (1986).

17. Moreover, the underlying model of human nature adopted in this approach differs fundamentally from that which is implicit in the retributivist account. It is assumed that lawbreakers are in no fundamental way different from those who adhere to the law. The reason why some break the law and others do not is because the perceived costs and benefits of alternative actions differ among individuals. Thus all individuals are potential lawbreakers. Compare this with retributivist notions. In the latter, offenders break the law either because their unique morality permits them to take " unfair advantage" of other members of society, or because in their ignorance they fail to recognize and fully appreciate the harm they do to others (or to themselves). In the retributive account a fundamental attitudinal change is required to reduce criminality, whereas in the economic account changing the costs and benefits of crime may suffice.

18. Even if the question of deterrence were ignored, a possible violation of retributivist principles results due to the reduced restoration of stolen property (or other forms of recompense for victims). Those victims whose property is not returned as a result of following the inefficient policy of equating risk could not be said to have

been treated equitably, relative to an efficient policy. Nor would spreading the costs via criminal victimization insurance schemes be the answer. Again, adopting inefficient policies unfairly "taxes" those who pay for the scheme, whether taxpayers or private insurers.

19. This appears to accord with D. Bruce Johnsen, "Wealth Is Value" Journal of Legal Studies, Vol. XV (June, 1986) 263-281. For an alternative view see Albert 0. Hirschman, "Against Parsimony: Three Easy Ways of Complicating some Categories of Economic Discourse," Economics and Philosophy, Vol. 1, (1985) 7¬21.

20. Before answering this question, it should be noted that the consequentialist position at least requires that the punishment of the innocent be considered as a possibility. Some philosophers have argued that this willingness to entertain the possibility of punishing the innocent, by itself, violates Kantian principles. Here I am ignoring this concern: no violation is presumed to occur unless the idealized legislature actually adopts, and not just considers adopting, a policy which results in punishing the innocent.

21. See for example, Richard 0. Lempert, "Desert and Deterrence: An Assessment of the Moral Bases of the Case for Capital Punishment,"

Michigan Law Review, (1981) 2(1172-1231), who argues against capital punishment partly on the grounds that execution of the innocent is inevitable. See the response of Larry Alexander, "Retributivism and the Inadvertent Punishment of the Innocent," Law and Philosophy, (1993) 2 (233-246). My position, clarified below, is that punishment of the innocent is not "inevitable," but that reducing the risk to levels approaching zero may require unacceptably large social expenditures.

22. A more complicated account provides for substitution among a range of activities. See

pp. 16-18 in Isaac Ehrlich, "The Optimum Enforcement of Law and the Concept of Justice: A Positive Analysis," International Review of Law and Economics (1982), 2 (3-27).

23. Assume that the technology for producing the subjective risk of punishment for the guilty depends upon the proportion of crimes cleared, whether by convicting the innocent (as secret scapegoats) or the guilty. In such circumstances a least cost way of increasing the perceived risk of capture for prospective offenders may be to convict the innocent of reported crimes. For example, suppose that the current risks of punishing the guilty and the innocent are 10% and 0%

respectively, whereas the optimal values are 11% and 0% respectively. To change the actual to the optimal at what appears to be least cost, the authorities secretly adopt a policy of clearing crimes by randomly apprehending and punishing citizens who are innocent. The result is that the newspapers, in effect, erroneously report an actual risk of punishing the guilty of 11% and an actual risk of punishing the innocent of 0%. The true probabilities are now,, say, 9.5% and 1% respectively., Since it takes fewer resources to punish an individual at random than to selectively find and punish the real culprit, such a policy may appear to be wealth maximizing. However , the cost of maintaining secrecy must also be considered (see text).

24. This assumes that revealing the information does not expose the actual offender to increased risk. If the authorities adopted a policy of punishing the innocent to smoke out or decoy the true offenders, then the punishment of the innocent could not be kept secretive, as initially premised. Such activity involves a technology where the two probabilities are non-separable.

25. See for example John R. Harris, "On the Economics of Law and Order," Journal of Political Economy, (January/February 1970) 165-174, who explicates punishment of the innocent in terms of

Type I and Type II errors. Harris' account does not explicitly distinguish the probabilities of punishment for the innocent and the guilty.

26. See Proposition 6 (page 7) of Ehrlich, supra, note 21.

27. It is the value of the reduced risk of being a homicide victim that is included here. See E. J. Mishan (for example, "Consistency in the Valuation of Life: A Wild Goose Chase?" in Ethics & Economics. edited by Ellen Frankel Paul, Fred D. Miller, Jr., and Jeffrey Paul (Blackwell: Oxford) 1985. On application to capital punishment see David L. McKee and Michael Sesnowitz, "Welfare Economic Aspects of Capital Punishment," American Journal of Economics and Sociology, (1976), pp. 41-47, and the response of Morgan 0. Reynolds, “On Welfare Economics Aspects of Capital Punishment”, American Journal of Economics and Sociology, (1977), pp. 105-111.

28. For Canada see Kenneth L. Avio, “Capital Punishment in Canada: A Time-Series Analysis of the Deterrent Hypothesis,” Canadian Journal of Economics. (November, 1979), pp. 647-676, and Stephen Layson, “Homicide and Deterrence: Another View of the Canadian Time-Series Evidence,” Canadian Journal of Economics, (February, 1983), pp. 52-73; for the U.S. see Isaac

Ehrlich., "The Deterrent Effect of Capital Punishment: a Question of Life and Death," American Economic Review, Val. 65, (1975) pp. 397-417; and for the U.K. see Kenneth Wolpin, "Capital Punishment and Homicide in England: A Summary of Results," American Economic Review, (May, 1978) pp 422-427.

29. Peter Passell and John B. Taylor, "The Deterrent Effect of Capital Punishment: Another View," American Economic Review, Vol.67 (1977) pp.445-451 and Lawrence Klein, Brian Forst and Victor Filatov, "The Deterrent Effect of Capital Punishment: An Assessment of the Estimates," in A. Blumstein, J. Cohen and D. Nagineds., Deterrence and Incapacitation: Estimating the Effects of Criminal Sanctions on Crime Rates, Panel on Research on Deterrent and Incapacitative Effects, National Academy of Sciences (Washington, D.C.). Also see the responses of Ehrlich: "The Deterrent Effect of Capital Punishment: Reply" American Economic Review Vol. 67 (1977) pp. 452-4589 and (with Mark Randall, "Fear of Deterrence: a Critical Evaluation of the 'Report of the Panel on Research on Deterrent and Incapacitative Effects'." Journal of Legal Studies, Vol. 6 (1977) pp. 293-316.

30. See "Crime and American Culture," The Public Interest (Winter, 1983), pp. 22-48. In

short, Wilson attributes the increase in age-specific crime rates in the 1960's and 70's to the ethos of self-expression and immediate gratification.

31. See "Capital Punishment in Canada: Statistical Evidence and Constitutional Implications" (undated manuscript incorporating my earlier paper) "Capital Punishment Again," University of Victoria Department of Economics Discussion Paper 84-1 [1984].

32. See for example William J. Bowers and Glenn L. Pierce, "Deterrence or Brutalization: What is the Effect of Executions?," Crime and Delinquency, Vol. 26 (1980) pp. 453-484, who examine homicide rates in the months immediately following executions, but neglect to control for any of the "standard" variables hypothesized as affecting the homicide rate. Also see Isaac Ehrlich, "Deterrence: Evidence and Inference," Yale Law Journal, Vol 85 (1975) p.220.

33. David C. Baldus, Charles A. Pulaski, Jr., and George Woodworth, "Arbitrariness and Discrimination in the Administration of the Death Penalty:

A Challenge to State Supreme Courts," Stetson Law Review, Vol. 15, No. 2 (Spring 1986) pp. 133-

261.

34. McCleskey v. Kemp, 55 LW 4521 (1987).

35. Kenneth L. Avio, "The Quality of Mercy: Exercise of the Royal Prerogative in Canada," Canadian Public Policy, forthcoming (September, 1987).

36. It is interesting that the Supreme Court, in a 5-4 decision, decided that the Baldus results, even if valid, did not invalidate the Georgia statute. The court's reasoning relied on a distinction between employment discrimination cases and criminal justice cases. The court said that since purposeful intent must be established from the statistics, one must inquire into the decision-making process itself. In employment discrimination cases, typically only a small number of persons are making the employment decision. In these circumstances it is plausible that the statistical evidence may establish purposeful intent. However, the Court reasoned that in criminal justice cases, where there are typically a very large number of actors involved in the final outcome, similar statistical evidence does not yield the same inference. The Court suggests that statistical evidence of the sort marshaled by Baldus et. al., regardless of the size of the adds-ratios, could never overcome the presumption that

the officials of the state are not engaged in a deliberate policy of discrimination.

My own study is illustrative of the type that may satisfy McCleskey concerns because unlike the Baldus study it addresses the capital punishment process at a single stage, and involves a relatively small number of decision-makers.

37. See Charles R. Lawrence III, "The Id, the Ego, and Equal Protection: Reckoning with

Unconscious Racism." Stanford Law Review, Vol 39 No 2 (January 1998). 317-388, who cogently argues that the courts should not require purposive intent in racial discrimination cases. Lawrence maintains that the current paradigm of racial discrimination as "crime" should be replaced by the paradigm of racism as "disease."

38. See Appendix e of Amnesty International, United States of America: The Death Penalty for a brief discussion of these cases.

39. See Barry Nakell, "The Cost of the Death Penalty," Criminal Law Bulletin, Vol. 14,

No. 1, Jan/Feb 1978, pp 68-80; "Capital Losses: The Price of the Death Penalty for New York State," a report from the Public Defense Backup Center (New York State Defense Association) to the Senate Finance Committee, the Assembly Ways and Means Committee and the Division of the Budget, April 1982; and J. R. Browning, "The New Death Penalty Statues: Perpetuating a Costly Myth," Gonzaga Law Review, Vol. 9, 651-705. The New York Report is the most comprehensive and comes the closest to the kind of calculation I advocate here. However, the Report is flawed in that it does not always indicate that it is the marginal cost (i.e., the cost over and above that for life imprisonment) that is being calculated. Moreover, costs are not discounted, and offsetting benefits go unconsidered.

40. There seems to be something fundamentally different between the commutation authorities deciding cases differently that are similar in all respects except date of murder, and the authorities adjusting risks of apprehension from year to year, even though both may be in response to efficiency requirements of the economic model. Perhaps the key to the distinction is that the identity of convicted murderess is known at the time the policy switch is made, whereas the identity of unapprehended murderers is unknown.

PART – III

THIRD WORLD PERSPECTIVES

CHAPTER
5

THE DEALTH PENALTY IN INDIA

F.S. Nariman*

There is a section in the Penal Code - S.302 which says that whoever commits murder shall be punished with death or imprisonment for life and shall also be liable to a fine. The handiwork of Lord Macaulay, (who was only thirty-five when he drafted it), the Indian Penal Code is a statute of Victorian vintage, - of the year 1860. With the advent of the Constitution in 1950 and the Chapter on Fundamental Rights, there have been frequent attempts to do away with the death penalty - at first, by legislation, later through the intervention of Courts. The attempts have not met with success.

First, a Bill to abolish capital punishment was introduced in the Lok Sabha (the House of the People) in 1956 - it was rejected. In 1961, a similar resolution was moved in the Rajya Sabha (the Upper House) but negatived by a voice vote. The next year a resolution for its abolition was once again discussed in the Lok Sabha. It was withdrawn only after Government assured the House that a decision would be taken after a detailed consideration of the matter. The question was then referred to the Law Commission of India (comprising judges and jurists). They submitted their report in 1967. After collecting as much available material as possible and assessing the views expressed by a cross-section of people, by abolitionists and by anti-abolitionists, the Indian Law Commission came to the conclusion that having regard to conditions in India, it could not "risk the experiment of abolishing capital punishment" - capital punishment, said this expert body, "should be retained in the present state of the country".

Being thwarted in the legislative field, the attempt of the abolitionists then shifted to the Courts. In 1973 - inspired by the opinion of some of the judges of the Supreme Court of the United States (in Furman's case) an appeal was made to the Supreme Court of India to rule the death penalty unconstitutional. It failed. In Jagmohan Singh Vs. State of Uttar Pradesh (AIR 1973 S.C. 947), it was argued that the right to life was basic to the seven freedoms mentioned in Article 19,2 and that no law could deprive a citizen of his life unless it was reasonable and in the public interest; capital punishment for the crime of murder was unreasonable and was not justified in public interest. A Constitution Bench of five Judges presided over by Chief justice Sikri unanimously rejected this plea. The Court relied not only on the findings of the Law Commission but on the plain language of Article 21 of the Constitution ¬which provides that no person shall be deprived of his life or liberty except in accordance with procedure established by law. The implication, said the Judges, was very clear - deprivation of life was constitutionally permissible in India if it was done according to procedure established by law. They found it difficult to hold that capital punishment as such was unreasonable or not required in the public interest.

But there was another and more serious argument advanced in Jagmohan Singh Vs. State of Uttar Pradesh (AIR 1973 S.C. 947). It was that the discretion conferred by section 302 of the Indian Penal Code to punish murder with death or life imprisonment was entirely unguided - in what cases should the judge sentence the accused to death and when should he impose the lesser sentence of life imprisonment? The statute offered no guide - and this unguided discretion must necessarily result in discrimination violating of Article 14.3 This contention was also negatived. The very wide discretion in the matter of punishment was to be found in all the offences prescribed by the Penal Code, said the Court. It has its origin in the impossibility of laying down standards. Since no two cases are alike, sentencing norms could not be statutorily prescribed. They had to be left to the discretionary judgement of the judge, to be exercised on what the court called "well recognized principles". This part of the judgement of the Court in Jagmohan Singh's case, albeit of five judges, has not convinced Indian penologists - it has rankled with some of the later justices of the Supreme Court.

In the year in which the decision in Jagmohan Singh's Case was handed down, the new Criminal Procedure Code, 1973, was enacted, replacing the provisions of the Criminal Procedure Code 1898. One of its provisions required that where an offence was punishable with death or in the alternative with imprisonment for life, the judgement should state the reasons for the sentence awarded and where the sentence awarded was a sentence of death, the judgement should state "the special reasons" for such sentence.4 Since 1973, the statutory rule is that punishment for murder is life imprisonment, death sentence being the exception. What are then these "special reasons" for imposing a death sentence? They are left undefined. Till now (and this was the traditional view) the Courts always looked to the nature of the crime - how heinous it was, how brutal or cold blooded the murder. But in 1979, in a batch of appeals, a Bench of three judges of the Supreme Court handed down a decision - a majority judgement (2:1), Mr. justice Krishna Lyer (the abolitionist judge) speaking for the majority. This judgment in Rajendra Prasad's Case (AIR 1979 S.C. 916) broke new ground. The "special reasons", said the majority, related not to the crime, but the criminal. Death is no longer the punishment for a brutal murder, if there is a reasonable prospect of reformation of the criminal. But Mr. justice A.P. Sen (the minority view), was sharply critical of this thesis. In one of the cases in the batch dealt with by the Court -a case from Kerala, a married man infatuated by the charms of a village girl brutally murdered his innocent wife and his two children when they were asleep. "If the death sentence was not to be awarded in a case like this", moaned Mr. Justice Sen, "I do not see the type of offence which calls for a death sentence". But he spoke only for himself - it is no secret, however, that he echoed the sentiments of some of the other members of the Supreme Court who had not participated in the decision. A few weeks after the judgment in Rajendra Prasad's case, the ratio was followed by another Bench of two judges. But when, a few months later another case (a case of a triple murder) came up before the Court - before the same Bench which decided Rajendra Prasad's case - justice Sen again dissented. The majority view in Rajendra Prasad's Case, he said, was not a precedent. In his opinion a decision on a question of sentence depending upon the facts and circumstances of a case could never be regarded as a binding precedent. What then was the law on sentencing in murder cases? Since judges spoke in different voices, and affirmed their respective views so strongly the question whether the death penalty should be imposed having regard to the nature of the crime or only if the criminal was beyond the pale of redemption, however dastardly the crime, stood referred to a larger Bench - again of five judges - so that the law could be declared with certainty. There was also another fall out from Rajendra Prasad's case. The majority doubted the correctness of Jagmohan Singh's decision on the constitutional question. Was not the death penalty arbitrary and discriminatory, they queried? and cited text-books and statistics in support. Well - whenever the decision of a larger Bench is doubted by a smaller Bench, litigants are quick to see the green light - an application was filed for reconsidering the decision in Jagmohan Singh's Case and taking a fresh look at the Constitutional validity of capital punishment. It was granted. Again a Bench of five judges (in Bachan Singh's Case (AIR 1980 S.C. 898) went through the motions and heard arguments afresh on the constitutional validity of the death penalty. It once again affirmed the decision in Jagmohan - not unanimously, but by a majority (4:1): Mr. justice Bhagwati (later Chief Justice of India) dissenting (the dissenting judgment. is reported in AIR 1982 S.C. 1325).

Why are Justices even of the highest Court divided in their views on this vexed question?

The truth is that the death penalty is not so much a legal or a constitutional problem, as a sociological one. It evokes divergent responses in different people - and judges being human are no exception. It even cuts across party lines. Politicians everywhere are always divided on this issue. There are the abolitionists, and (for want of a better word) the retentionists. In Britain where capital punishment stood abolished, a resolution was proposed in the House of Commons in July 1983 for restoring it (at least for terrorists and for murderers of police officers). The resolution was lost, but it was a close vote 362:243. The Prime Minister Mrs. Thatcher voted for restoration of the death penalty, the Conservative Party Home Secretary Mr. Whitelaw voted against it; James Calaghan the former Labour Prime Minister and the Leader of the Opposition voted with Mr. Whitelaw. That venerated British historian, Arthur Bryant wrote in indignation:

"I believe as a historian that this decision (of Parliament) is against the permanent lesson of history which points strongly to the deterrent effect in all ages of the death penalty on law breakers of habitual violence who, in its absence, are ready to resort to murder....... The sole justification for the death penalty is not to punish murderers but to prevent murder."

In my country there has always been a cleavage of opinion. For some, it has been a matter of conscience. I remember my senior leader of the Bombay Bar (Sir Jameshedji Kanga) telling us in the fifties about a senior District Judge Mr. Khareghat who was due to be elevated to the Bombay High Court Bench. He declined the honour on the ground that he would never be a party to the death sentence. He would rather not be a High Court Judge. In those days the capital sentence could only be imposed by a judge of the High Court.

The abolitionists have a strong lobby. Recent events in various countries (especially in the developing world) have driven many to the conclusion that murder will never cease to be an instrument of politics until the execution even of proved murderers is regarded as immoral and wrong. In the world of today there are fewer and fewer men condemned to death for murder, and more and more executed for political views. As long as death remains a permissible instrument of Government, those in power will always justify its use. Besides, (and this is a particularly pertinent point) the hangman's noose ends the search for truth - what if the judge is wrong? The haunting question plagues our consciences.

Judgements of Courts can always be recalled and reviewed; execution of sentences of death, never.

But then there is the other side of the coin. In our obsessive concern for the criminal and his reformation, we are often apt to forget the victim and those that the criminal's act have left destitute. An eye for an eye and a tooth for a tooth, hallowed by Biblical injunction does sound just to those who are irretrievably hurt. It is sanctified in boh religious and secular legal tradition. In England the hate engendered by the crime is assuaged by generous awards of compensation by the State. The Government in U.K. funds in every year large amounts and places them at the disposal of an administrative agency - the Criminal Injuries Compensation Board - to be paid over to the victims of violent crime. Where this system of social welfare is lacking (as in India) there is a feeling that if the victim's family cannot be generously compensated for the loss, they should have their revenge at least through the courts - by invoking the awful majesty of the law. In August 1986, the New York Times in an editorial said: "the sentence of death is an expression of vengeance and it is still barbaric".

Both parts of this condemnation are applicable to India. Vengeful, yes. But on the plea that it was barbaric the Supreme Court of India has held in Bachan Singh that death by hanging is not an "unreasonable, cruel or unusual punishment". Roma Locuta est causa finita est (Rome has spoken the cause is ended). At least for the present.

Should revenge be the basis of a civilized system of criminal jurisprudence? Another Biblical quotation mocks the earlier one 'Revenge is mine", saith the lord, "I will revenge". But all this is theology, not law.

The main plank of the retentionists is that the death sentence has a deterrent effect - not by the fear of death but exciting in the community a deep feeling of abhorrence for the crime of murder. I remember in 1973 when Jagmohan Singh's case was being argued, Chief justice Sikri said (in the course of arguments), that he was certain that if the death penalty were abolished, entire villages in the Punjab would be wiped out in a wave of crime. He spoke with the voice of experience having been the Advocate-General of that State for many years. Other justices from this and other States have expressed similar views. But contrary views are also held and equally emphatically expressed, none more persuasively that by a Professor of Law at Stanford University. He summed up the creed of the abolitionist in a trenchant searching question: "Do we really need to kill people in order to teach people that killing people is wrong?"

In the end, the life-and-death question cannot be resolved by arguments - neither the abolitionists nor the retentionists will convince one another. But this easy escapist view is not for Courts. The Courts - especially the highest Court - must declare the law with certainty. The Supreme

Court of India has declared the law: at first (in 1973) unanimously, later (in 1980) with less certainty, one of its senior judges in a powerful dissent harkening to "the brooding spirit of the future". The dissent has helped. In a judgement of the Constitution Bench of the Supreme Court on 7th April, 1983 (Mithu Vs. State of Punjab (AIR 1983 SC 473) the Court struck down Sec. 303 of the Indian Penal Code which provided a mandatory death sentence for the crime of murder committed by a life convict - "whoever being under sentence of imprisonment for life commits murder shall be punished with death".

The Court held that Sec. 303 violated the Guarantee of Equality contained in Art. 14 of the Constitution, as also the right conferred by Art. 21. - "No person shall be deprived of his life and personal liberty except according to procedure established by law".

The Section was originally conceived to discourage assaults by life convicts on prison staff, but the language chosen far exceeded the intent. The Section assumed that life convicts were a dangerous breed of humanity and condemned them as a class: the assumption and condemnation was not supported by any scientific data.

There are many in my country who would like to see the Supreme Court of the future echo the optimistic sentiments of Justice William Brennan of the U.S. Supreme Court (sentiments expressed in September 1986):

"I believe that a majority of the U.S. Supreme Court will one day accept that when the State punishes with death it denies the humanity and dignity of the victim...... That will be a great day for our country and our Court."

Till then, we in India must live with the death penalty the highest Court assuaging its collective conscience with the assurance that the sentence would be imposed only "in the rarest of rare cases."

NOTES

* Fari S. Nariman is an advocate in the Supreme Court of India

1. Senior Advocate, Supreme Court of India; Vice President, Bar Association of India; Member, International Commission of Jurists.

2. Article 19 lists the seven freedoms in these words: All citizens shall have the right:

a) to freedom of speech and expression;

b) to assemble peaceably and without arms;

c) to form associations or unions;

d) to move freely throughout the territory of India;

e) to reside and settle in any part of the territory of India; 11(and)

f) right to acquire hold and dispose of property

g) to practise any profession, or to carry on any occupation, trade or business.

Clause (f) was deleted by the Constitution 44th Amendment Act 1978.

3. Article 14 Provides: "The State shall not deny

to any person equality before the law or the equal protection of the laws within the territory of India."

4. "The death penalty is being retained but its imposition will be restricted to extreme cases" said the Minister of State for Home Affairs when introducing the Criminal Code Amendment Bill in December 1972.

CHAPTER 6

THE GRENADA MURDER TRIAL: NO CAUSE FOR HANGING

Tony Gifford, QC, U.K. *

On the 4th of December 1986 a jury sitting in the Richmond Hill prison courthouse in Grenada returned guilty verdicts against thirteen men and one woman charged with the murder of eleven people, including Maurice Bishop, Prime Minister of Grenada from 13th March 1979 until his death on 19th October 1983. The fourteen were sentenced to the mandatory sentence of death. Three other men were convicted of manslaughter, and were sentenced to terms of 45 and 30 years imprisonment.

The trial was one of the most momentous in recent history. If one looks at the names of the victims in the murder indictment, and of the defendants accused of murdering them, between them they include nearly all the leadership of the Peoples' Revolutionary Government of Grenada (PRG) and of the New Jewel Movement (NJM) party - a leadership which had been a beacon of progress in the Caribbean; which had proved that there could be a real and popular alternative to neocolonialism; and which therefore had attracted the implacable hostility of the United States government.

Those dead included Maurice Bishop, a leader loved by his people and respected right across the world; Jacqueline Creft, the Minister of Education; Unison Whiteman, the Foreign Minister; Norris Bain, the Housing Minister; and Fitzroy Bain, leader of the Agricultural Workers.

Those on trial included ten members of the Central Committee of the New Jewel Movement. Among them were Bernard Coard, Deputy Prime Minister and Minister of Finance; Selwyn Strachan, Minister of National Mobilization; Hudson Austin, Minister of Communications and Commander of the Peoples' Revolutionary Army (PRA); and Phyllis Coard, Head of the National Womens' Organization. These were people who had been at the heart of the Grenada revolution.

At the center of the trial were the shattering events of 19th October 1983. Some of the events of that day were known to the world: that Maurice Bishop had been confined to his home by the NJM Central Committee; that a demonstration of Grenadian people came and released him, and marched with him to the capital St. George's; that the crowd took over Fort Rupert, the headquarters of the PRA, and ordered the soldiers to disarm; that a PRA detachment of three armored cars was sent from Fort Frederick, another army post, to Fort Rupert; that there was sustained firing in which people, including four soldiers, were killed; that the PRA took control of Fort Rupert, and that eight people were executed in an upper courtyard of Fort Rupert and their bodies burned during the night. But whilst those facts were reasonably clear, many questions remained completely unanswered. Had the situation been manipulated by agents of the CIA, and if so how? Who had taken the decision to march on the army headquarters, rather than, as many in the crowd had expected, to hold a meeting in the market square? What orders were given to the PRA officers who drove from Fort Frederick? Who opened fire when they reached Fort Rupert? Above all, what was the chain of command which ended in the execution of Maurice Bishop and the other seven? Did the execution order, as alleged by the prosecution, come from a meeting of the ten NJM Central Committee members at Fort Frederick?

1. ANALYZING THE TRIAL

I approached the trial with a particular experience. I had visited Grenada twice since the U.S. invasion in order to take part in the defense team. On each occasion I had been refused admittance to the Grenada Bar. But on the basis of my experience in Grenada I approach an analysis of the trial on the basis of certain principles.

First, it is necessary to understand the trial against the history of the invasion and subsequent occupation of Grenada by the United States. That invasion was a flagrant violation of International Law. The justifications advanced by the Reagan Administration were fabricated. It was said that U.S. citizens were in danger - they were not. It was said that the Governor General had asked for the intervention - he had not. The United States had in truth been planning for a long time to crush this new example of socialist development in the Caribbean. Ronald Reagan had even claimed that tiny Grenada was a threat to the security of the United States. He struck on 25th October

1933 because an opportunity had been presented to him to flout International Law with the minimum of adverse reaction.

Once in control, the United States and their Caribbean allies were determined to extirpate all the gains of the Revolution. I well recall the helicopters, the constant jeep patrols, and the vulgar soldiers off-duty who were the visible signs of the occupation in February 1984. The leaders and activists of the Revolution were put in jail, and a massive propaganda campaign was launched to brand them as the murderers of Maurice Bishop and the betrayers of the Grenadian people.

In those circumstances the motivation of the charges, particularly against the Central Committee members, was clearly to ensure their elimination as a potential force of political

resistance in Grenada, by means of judicial verdicts and executions, irrespective of their guilt or innocence on the charges.

On the other hand, the trial could not be seen as an sham. Inexcusable crimes had, in fact, been committed. NOTHING, in my view, could justify the deliberate execution of Maurice Bishop and the other seven who were shot in the upper

- DR. MUNYONZWE HAMALENGWA

courtyard. The perpetrators of that deed had killed a dedicated and inspirational leader whom the whole progressive world mourned. They had dragged seven others into the firing line without any time for reflection, let alone due process of law. The world had an interest in knowing who had committed or authorized these crimes. The support given to the defendants could not be unconditional.

2. POLITICAL ERRORS OR CRIMINAL ACTS?

There is a distinction between the criminal act of execution and the political errors which led to the 19th October confrontations. For there was another central question hanging over the trial - how was it that the leadership of the NJM became so fatally ruptured that the trauma of 19th October could happen at all? On this question there have been many commentaries, but until recently the voice of those in jail was not heard. Now, from their statements in court and from a book to be published, their account is known.

My own belief is that serious mistakes were made in the handling of the proposal made in September 1983, that there should be joint leadership of the NJM by Maurice Bishop and Bernard Coard, although I totally reject the US propaganda that this proposal was an attempt by the "Marxist Coard faction" to overthrow the "moderate Maurice Bishop". There is no evidence for that story, which is an offence to the integrity of both men. The argument was not about the direction of policy, but over the weak state of the NJM as a party.

The joint leadership proposal was made and accepted by Maurice Bishop as a cure for the NJM's weaknesses. That was simplistic in itself, for the problems lay more with the lack of participation at the grass roots than with the precise character of the leadership. When Maurice Bishop had second thoughts about how the proposal would work in practice, the majority on the Central Committee reacted with impatience and intolerance, insisting on adherence to the original decision rather than pausing to weigh up the situation and to maintain unity. The house arrest of Maurice Bishop, while prompted by genuine fears, was the final act which set the Central Committee majority against the Grenadian people, who could not understand what was going on.

Mistakes were also made in that period by Maurice Bishop and those with him. They stirred up opposition to the joint leadership decision while abroad on a trip to Eastern Europe,

instead of waiting for further discussions back in Grenada. They allowed rumors to be put about that Bernard and Phyllis Coard were plotting to kill Maurice Bishop - rumors whose exact source is still unclear, which may well have been put about malevolently by CIA agents in order to inflame the situation.

There are many lessons to be learned from that crucial time. The essential point for an analysis of the trial is that the defendants should not be left to hang because they may have mishandled the situation in their party. The issue must be whether a fair, judicial process has found them guilty of murder. On that issue my conclusions, in this paper, are that the process has not been fair, and that the case against the NJM leadership is flimsy. That is why there must be a campaign to save their lives.

3. AVOID SIMPLE PREJUDGEMENTS

It follows that an objective analysis of the trial must avoid two errors into which different progressive groups have fallen over the last three years. On the one hand there are those who are so incensed at the death of Maurice Bishop and by the destruction of the Grenadian revolution, that they spit upon the defendants on trial and care not if they are executed. Such people are playing the game of imperialism. If the defendants were executed, almost the whole leadership of the NJM would be liquidated, and the forces of reaction and exploitation would be delighted.

On the other hand, there are those who are so outraged by the US invasion that they denounce the whole trial process as being inevitably corrupt, and act as if all the defendants must, by definition, be innocent. The danger of applying to the trial such uncritical labels as 'kangaroo court' or 'Yankee court' is that they obscure a more complex reality. The trial in the Richmond Hill courtroom did bear most of the hallmarks of due process. The accused had the right to lawyers of their choice under legal aid. The evidence against them was supplied to them in advance, and was given in public. They had the right to cross examine the witnesses and to present their own defense. The verdicts were delivered by a jury of Grenadian citizens.

However the trial, while superficially normal, was fundamentally flawed. It was held in an unconstitutional court, from which the constitutional safeguard of an appeal to the Privy Council was missing. It contained a number of grossly irregular features. As a result I shall argue that it cannot be considered to be a fair trial. I shall argue further that, on the basis of the evidence as presented, a fair trial may have ended in very different verdicts. Tragically, the trial has not provided answers to the key questions which are posed by the tragedy of 19th October.

4. THE UNCONSTITUTIONAL COURT

Under Grenada's Independence Constitution, the court having jurisdiction over Grenada is the Supreme Court of the Eastern Caribbean States (ECSC). From there an appeal lies to the Appeal court of the Eastern Caribbean States from which there is a final right of appeal to the Privy Council in London.

Following the Grenada revolution in March 1979, the other Eastern Caribbean Governments, out of hostility to the PRG, unilaterally withdrew the facilities of the ECSC court system from Grenada. The PRG was therefore forced to set up its own court system, the High Court and Court of Appeal of Grenada. The judges of these courts enjoyed full security of tenure and remained wholly independent of the government. It is significant that since the invasion the President of the Appeal Court, Mr Justice Haynes, has said that during the period of the revolution, "fair trials did take place". Since the invasion, the Grenada government has claimed to respect the provisions of the 1973 constitution. It has restored every other clause EXCEPT the clauses designating the court system of Grenada.

Why has the constitutional court system not been restored? One can see no reasons of administrative difficulty, for until March 1979 the ECSC court system worked smoothly to administer in Grenada. Indeed, if one looked only to administrative convenience, the arguments would be strong in favor of returning to the ECSC court system as soon as possible. For of the two judges sitting in the High Court of Grenada, Chief Justice Nedd retired in December 1985, and Mr Justice Patterson was obliged to disqualify himself from hearing the murder trial because of a highly prejudicial speech made in Jamaica in 1984, in which he called the defendants "Satans". By the start of 1986 there were therefore no judges available in the High Court of Grenada to preside over the trial.

Meanwhile in 1985 the Grenada Court of Appeal had made a ruling, in an application

made by the murder trial defendants, on the legality of the existing Courts. In its ruling the

Court of Appeal granted the High Court of Grenada a temporary validity on the grounds of necessity. However, it accepted the argument that the High Court was unconstitutional, and it expressed the expectation that the Grenada government would act with "reasonable despatch" to restore the Court system embodied in the Constitution.

In November 1985 the Constitution Commission set up by the Grenada government itself reported, and recommended a return to the ECSC court system, including the right of appeal to the Privy Council.

But the Grenada government took no steps to rejoin the ECSC. Instead Mr Justice Dennis Byron was seconded from the ECSC for a temporary period to be "acting Chief Justice" of Grenada. The Official Grenada government gazette of 30th January 1986 stated that he was appointed to "hear certain matters". The local press revealed that his appointment was to last for three months.

The position, therefore, was that a temporary Judge was sitting in a temporary court and the inference was irresistible that the government of Grenada was deliberately manipulating the judicial arrangements in order to deprive the accused of the much stronger legal protection afforded by the ECSC. In particular the ECSC would provide:

(a) the right of appeal to the Privy Council;

(b) the opportunity for the accused to apply for the trial to be held in another island if the local prejudice against the accused was thought to be so overwhelming as to prevent a fair trial in Grenada;

(c) the right to be tried before a judge whose appointment and tenure did not depend on the Grenada government.

5. FAIR TRIAL MOTION

In September 1985, the defendants had filed a constitutional motion in which there were two main elements:

First, the defendants submitted that their constitutional right to a fair trial could not be granted to them because of the massive prejudicial pre-trial publicity campaign, which had been directed against them from the time of the invasion onwards.

Secondly, and because of the ruling of the Court of

Appeal that the High Court was only of temporary validity, the defendants applied to have the fair trial issue referred to the ECSC, which they claimed must now be the only court which could have legal jurisdiction.

After considerable delay, because no judge was able to hear the case, the motion came before Mr Justice Byron in March 1986. On 25th March he ruled that he would not have the Fair Trial Motion referred to the ECSC, and that the Grenada High Court was competent to hear it. The defendants immediately appealed against this ruling to the Grenada Court of Appeal which was due to sit in May. The position then was that the Court of Appeal would determine the issue of the reference to the ECSC, and then, depending on their decision, the Fair Trial Motion would be heard. It was clearly desirable that those matters should be dealt with before the actual murder trial began. But on 7th April Mr Justice Byron announced that the trial would proceed immediately. The defense applied for a stay of the trial pending the ruling of the Appeal Court, but on 9th April the Judge refused the Application for a stay. He ordered that the Jury should be empaneled to hear the trial on 11th April.

6. THE WITHDRAWAL OF DEFENSE LAWYERS

It was at this point, on 11th April 1986, that the defendants, after consulting with their lawyers, instructed them to withdraw from the trial. Ian Ramsay QC, the leader of the Defense team, said to the Court:

"We will not co-operate with this part of the proceedings which we see as having the effect of preempting the Court of Appeal proceedings, and to face the Court of Appeal with a 'fait accompli' when the applicants' appeal comes on."

In a subsequent letter to all the Commonwealth Heads of Government, Mr Ramsay said:

"As lawyers trained in England and brought up in the principles of the Common Law, we are unable to take part, nay prohibited, from legitimizing in any way a 'trial' in or by an admittedly unconstitutional court."

He also claimed that it was quite unrealistic for the Defense team to prepare complex written submissions for the Court of Appeal and at the same time to be devoted to the defense of people on trial for their lives.

The withdrawal of the lawyers was followed by a

decision made by nearly all of the defendants to take little further part in the proceedings, and to protest with chants of "this is a Yankee court", "Why are you afraid of a constitutional court?" and "No trial in a Reagan court".

There is no doubt that this strategy had decisive and devastating consequences. In the firstplace, the evidence of all the prosecution witnesses went completely unchallenged. As we shall see, there were a number of witnesses called on behalf of the prosecution whose evidence was confused and contradictory, and whose credibility might well have been destroyed by cross-examination. Secondly, the defendants were completely unprotected when, in the weeks following their change of strategy, they were treated to a judicial sentence of Contempt of Court, and a number of extra-judicial and illegal beatings and harassments which are described below. Thirdly, they were unable to argue a number of legal points which arose during the trial concerning the jury, the court procedures, and the law relevant to the murder charges. Finally, their possibilities of exposing to the outside world the nature of the trial and of the evidence brought against them, and their answer to it, were severely restricted.

For all these reasons, I feel bound to question the wisdom of the decision which was taken to withdraw the lawyers from the case and to disrupt the proceedings thereafter. Later the defendants claimed that they were in "an impossible 'no win' situation", and they were surely right in concluding that every obstacle was being put in their way in order that convictions could be secured. Even so, it is possible and necessary in political trials to use every weapon available to win the battle for international public opinion. Whatever the prejudices of the judge and jurors, it was possible and necessary to expose to a wider public the truth of what was happening before, during and since 19th October 1983.

However, the fact that the defendants adopted this strategy does NOT mean that they are guilty of the charges, still less that they must be allowed to hang. On the contrary, they have asserted that they would be anxious to establish their innocence in the course of a fair trial, and in the course of their statements from the dock many of them set out what their defense would be. They spoke of the torture to which some of them had been subjected in order to extract "confessions of guilt". They analyzed the impossibilities in the evidence of some of the key witnesses. In spite of all the limitations caused by the absence of the lawyers, it is still possible and necessary to analyze whether justice was done in this trial.

\- DR. MUNYONZWE HAMALENGWA

7. STILL NO CONSTITUTIONAL COURT

In the event, the defendants lost their attempt to have the case referred to the ECSC. On 17th May 1986 the Grenada Court of Appeal declared that Court did not exist in Grenada, and it was therefore an abuse of the process of the court to attempt to refer a motion to it.

On 19th June 1986, a hearing took place before Mr. Justice Patterson who ruled that he had no jurisdiction to hear the Fair Trial Motion when the trial itself was proceeding in another court. That ruling was successfully appealed, and on 25th July 1986 the Grenada Court of Appeal referred the Motion back to Mr Justice Patterson. But by the end of 1986 the Fair Trial Motion had not been heard. it has to be said that given Mr Justice Patterson's known views, and the fact that the trial has now concluded, it would be unlikely in the extreme for the defendants to get anywhere by having the motion heard.

In its ruling on 17th of May the Grenada Court of Appeal expressed itself in strong terms about the delays which had taken place in the return to the ECSC. Mr Justice Haynes, the President of the Court, said that while their 1985 judgement, which gave the Grenada High Court its temporary validity, was still in effect, "we cannot escape the fact that a year has passed since the judgement and nothing has been done. We should not leave the matter so. We cannot."

Mr Justice Haynes made an order that the Grenada courts remained valid and unchallengeable, but continued:

"We, however add this, that this Court recognizes and records the urgency of the matter and demands that active steps be taken to regularize the judicial system of Grenada, and this Court expects to be advised as to the position of the negotiations at its next sitting which is fixed for Monday 21st July 1986."

Faced with this clear directive from the Court, the Grenada Cabinet in July 1986 took a formal decision to authorize the Minister of Legal Affairs to apply for Grenada's re-entry to the ECSC. But, yet again, months have dragged by, and there has been no further announcement of which I am aware. The inference seems clear, that the Grenadian authorities are seeking to delay any final arrangement with the ECSC court until after these defendants have had their last appeal and been executed. They do not wish to allow the defendants the right of appeal to the Privy Council.

On the issue of the Privy Council appeal, there is no doubt that any independent Commonwealth State has the full right to opt out of what is, in many ways, a colonial anachronism. But that is not Grenada's position; they wish to reinstate the Privy Council appeal, but not yet. Is that because they fear the scrutiny of an independent judicial body, external to Grenada? It is for that reason that an appeal has been made by myself and others to urge the Government of Grenada to return to the constitutional court system in time for the murder trial defendants to have the benefit of it.

8. THE PREJUDICE OF THE JURY

On 11th April 1986, when the defense lawyers announced their withdrawal, the array of 140 potential jurors were present in court, waiting for the time when 12 of their number would be empaneled as the jury. They were present when Mr Justice Byron, rather surprisingly, threatened the lawyers with charges of contempt of court. One of the defense lawyers, Mrs.

Jacqueline Samuels Brown described the scene which followed in an affidavit:

"Immediately after Mr Justice Byron intimated

contempt proceedings, there was widespread clapping by jurors as well as jeering and booing.... during the adjournment the jurors continued to make hostile comments in relation to the accused and their counsel...."

"On resumption of the session the presiding judge announced that he would postpone his decision in relation to possible contempt proceedings until the following Monday, and he adjourned the day's session of the court .... on this adjournment the array of jurors hurled further hostile remarks, threats and jeers at the accused and their counsel..."

"As buses filled with jurors left the compound, a large number of them raised their fists threateningly and menacingly at the defense counsel who were in the prison yard, saying, among other things, 'they going get a cut-arse and you too'..."

"From this array 12 persons were subsequently empaneled to sit as the trier of fact in this trial."

A panel of jurors which displayed such open prejudice ought to have been disqualified from sitting. It was inevitable that many, if not all, of the potential jurors in this trial would have been infected by a degree of hostility and prejudice.

Ever since the invasion there has been an orchestrated propaganda campaign, initiated by the United States government, labeling those now accused of murder as "power seekers", "thugs" and "murderers". Even following the laying of charges and the preparations for trial the propaganda campaign never died down. The defendants, who have analyzed the local media closely, state that during 1985 one hundred and twenty seven prejudicial references to the accused were in two of the five local newspapers, including emotive articles and editorials and "Letters to the Editors". No action was taken to curb this publicity, just as no action was taken in court on 11th April when the jurors made their outbursts.

Complaints have also been made about the method of selection of the panel of jurors. On the 5th March 1986 the Registrar of the Court had been abruptly dismissed, and on the following day replaced by a woman, who until then had been a member of the prosecution team. The defendants, not surprisingly, found this replacement extremely suspicious. It was believed that the former Registrar had selected an array fairly and in accordance with the law, and that he had been criticized for this. The final array was selected by his successor.

It is impossible to judge on the material available

whether this jury was chosen from a genuinely random sample of Grenadians or not. The trial judge dismissed a challenge to the array of jurors which had been made by the lawyers before their withdrawal on the basis of the presence of the former member of the prosecution team as Registrar. Much later on, a detailed analysis of the jurors was done by Phyllis Coard in her statement from the dock. She described "a truly amazing and baffling situation", in which many hundreds of potential jurors had been passed over without any apparent reason. She. concluded that "the array of jurors was carefully handpicked". However, it should be noted that the defense legal team, which was still in Grenada when the array of jurors had been selected, did not allege that the actual selection was biased, only that justice was not being seen to be done by the appointment of the new Registrar. The truth may well be that the authorities did not need to rig the jury - their propaganda had ensured that almost any group of Grenadians would, at least until they heard the other side of the story, be affected by feelings of intense hostility towards the accused.

9. THE RIGHT TO CHALLENGE JURORS

The final selection of a panel of 12 jurors was made on 18th April 1986. Seventeen of the defendants had by then been sentenced to 7 to 10 days imprisonment for contempt of court, after disrupting the proceedings. They were not present when the jury was selected, and had no opportunity to exercise their right to challenge prospective jurors. This, in my view, was fundamentally wrong. The right to challenge jurors is deeply entrenched in the system of jury trial. It may well be that their disruption entitled the judge to hear evidence in their absence. It did not entitle him to have the jury picked in their absence. This will certainly be one of the matters to be argued on any appeal.

In the event, the prosecution played a major part in the selection of the final jury. Forty- three names were called before 12 jurors were sworn. Twenty-nine of them were made to "stand by" by the prosecution, and 2 were discharged for other reasons. Fifteen further people were made to stand by the prosecution before 6 alternate jurors were selected.

This right for the prosecution to "stand by" jurors exists also in England, but is very rarely used. The right is limited to standing jurors by until the whole panel is exhausted. It would have been possible, therefore, for the defendants to have secured the presence on the jury of some of the jurors who had been stood by, if they had used their right of making challenges so frequently that all the 140 jurors had either been challenged or stood by. It would then have been necessary to recall the jurors who had been stood by. The complete absence of the defendants, with the exception of Fabian Gabriel and Raeburn Nelson, meant that none of this could take place. I presume that the prosecution had good reason for their decision to stand 29 prospective jurors by. In a small society like Grenada they must have had information as to which of the jurors was most likely to be favourable to the prosecution case.

10. CONTEMPT OF COURT

As soon as the lawyers left the case, the pressures upon the defendants escalated. Food from their families, visits and letters were stopped. The defendants were refused the possibility of meeting together to discuss their defense - a right which had been accepted in a court order made by Chief Justice Nedd in 1985. For some weeks families were even stopped from entering the court. The Director of Public Prosecutions informed the Court that the defendants had "broken a prison regulation" on 11th April, and that therefore all their "privileges" were withdrawn.

Matters became worse on 16th April, and again on 18th April, when the judge cut short defendants who were making protests about their treatment. The judge countered by sentencing them to imprisonment for the offence of contempt of court, at first for one day, then on 18th April to sentences of between 7 and 10 days. All defendants were sentenced except for Fabian Gabriel, who was soon to turn Queen's evidence, and Raeburn Nelson, who objected on conscientious grounds to making any disruption of the court.

The effect of the contempt of court sentences was that the prison authorities took the opportunity to treat them as convicted prisoners rather than as untried prisoners on remand. Their hair and beards were forcibly shaven, a move designed both to strip them of their dignify and to give them the appearance of convicts before the jury.

These contempt of court sentences were unnecessary and deplorable. A judge presiding over a trial normally has the right to order a defendant to be removed to the cells if he disrupts the proceedings. It may also be appropriate to sentence a defendant for contempt of court AFTER the trial has ended. But during the trial, the right of the defendants to have the facilities for their defense must be paramount.

11. THE ABSENCE OF THE DEFENDANTS

The defendants have stated that "by April 18th it had become clear that a free and fair trial was not to be had in Grenada". From then until the close of the prosecution case they refused to participate in the trial. When brought into court at the beginning of each day, they chanted, clapped and shouted until the Judge ordered them to be removed back into the cells. After each witness had given evidence, the defendants were brought into court individually to have the evidence read to them and to be given the opportunity to ask questions. Again they continued with their protests.

The defendants have argued that according to the Grenada constitution they have an absolute right to be present at their trial. Presumably this argument means that a defendant who was determined to disrupt the proceedings would have to be gagged or straight jacketed in order that the proceedings could be heard in his presence. The argument depends on the interpretation of the words of the constitution, and is by no means straight forward. It will presumably be fully explored in any appeal.

12. PHYSICAL BEATINGS

On 25th April, after being charged and sentenced for contempt of court for the third time, 8 defendants, including Bernard Coard, Selwyn Strachan, Leon Cornwall and John Ventour were beaten by a group of policemen attached to the court. The beatings began immediately outside the court, actually within the precincts of the court. They were thrust into a car, and were beaten again all the way back to their cell block. They were then denied medical attention for more than 72 hours, and appeared in court on 28th April, the following Monday, with obvious injuries. Selwyn Strachan's eye was so obviously swollen that it was almost closed. He said that he had been beaten about the head, shoulders, arms and legs. The Judge ruled that "this is not a suitable court to investigate the matter", and left it to the Director of Public Prosecutions to investigate. But no charges were ever brought against the police officers responsible.

13. REMOVAL OF DOCUMENTS

The contempt of court sentence an 18th April had the further consequence that the defendants' pens, paper and other writing materials were seized by the prison authorities. Their documents and legal notes were taken away. When they complained about this on 29th April the Director of Public Prosecutions argued that they were now convicted prisoners, and that therefore the "privileges due to remand prisoners" had been taken away. Even the Judge could not accept this, and ordered the immediate return of the documents.

However, five documents were never returned. They included a detailed analysis of the contradictions in the evidence of prosecution witnesses, and a list of potential defense witnesses. Each of these two documents would have been extremely interesting to any prosecuting authority unscrupulous enough to want to thwart the tactics of the defense by underhand means.

Other vital documents were never received by the defendants at any time. From early 1984 onwards they had requested, through their lawyers, the production of documents and tapes which had been seized by the United States military during the invasion. They included Minutes of NJM meetings; the diaries from various army camps (for example the Fort Frederick camp diary for 19th October 1983 would have recorded all movements in and out of the camp and would have been absolutely essential in rebutting the accusation of a Central Committee meeting at the

Camp on that day); and a tape recording and statements made by the key prosecution witness Cletus St. Paul during investigations made prior to the invasion.

The prosecution did not deny that these documents and tapes existed, but merely stated that they were in the possession of the United States which was claiming diplomatic immunity in refusing to provide them. The Judge ruled that he had no jurisdiction to compel a foreign government to produce the documents. Thus conveniently the United States and Grenadian authorities between them were able to prevent the defense from obtaining material which the law entitled them to have.

14. THE COURTHOUSE

The most conspicuous impropriety in the proceedings was the place of trial itself. In the capital, St Georges, there is a court building in the center of town with two large court rooms. In February 1984 the defendants had been brought into the court building to be charged with the murder charge. I was present on that occasion, which passed off without there being any serious security problem. A large crowd had gathered in the streets outside and they were cordoned off from the area of the court house without difficulty by the police. The court room which was used was big enough to provide room for the defendants and their lawyers, as well as for a large public gallery.

Instead of using the court house, a special court was constructed on Richmond Hill, within the precincts of the prison, just outside the main prison doors. To reach it meant a long journey out of town, through a number of police check points. Space for the public was limited, and tickets had to be applied for by relatives of the defendants.

The difference in atmosphere was obvious, and was intended. A trial in the normal court house would have given the opportu¬nity for Grenadians to drop in and listen, to have heard the defendants presenting their defense, to have understood that there were two sides to the story. The removal of the trial to an inaccessible hill top reinforced the impression that these were dangerous criminals on trial, and allowed the harassment of the defendants to go virtually unobserved.

15. THE EVIDENCE AT THE TRIAL

Any attempt to analyze the evidence given at the trial meets two obvious difficulties. First, there is no complete record of the trial proceedings. I have relied on a series of reports which were written in the Barbados Daily Nation, the Grenadian Voice, and the Grenada Newsletter, but they are far from complete. In particular there is a very inadequate record of the summing up, which would normally provide a useful summary of the factual and legal issues in the case.

Secondly, as indicated above, the evidence of the prosecution witnesses was not challenged or tested in cross examination. The defendants' statements from the dock, many of them extremely detailed, give an indication of some of the issues which would have been explored in cross examination. But one can only speculate as to what the strength of the evidence would have been if it had been put to that test.

It may be useful to summarize some of the key figures in the case. There were eleven victims alleged in the murder indictment, and from their mode of death they fell into two categories:

(i) the eight victims of execution, who were Maurice Bishop, Jacqueline Creft, Unison Whiteman, Norris Bain, Fitzroy Bain, Brat Bullen, Evelyn Maitland and Keith Hayling. The evidence from a number of eye witnesses was that after the PRA detachment had retaken Fort Rupert, these eight were lined up against a wall in the upper courtyard of the Fort and executed by a firing squad. In their case anyone who ordered their execution or who assisted in carrying it out, would in law be guilty of murder. The central issue for the jury would have been who was involved either in the ordering or the carrying out of the execution?

(ii) Avis Ferguson, Jemma Belmar and Vincent Noel, who were killed earlier on in the course of the shooting, after the PRA detachment arrived from Fort Frederick to retake Fort Rupert. In this case, the questions to be answered were more complex:

(a) who had given the orders for the operation? Here the same issues arose in relation to most of the Central Committee members as in the case of the executions, ie) were they meeting as a Central Committee at all and if so what did they order?

(b) was it a lawful military operation to seek to take back Fort Rupert after it had been taken over by a crowd of civilians? Ewart Layne, who admitted giving the orders to the PRA detachment, argued strongly that he gave lawful orders for a lawful mission.

(c) who fired first at Fort Rupert? If the PRA detachment had fired first, then it probably would be responsible for using excessive force. But, if, as many defendants claim, the firing was started by those inside Fort Rupert, then the soldiers could argue that they used reasonable force to accomplish a lawful mission, and that they were therefore not guilty of murdering those who died in the cross-fire.

16. THE DEFENDANTS

The defendants also fell into different categories:

(1)(1 The ten numbers of the Central Committee of the NJM: Hudson Austin, Bernard Coard, Liam James, Leon Cornwall, John Ventour, Dave Bartholomew, Ewart Layne, Kamau McBarnett, Selwyn Strachan and Phyllis Coard. No one suggested that they were at Fort Rupert when any of the deaths occurred. The case against them was that they met together at Fort Frederick and gave the orders. By ordering the storming of Fort Rupert by force, it was said that they were guilty of the murders of the three who died in the fighting, and it was further alleged that they gave a direct order for the execution of Maurice Bishop and those who were with him.

Among the Central Committee members a particular and prominent part was taken by

Ewart Layne. He accepted that as Second in Command of the Army he had given orders to the PRA detachment to recapture Fort Rupert. Important questions therefore arise as to what orders he gave, and as to whether he was acting alone as a military commander, as he claimed, or following orders from the Central Committee.

These ten defendants were all convicted of all the murders and sentenced to death.

(2) Christopher Stroude, Lester Redhead and Callistus Bernard (usually known as Abdullah). These were all senior PRA officers who according to some of the evidence (although it was very contradictory) had been in positions of command at Fort Rupert at the time of the executions, and had taken some part in giving the orders to fire. They were all convicted and sentenced to death. Lester Redhead and Christopher Stroude, who were already at Fort Rupert at the time of the capture were found guilty only of the murder of the eight who were executed.

(3) Andy Mitchell, Vincent Joseph and Cosmos Richardson. These were three PRA soldiers who, according to the evidence (although again it was contradictory), had actually fired upon the eight who were executed. They were each found guilty of manslaughter only. The basis of the verdict is

not clear. The prosecutor had suggested in his speech to the jury that any soldier who mistakenly acted in the belief that he was carrying out lawful orders could be found guilty of manslaughter, but I do not know whether this line was adopted by the Judqe. It seems more likely to he the case of a merciful verdict by the jurors. Vincent Joseph and Cosmos Richardson were sentenced to 45 years imprisonment and Andy Mitchell to 30 years.

(4) Cecil Prime, who was a soldier on duty at Fort Rupert, and who hardly appeared in the evidence at all. According to Fabian Gabriel, he was present in the top square at some time before the executions, but is not said to have taken any part. He did not make any confession to the police. Yet he was convicted and sentenced to death. His conviction is particularly iniquitous, for he would appear to have had every chance of being acquitted if the trial had been properly contested.

(5) Raeburn Nelson, who was part of the PRA detachment sent to take Fort Rupert, but against whom also there was very little direct evidence. He took no part in the disruption of the court proceedings, but sat silently throughout the trial. He said

that he had had "friendly encounters" with the investigating police officers. He was acquitted on all of the charges and released.

17. THE DEFENDANT TURNED CROWN WITNESS

The last of the original 19 defendants was Fabian Gabriel , a PRA sergeant who was in charge of logistics at Fort Rupert. On 22nd April 1986, the day before the prosecution opened its case, the Director of Public Prosecutions announced that Fabian Gabriel had been given a "conditional pardon". She said that the pardon could be canceled, and he could still be tried for murder, if he did not "testify fully and truthfully".

During the remand period there had been intense pressure brought to bear against some of the defendants and their families to induce them to give evidence against their fellow

accused. For instance, Kamau McBarnette said in his statement from the dock:

"I was promised a house. Those people said to me that measures would be taken to guarantee my safety. These promises and enticements did not work and when they failed they resorted to threats such as I would be hanged, or I would spend many years in prison if I did not co-operate."

It is to be regretted that no one was able to cross-examine Fabian Gabriel in order to extract from him information as to exactly what pressures were put upon him and what

deal was done. Experience from the "Supergrass" trials in Northern Ireland indicates that such witnesses are extremely vulnerable in cross-examination, and extremely

suspect in their reliability. With a witness like Fabian Gabriel, one can never know

whether he is implicating people because they are guilty, or because he has promised, as part of the deal with the authorities, that he will implicate as many people as possible.

Fabian Gabriel was only able to give evidence as to what was alleged to have happened at Fort Rupert, although there his evidence against several defendants was crucial. However, the authorities must have been furious not to have also secured a "supergrass" within the Central Committee, where we shall see their case was extremely weak.

18. THE EVIDENCE

The prosecution evidence fell broadly into five categories:

1. evidence as to the history of the crisis

2. evidence as to the takeover of Fort Rupert by the crowd and its subsequent capture

3. evidence as to the executions

4. evidence as to the role of the Central Committee

5. evidence from police officers as to the alleged confessions of the defendants

19. THE HISTORY OF THE CRISIS

George Louison, a former member of the Central Committee of the NJM, gave extensive evidence about the buildup of tension within the NJM during September and October 1983. He spoke of his return with Maurice Bishop from the Eastern European trip on 8th October. They were met at the airport by Selwyn Strachan alone, who said that the joint leadership issue would be back on the Central Committee agenda on 12th October.

He spoke of the meeting on 12th October, when he

himself was charged with influencing sections of the Party against the Central Committee decision, and was expelled from the Central Committee. Maurice Bishop was accused at the same meeting of circulating the false rumor of a plot by the Coards against him, which he denied. He spoke of the general meeting of Party members, about 250 - 300 people, which was held on 13th October. He said that Selwyn Strachan made the announcement that Maurice Bishop was under house arrest for spreading false rumors.

George Louison went on to speak of a series of meetings held between Bernard Coard,

Selwyn Strachan, Unison Whiteman. and himself. He said that Bernard Coard was proposing that Maurice Bishop should leave the country and go somewhere else, maybe Cuba and cool it for a few years. George Louison and Unison Whiteman were arguing that the people were becoming increasingly angry over the house arrest of Maurice Bishop and were likely to protest through mass demonstrations, and that the only solution was to restore Maurice Bishop to the position of leadership. Bernard Coard and Selwyn Strachan said that they would take their views to the Central Committee, but by 18th October there had been no decision and on that day George Louison was arrested.

Cletus St Paul, Maurice Bishop's head of security, also gave evidence about the October days. He had been with Maurice Bishop all the time during the Eastern European trip and after the return to Grenada on 8th October. On 12th October he was accused by Liam James of circulating the rumor about a plot and he was put under arrest.

These two witnesses were both accused of telling lies by the defendants, but were not directly cross-examined. They were both key actors in the unfolding drama. Cletus St Paul has been directly accused by the defendants of being an agent for the CIA. George Louison was believed by them to bear a heavy responsibility for stirring up animosity against the Central Committee majority during the Eastern European tour. George Louison's account of the final days presents a very different emphasis to that later given by Bernard Coard to the Court. According to Bernard Coard, the crisis was tragically close to being satisfactorily settled, and the Central Committee had conceded many of the points which Maurice Bishop was insisting on. So the testing and probing of the evidence of George Louison and Cletus St. Paul by cross-examination could have been extremely significant in helping Grenadians to understand the development of the crisis.

20. EVIDENCE FROM FORT RUPERT

A number of witnesses had taken part in the demonstration at Maurice Bishop's house and went with him to Fort Rupert. Pamela Cherubin said that she was part of the crowd chanting, "B for Bishop, C for Coard and C for Communism". Sylvia Belmar spoke of Maurice Bishop asking Christopher Stroude to disarm the soldiers at the Fort. She said that Maurice Bishop had asked two of the soldiers to reconnect telephone lines so that he could speak to Grenadians and to the rest of the world.

These and other witnesses then described what happened when the three armored cars arrived from Fort Frederick. Ann Fleptune, a student who lost her left leg during the firing, was near the entrance to Fort Rupert:

“I saw the armored cars coming up towards the Fort and heard gun shots coming from the direction of the armored cars. I started to run towards a building not far from behind me but I fell. Before I fell my left leg was paining.”

Sylvia Belmar was one of the witnesses in the operations room. She said that there were continuous explosions for about 15 to 20 minutes. It was during that time that Avis Ferguson was killed and Jemma Belmar and Vincent Noel received fatal injuries.

Later the defendant Abdullah, in a full statement from the dock, gave his account as commander of one of the armored cars. He said that he was going on a lawful mission, without any idea that they would be shot at. He said that when the first armored car arrived at the entrance to Fort Rupert the unit was ambushed by rifle fire and one of the soldiers fell dead. Rifle fire was coining from the Fort over his head. Officer Cadet Mayers, who was in command of the detachment, was killed. He said:

"When we arrived there I gave the order to disembark from the transport. The objective of my unit was to control the Fort. It was not possible to advance to the square immediately because hundreds of people were streaming down from the Fort because of the battle which followed after the civilians opened fire and ambushed the unit. People were streaming down from the Fort with their hands in the air and the army did not open fire on them. There are photos of this. We were bogged down for some time, it could be about two to three minutes, by the civilians streaming out of the Fort."

It is clear that if there had been cross examination, a number of questions would have been asked about the unfolding of the events of 19th October. The issue of how and why and at whose instigation the crowd went to Fort Rupert at all, was never opened up. It would appear that there were people among Maurice Bishop's followers who had decided that a military solution to the crisis was necessary. It is equally clear that the Army Command considered it necessary that they should regain military control. The tragic outcome described by the witnesses was perhaps inevitable once these positions had been taken up. But whether those who ordered and carried out the action were guilty of the murder of those who died in it is a question on which it is impossible, on the limited evidence available, to give a complete legal answer. It could certainly be argued, as a matter of law, that the legitimate army command has the right to eject civilians who have taken over the central headquarters of the army itself, even though the Prime Minister of the country is one of those responsible - at least as long as no unreasonable force is used by the army in its action.

21. WITNESSES TO THE EXECUTIONS

Three witnesses claim to have actually seen the executions: Beverley Charles, Walter Charles and Fabian Gabriel.

Beverley Charles, a PRA soldier, said that she was watching from a window in the barracks overlooking the upper square. She had seen seven of the victims in the square facing a wall with their hands on their heads. Andy Mitchell, Fabian Gabriel, Cosmos Richardson and Keith Hayling were with them. Andy Mitchell ordered Keith Hayling to be disarmed and told him "to join the other criminals across there."

She said that a little later she saw Lester Redhead coming across the Square. He spoke to Andy Mitchell, Fabian Gabriel and Cosmos Richardson. Shots were then fired from three directions. Andy Mitchell was in one direction and Fabian Gabriel on the second. She could not see the other direction. After the firing the victims fell to the ground.

Beverley Charles was adamant that Abdullah was not on the square at this time. She knew him, and said that she saw him later, when he threatened to shoot the wounded Vincent Noel.

Walter Charles was also watching through a

window in the barracks. He said that the victims were led by Abdullah and Christopher Stroude up to the top square. He says that he saw Abdullah, Cosmos Richardson and Vincent Joseph carry out the executions with machine guns. He said that before the firing Jacqueline Creft had pleaded with Cosmos Richardson that she was a pregnant woman.

Fabian Gabriel succeeded in naming all the eight accused, other than the Central Committee members, as having been involved in some way. He said that Maurice Bishop and five of the other victims were being guarded in the top square by Lester Redhead, Christopher Stroude, Abdullah, Vincent Joseph, Andy Mitchell,

and Cosmos Richardson. They were ordered by Lester Redhead and Abdullah to go to the waI1 . He said that Lester Redhead then pointed to Keith Hayling and Evelyn Maitland, and then said:

"You Hayling, join the fucking line, and you Maitland, join the fucking line too. You also are bourgeois."

There then followed a question and answer which are significant as being the only evidence implicating Cecil Prime in the executions:

Gabriel:"I noticed Abdullah and Redhead leave

the top square leaving Vincent Joseph on top of the tunnel on the top square with the machine gun."

Hudson-Phillips: “Did you see anybody else on top there?” (prosecutor)

Gabriel:“At that time I saw Cecil Prime also.”

Fabian Gabriel said that Abdullah and Redhead returned again after about an hour. Gabriel was one of those who were guarding them. At one point the Prime Minister asked for a cigarette, but Andy Mitchell refused to allow him a light.

When the actual executions occurred, Fabian Gabriel said that he was in his office on the top square “preparing a menu for the next day.” He heard the voice of Abdullah saying: “¬Comrades, turn around. This is an order from the Central Committee, you shall be executed by fire. It is not my order, it is the Central Committee’s.”

He said that Abdullah was reading from a piece of white paper. He then said that Jacqueline Creft pleaded that she was seven months pregnant, but Andy Mitchell replied saying, "no fucking comrade at this time." Abdullah then gave the order, "prepare to fire" and counted to three. Gabriel said that after that he witnessed "rapid firing that was on the bodies against the wall" lasting for "at least ten to fifteen minutes, I'll say ten minutes." He said that Vincent Joseph, Andy Mitchell and Cosmos Richardson were firing and Abdullah and Christopher Stroude were also present. He said that he "noticed Prime" at the tunnel on the top square, but again gave no evidence as to what Prime was doing.

Afterwards he said that Christopher Stroude called all the soldiers together, and said that Maurice Bishop was not true to the revolution. He was a traitor and that was why he had to be executed. He said that after that he helped to move the bodies. Abdullah

told him to "finish" one of the bodies and he fired a single bullet at it. He claimed that:

"That is the only time that I, Fabian Vernon Gabriel, ever held a weapon in my hand."

Reading over the eye witness evidence, I felt two reactions. First, even if it was only approximately true, the callousness of the operation was sickening. But the second reaction looking at the evidence in its detail, is that it is riddled with contradictions and inconsistencies. These are apparent from the summary given above. The three witnesses give different evidence on such vital matters as who was in charge of the lining up of the victims; who gave the orders to fire; who carried out the firing; who swore at Jacqueline Creft; and who was present at the time. Penetrating cross-examination may well have served to heighten the differences and to have made it quite impossible for the jury to reconcile the three accounts. While it seems undeniable that a number of those in the dock had taken part in the execution, one must remain extremely concerned at the

blanket conviction of all eight soldiers without there having been a detailed analysis of the strength of the evidence against each.

22. THE CASE AGAINST THE CENTRAL COMMITTEE

Two members of the Central Committee, Ewart Layne and Kamau McBarnette had made "confessions", which I deal with below. According to the law of evidence, those confessions could only be evidence against them. As against the other members of the Central Committee, the single witness was Cletus St. Paul.

Cletus St. Paul's account of the events of 19th October was that he was under arrest at the army camp at Calivigny, when Ewart Layne came to the camp. He spoke to Officer Cadet Myers, and then the soldiers at the camp who were in combat wear were made to board a military truck. He was made to board the truck as well, and it drove to Fort Frederick. He said that on his arrival , he came off the truck and went and sat on some ammunition boxes on a verandah "in the second building located at Fort Frederick from the Mental Hospital gate." He said that Liam James then arrived and told the soldiers that the masses had freed Maurice Bishop and were taking him to the city. Liam James said:

"As a result things are getting dread in the country, and as a result the Central Committee will be arriving shortly to take a serious decision."

Cletus St. Paul then said that he saw the Prime Minister's car arrive with Bernard and Phyllis Coard in the back. He said that Bernard Coard had a brief case in one hand and a Makarov pistol at his side. Other members of the Central Committee then arrived. He named Selwyn Strachan, Hudson Austin, Ewart Layne, Leon Cornwall, John Ventour, Dave Bartholomew and Kamau McBarnette. The cars came to the bottom level of Fort Frederick, by the mental hospital entrance.

In the following exchange Cletus St. Paul then

described the suggested "meeting" of the Central Committee:

Q. "Tell these persons, having arrived there, what else did you observe?"

A. "They joined the company of Liam James, Bernard Coard and Phyllis Coard. They conversed amongst themselves for a while."

Q. "Were you able to hear what they were saying?"

A. “No.”

Q. "What made you say they were conversing?'

A. "They were in a group shaking heads and making signs with their hands."

Q. “What next happened?”

A. "After that Leon Cornwall left the group and spoke to the soldiers ... in a commanding tone of voice."

Q. "When he spoke, could the other members of the Central Committee hear?"

A. "Yes. ... he told the soldiers that because of a rumor, a vicious rumor, spread by Maurice Bishop, counter revolutionaries, big businessmen seized the opportunity to create trouble, free

Maurice Bishop from house arrest, and as a result these elements must be liquidated."

Q. "When he said this, was this in the presence and hearing of the Central Committee members?"

A. "Yes."

Q."What Happened?"

A."He started shouting 'Central Committee orders', the other members of the Central Committee shouted, 'Central Committee orders', and the soldiers said,.'We obey, we obey'."

He said that the other members of the Central Committee went to the second level of Fort Frederick, while Ewart Layne gave orders to Mayers, Abdullah and Nelson. The three vehicles then left Fort Frederick and he heard loud explosions and bursts of gunfire. After more gunfire he saw a "yellow flare in the direction of Fort Rupert". He heard Hudson Austin shout "mission accomplished". Other members of the Central Committee had been shouting "Long live the revolution, long live the Central Committee".

On the face of it this was an extraordinary piece of evidence. For the ten members of the Central Committee to hold a meeting in full view of a close associate of Maurice Bishop, who they had themselves arrested, was unlikely. In the event, it conflicted sharply with other evidence which was given. Joseph St Bernard, a worker at the mental hospital nearby, told the court that he saw various Central Committee members arriving in cars at Fort Frederick. He said that they went immediately to the upper level of the Fort, and therefore he did not witness any "meeting" in the courtyard.

Several of the Central Committee defendants in their statements from the dock denied altogether that there had been any meeting at Fort Frederick or that they had any advance knowledge of the executions. Phyllis Coard, as mentioned below, described vividly how she had arrived with a suitcase in her hand, and not in the Prime Minister's car, having been asked by Bernard Coard to pack their bags because they were leaving the island. Bernard Coard stated that he and others were "paralyzed" by the development of the situation.

Yet on Cletus St. Paul's evidence alone ten people have been sentenced to hang. At best he was a witness who had every reason to be biased against them. At worst, as the defendants allege, he was an agent. His claim to have observed a meeting going on under his very eyes, and to have heard the orders given directly afterwards with his ears, was extraordinarily convenient for the authorities who otherwise had no case against the majority of the Central Committee. It is quite unacceptable for death sentences to be carried out on the basis of such evidence.

One naturally has to look at the whole sequence of events on that day to see what explanations there could be for the ultimate executions. There are three possible explanations:

(1) that the officers on the ground at Fort Rupert carried out the executions on their own initiative as part of their mission to restore order at the Fort. One would think that this was unlikely, and that such a momentous action would have to have some order from higher authorities.

(2) that the whole operation, including the executions, was ordered and carried through by some or all of the senior military command. This I consider to be a very real possibility. The retaking of the Fort was a military operation, by military men for a military objective. It was carried through with a degree of violence which may well have been excessive. It is not at all unlikely that senior military officers may have given the execution orders in the name of the Central Committee to their subordinates, or that

the civilian leadership was bypassed, particularly if it appeared to be dithering. Indeed many of the events of the day, including the disposal of the bodies and the subsequent curfew announcement, indicate a considerable extent of military ruthlessness in charge. I am not prepared to believe, without much stronger evidence, that the whole membership of the Central Committee had approved the fateful decision.

(3) The third possibility is, of course, that the prosecution is right and that the Central Committee did approve the action. It may have been in their minds that if Maurice Bishop remained alive and regained control of Grenada their own liberty was in danger, and perhaps their lives. It must remain a real possibility; but it certainly has not been proved satisfactorily to be true by the evidence given at this trial.

23. TRUE CONFESSIONS OR STATEMENTS UNDER TORTURE?

A number of the defendants had been interrogated by a team of Barbadian police officers, mostly during November 1983. Of the soldiers at Fort Rupert, Vincent Joseph, Abdullah, Christopher Stroude, Lester Redhead and Andy Mitchell were alleged to have made "voluntary" statements which amounted to full confessions that they had direct responsibility for the executions. Of the Central Committee members, Ewart Layne had made a "voluntary" statement in which he said that he had taken sole responsibility for giving orders to "liquidate" the leaders if they resisted. Kamau McBarnette was alleged to have said that after the army had retaken Fort Rupert, Abdullah returned to Fort Frederick and spoke to Ewart Layne; and that the Central Committee THEN held a meeting and decided that "Maurice Bishop and his clique must be executed." (It will be observed that this account is quite different from that of Cletus St. Paul, who had the Central Committee meeting BEFORE the army departs to retake the Fort.) Finally, Selwyn Strachan made a statement in which he said that Ewart Layne told him that a unit had been sent to recapture Fort Rupert, but that he was not aware of any instructions to execute, and there was no Central Committee meeting on the 19th of October.

When the Barbadian officers came to give evidence at the making of these statements, the accused made statements to the court in which they said that the statements had been obtained after they had been tortured and beaten. The Judge then held a "trial within a trial" in order to determine whether the statements were voluntary, and in each case decided that they were, and that they therefore should be admitted in evidence. When Inspector Watson came to give evidence, many of the defendants singled him out as one of those principally responsible for torture. Christopher Stroude claimed that he was the "victim of psychological and physical torture at his hands". Selwyn Strachan denounced him as a "torturer and henchman". John Ventour described him as the "king of them all". When he took the witness stand, all the defendants except Raeburn Fielson chanted "torturer, torturer" until they were removed from the court. Inspector Watson then said in evidence:

"I have never beaten or brutalized any of the accused persons ... during the investigations, I found that the accused persons were very co-operative. They were all eager to assist. I am now totally surprised at their allegations of brutality."

In his statement from the dock, Abdullah gave graphic details of his interrogation by Inspector Watson and by Sergeant Ashford Jones. He said that he was sat on a chair, handcuffed behind his back, from 9.00 am till 12.00 midnight. He was questioned without a break by the officers taking turns. He continued:

"At about 12:00 midnight, I sort of drifted in

sleep. Suddenly I found something around my neck! I jumped up. Sergeant Ashford Jones had taken a bath towel, tied it round my neck and start choking me by pulling it tight! I got up. He said, 'You ready to talk?' I remained calm. I sort of choked. He eased up, then tightened it again! He did that three times. Your Lordship, you can imagine the frame of mind I was in. These people could have killed me easily. They were a law unto themselves..."

"Ashford Jones realized that this choking business was not working so he dragged me in one corner. ... I was grabbed by about 7 policemen who started cuffing me with their fists to my head, groin and other parts of my body. They also used their feet. The physical pain was great. In retrospect, I feel that I should've resisted the torture some more, I should have stood up more and fight them more. But I was faced with a difficult situation. It was like a man who had worked for 15 years to accumulate some money and after that a robber stick him up with a gun and said 'Your money or your life'; and the man has decided and eventually he reasons 'I would give the money because after I can work another 15 years and get that money back one way or another."

"After I was stamped in the face, my eyes were

bleeding, I was completely disoriented. What to do? What should I do? In the end, although in some ways it is very hard for me emotionally to say this, I did sign a statement of lies incriminating myself that I Abdullah, did all sorts of fantastic things."

Christopher Stroude claimed that he had been kept at the police headquarters from 9.00 am on 15th November 1983 until around 3.00 am on 16th November and that he was tortured throughout the day on the 15th until he finally broke in the early hours of the morning of 16th. The statement itself records that it was written between 4.15 and 7.05 am, which is an unlikely time for a normal interrogation. He called for the prison diary which would prove that he had been at police headquarters between the times which he stated. Unaccountably it turned out to be "missing", and despite repeated complaints it was never provided.

In five cases the prison doctor was able to confirm the defendants allegations by testifying that he had observed injuries such as abrasions to the chest, abdomen and genitals, on the day following their questioning at CID headquarters. But in four of the cases the doctor maintained, and the Judge accepted, that the injuries could have been "self-inflicted". In the fifth case even the doctor could find no other explanation for swollen and injured testicles, but this did not prevent the Judge from accepting the statements in every case as "voluntary".

Finally, it should be noted that there are blatant contradictions both between one alleged "confession" and another and between the "confessions" and the evidence given by eye witnesses. In particular, in the "confessions", all the accused soldiers maintain the victims were told this was an order of the Central Committee. The defendants, in their oral statements to the court, stress that this was the point on which the interrogators were most insistent, and on which they had been tortured for several hours. They said that the Barbadian officers were determined that they MUST all say that the NJM Central Committee issued such an order, and that this was communicated to the victims before they were shot. Fabian Gabriel in his evidence also put forward this version. But neither of the other two eye witnesses referred to Central Committee orders.

Where does the truth lie? There can be no doubt that all over the world, when experienced and ruthless interrogators are working under pressure to obtain a confession, the resort to physical violence is common, and it can be very effective. One of the most controversial cases in recent

British criminal history is the Birmingham bombing trial, where the defendants have consistently alleged that such violence was meted out to them. In Grenada in November 1983 the pressure to get "evidence" on which to try the NJM Central Committee was intense. The defendants have consistently alleged that these tortures took place. In these circumstances, it would be quite wrong to rely on the "voluntary" statements as being reliable evidence of the truth.

24. INCONSISTENT WITNESSES

On several occasions during the trial, particularly when defendants were making their statements from the dock, they tried to point out to the jury that witnesses had said one thing in their evidence and another thing in their evidence to the preliminary inquiry. Mr. Justice Byron, although he must have noticed the differences, had not pointed them out when the witnesses gave evidence. When the defendants mentioned them, he ruled that the evidence given at the preliminary inquiry could not be referred to in open court.

In strict law the Judge was right in his ruling. In the adversarial system of justice it is for the defendants or their lawyers to question witnesses about inconsistencies between their evidence and any previous testimony. Had they been present, the defense lawyers could have probed these differences to see whether they were caused by perjury or by a lapse of memory. Whether in the absence of defendants and lawyers it was the duty of the Judge to explore such differences, is a matter which may have to be argued on the appeal. Certainly it was another way in which the tactics of the defense make it difficult to evaluate the strength and credibility of the evidence against them.

25. THE DEFENDANTS ADDRESS THE COURT

Many of the defendants exercised their right to make statements from the dock, some extending over many days.

CALLISTUS BERNARD (Abdullah) said that after the demonstration had over-run the military guards at the Prime Minister's house, he himself went to Fort Frederick. He described the general scene:

"There was a state of chaos, confusion and uncertainty. There was a state of paralysis among a number of key leaders of the Party and army who were around on that day. Some people were in a daze - what next, where do we move from here?"

He and other officers realized that the civilians had taken over the operations room of the army, the "nerve center of the armed forces, where all the security plans and documents of the army are kept". He learned that the civilians were being armed and some of the women soldiers had been stripped and beaten. He claimed that although the majority of the demonstrators were ordinary hard working and honest Grenadians among them were "spies, saboteurs, anti-social elements, CIA plants and instigators." There was a big poster among the demonstrators saying "God Bless America". He continued:

"Those elements within the crowd were instigating ordinary Grenadians to do a number of acts that they did not understand the consequences for and the deep and far reaching implications of. They wanted a clash between the army and people to create the conditions for invasion."

Abdullah spoke to Officer Cadet Mayers, who gave him the instructions which he had received from the day to day Commander of the Army, Lt Col Ewart Layne:

“The orders were for us to move to restore order on Fort Rupert and to get the civilians off the Fort; to organize the defense of the headquarters. To make an assessment of the damage and to see what crisis measures could be taken to straighten the situation and put it back to normal.”

As mentioned earlier, he said that there was no thought that the unit would be shot at, but in fact it was ambushed. He described how, as a result of the ambush, Warrant Officer Raphael Mason and Officer Cadet Mayers had been killed, and another soldier Martin Simon was seriously wounded. He insisted that "we did not go on Fort Rupert with blood in our eyes. We went there as officers on a legal mission to restore order."

Finally, Lt Bernard made a brief reference to the circumstances of the execution:-

"there was confusion, chaos ... soldiers had been stripped and all kinds of things had happened. It was in this atmosphere, in this context; it was in this way that a number of soldiers who went there to restore order, including myself, held a number of people prisoner, and it was in this atmosphere - in a situation of anger and rage - in this situation of chaos and confusion, that a number of people died at Fort Rupert. It was in this tragic situation of rage, confusion, problems. I think this is the most honourable position I can take at this time to explain the situation to Grenadians."

This was a very significant statement. If true, it indicated that the final decision was a military one, taken either by the officers on the ground or their immediate superiors. It does not indicate a decision taken by the Central Committee.

CHRISTOPHER STROUDE in his statement from the dock denied any part in the executions. He said that far from being responsible for the deaths, he had prevented a blood bath from taking place on the Fort, by disarming the soldiers when civilians arrived there and had started to tear off their clothes.

As to the executions Stroude said that he was outside after the Fort had been retaken, helping to get the fire brigade in. He told a soldier to move an armored car so that the fire truck could come up. He told Inspector Williams, the fire chief, to hurry up to prevent the fire from spreading. He then heard a gunshot from the upper level of Fort Rupert. He went upstairs and saw soldiers on the step with the body of Maurice Bishop. He was shocked because Maurice Bishop was the "hero" to many people.

EWART LAYNE in his statement from the dock,

confirmed that he had given the orders to the soldiers to recapture the Fort. He said:

"I decided to send the military unit to recapture the Headquarters of the army and restore order there. I was authorized to issue such instructions. The unit which left Fort Frederick, left with lawful orders on a lawful mission to recapture the Headquarters from civilians, and they left under my lawful instructions. He said that the Central Committee had nothing to do with the decision to send troops to recapture Fort Rupert. I was the only person, besides General Austin who was authorized to move forces at any time, place the army on alert or for combat battle."

He described Cletus St Paul's evidence as a pack of lies.

HUDSON AUSTIN, commander of the PRA, agreed that it was Ewart Layne, rather than himself, who was in charge on the day. He said that he had been at Maurice Bishop's home until after midnight on 18th/19th October. Maurice Bishop had agreed to have a meeting with a special delegation of the Central Committee on the 19th October at 10.00 am. Hudson Austin said that he left with the understanding that everything would be settled the next day. When he came to Maurice Bishop's home on the next day as planned, he saw the crowd of demonstrators break open the gates and take him away. He believed that Bishop was going to talk to the people in the Market Square.

Hudson Austin said that he was at home on sick leave when a soldier drove up in an army jeep, hurriedly ran up the steps and handed him a note, which stated that the late Prime Minister had been killed and that he should report immediately to Fort Frederick.

"I was shocked. I could not believe that note. I could not believe it. I left just as I was and went along in the jeep with the soldier to Fort Frederick."

There he was told by Ewart Layne that when he dispatched troops to recapture the military installations, the Prime Minister and his colleagues were killed in cross-fire. He said that "I never in my wildest dream thought that any such thing as what occurred would have happened."

LEON CORNWALL said that he had stopped at Fort Frederick and had watched the demonstrators going towards Fort Rupert. He saw the three armored cars leave the fort.

"After the armored cars left, I heard firing. What

struck me was that the firing was somewhat prolonged. When I asked Layne about the firing, he told me armored cars had gone there to take control of the Fort." He said that when he got the information about the deaths he was "genuinely stunned". "I could not imagine how this could happen, how such a situation could take place. I still feel the pain and sorrow of what took place on Fort Rupert. It is something that has affected me seriously."

JOHN VENTOUR said that he had no motive whatsoever to kill Maurice Bishop and his colleagues. Bishop and others of the victims were extremely close to him. "It will take several, many, many years for the psychological woes, emotional woes, to heal."

He said that around two o'clock a trade union colleague came to his home in a distressed manner informing him that Bishop and others were injured, following shooting at Fort Rupert.

"I was shocked. I could not believe what he was saying. I thought he was joking, but when I saw the distressed look on his face, I knew he was serious." Realizing that his telephone was out of order, John Ventour left home and headed for Fort Frederick. On his arrival he met Layne who told him the dreadful news of Bishop's death.

BERNARD COARD made a statement from the dock which lasted for over twenty-five hours, covering six court days. He reviewed the whole history of the crisis. He said that George Louison, Cletus St. Paul, Don Rojas and others had been with Maurice Bishop on the eastern European tour:

"They pushed all kinds of lies and conspiracy into his head. They bombarded him for two weeks in eastern Europe. They did a job on him. They greatly aggravated the situation and turn¬ed it into a crisis of grave proportions which ultimately led to the tragedy."

Only parts of Bernard Coard's long statement are available, but passages from his account of the events of 19th October 1983 are worth quoting in full:

“In my opinion, no event in this century has ever been more tragic and traumatic or devastating for the future of this country than the death of comrade Maurice Bishop. It is not only a stunning blow to the entire people of Grenada, one which 1, personally, along with most, if not all Grenadians, have not yet fully recovered from and may never recover from.”

"It is hard to describe the sense of paralysis I felt

that day. It was deep."

He referred to the widespread propaganda portraying him as wanting to take over the leadership, which had been published between 14th and 18th October, and he continued:

“I was profoundly affected by this. The final straw was seeing the commotion of the chanting and placards of demonstrators outside my home and actually the smashing of-the gate and the taking away of comrade Bishop. I took the decision that the only way to put to rest the propaganda was for me to leave the country. I actually announced that decision to leave the country on the morning of October 19th."

He told his wife and children about the decision, and his wife began packing suitcases for their departure. The telephone lines were not working, and he could not make the travel arrangements. Because of the hostility of the demonstrators, security personnel took him and his wife from their home to Fort Frederick Army Headquarters for their own safety. While at Fort Frederick he heard shots from Fort Rupert, and later he was informed of Bishop's death.

“Memories of that afternoon and days and weeks to follow are tragic ones for me. What made that day even more than emotional trauma, was the fact that expectations were so high, that problems in the crisis were about to be resolved. Then came this series of stunning events."

As to the events as a whole, Bernard Coard told the court that documents relating to cabinet meetings in Barbados while Tom Adams was Prime Minister would show the conspiracy between Adams and President Reagan to plan the massacre. He said that Washington and Bridgetown collaborated to ensure a shoot-out, violence and bloodshed between the Army and civilians. The conclusion of the trial would mark the beginning of the case, since at the end the defendants would ensure that an international team of jurists conduct a commission of inquiry to determine what really happened at the Fort.

"Far more important to me than my life is my reputation and character. You can kill our bodies but you would not be able to kill the truth forever."

Bernard Coard referred to the role of Don Rojas, who he hinted had been planted on the island by the enemies of the Grenada revolution. He said that after Maurice Bishop had been freed, Rojas went to the telephone company and held workers there at gun-point, ordering them to disconnect the lines of several key government and military personnel, as well as army camps. He continued:

"As more and more revelations unfold in the years ahead, many of the words I speak today would take on meaning for Grenadians. I believe that people will one day understand the full picture ... It is very important that we understand very carefully that the United States government and its agents did ¬everything else on October]9th but pull the trigger."

PHYLLIS COARD's statement from the dock has been published in full. She gave a detailed account of her movements on 19th October. She had been at home with her three children during the morning. After observing the demonstration her husband decided that "since he was being used as a scapegoat by those who wished to stir up divisions and confusion in the country, we ought to leave Grenada immediately. I agreed with him. He asked me to pack suitcases for our children and ourselves and I did so." She described how photographs and other possessions were packed:

"In a free and fair trial I will put these photographs to a jury and ask them to judge whether a woman who is so obviously leaving the country that she even pack her most treasured photos of her husband and children, is going to stop off somewhere on her way out of the country and casually take a decision to kill people! What possible reason could there be for such an action? This is just one of many facts which makes nonsense of Cletus St. Paul."

She said that she was taken by security officers in an unmarked car to Fort Frederick after being informed it was no longer safe to remain at her home. She said that in a free and fair trial she would call the driver who drove her to Fort Frederick. She said that the duty Officer's diary for Fort Frederick for 19th October would show that the evidence of Cletus St. Paul was a "complete perjury". "That is why the Americans have so far refused to return it!"

She arrived at Fort Frederick with a suitcase. Soon afterwards the news of the tragedy was given:

"It was like one of those nightmares over which one has no control. I can remember clearly the feeling of disbelief I felt upon learning that comrade Maurice Bishop was dead. It was unreal. I could not believe it."

She said that the feeling of unreality grew worse as she learnt of other deaths of people who were very close to her. She spoke of their children:-

"One of the greatest cruelties that the American government has inflicted is their cruelty against the children of those who died, with this lie that their parents' friends killed their parents."

She said that for several hours she was unable to do anything. She was in a state of shock.

"The truth is that nothing in my entire life had prepared me for such a trauma as what took place on October 19th, 1983. To lose so many friends at one blow! To know what their families must be suffering, what they must be going through; to know that other women were injured, including some of my own two sisters, also that school children must have been injured or perhaps killed, as I saw some of them in the demonstration at Mount Weldale earlier on in the morning. To know also that soldiers were killed, and to know that some of them would have had young children, families dependent on them and so on. It was indeed a most horrifying, a most unbelievable situation."

Phyllis Coard's statement ought to be read in its entirety. It is a most eloquent statement of her own innocence, and of her concern for all the victims of the tragedy, particularly the children.

26. ANALYZING THE DEFENSE STATEMENTS

Apart from the statements of Callistus Bernard and Phyllis Coard, the statements of the accused are only available in patchy extracts. It may well be that other defendants, not mentioned above, put forward the reasons why they were innocent. In those circumstances it is impossible to make any definitive judgements about their credibility or truth. My impression on reading the material which is available is that while some defendants did not address some of the central issues, and while some gave

explanations which are difficult to accept, in the case of others there is the ring of truth. Certainly the statements indicate that many of the defendants had a clear and complete defense to put forward.

27. CONCLUSION - WHAT WE MUST DO

The clear conclusion which comes from a study of this trial is that a campaign MUST be urgently waged to prevent those sentenced to death from being hanged. The campaign is justified for many reasons:

(1) because the trial took place in an unconstitutional court;

(2) because the jury which convicted them appeared to be affected by intense prejudice and hostility;

(3) because the defendants, once their lawyers had withdrawn, were subjected to serious violations of their right to a fair trial;

(4) because the case brought against them was contradictory and in the case of most of them extremely weak;

(5) because the case against Central Committee members, in particular, is riddled with doubt;

(6) because the evidence against the defendants was never tested or challenged;

(7) because there is substantial reason for believing that the "confessions" which many of them made were gained by the use of torture;

(8) because the motivation of the prosecuting authorities has been clearly to eliminate the leadership of the Grenadian revolution, irrespective of the guilt or innocence of the defendants.

In those circumstances there are a number of demands to be made:

First, that the Grenadian government must stop

dragging its feet on the return to a constitutional court system, and must restore to the defendants their right to an appeal within the constitutional framework.

Second, that whether through the appeal process or otherwise, a new trial must be ordered in a constitutional court at which the evidence on both sides can be freely and fairly examined.

Third, that whatever the outcome of any appeal the barbaric death penalty must not be executed against any of those sentenced to hang.

No one should be in any doubt that the execution of the defendants in this case would be a massive victory for the forces of imperialism. They would have achieved by judicial means what they have been plotting for years - the final elimination and burial of the Grenadian revolution.

Editor's Note:

The accused in this case were never hanged because of international outcry.

NOTES

* Tony Gifford, QC, U.K.

CHAPTER 7

THE DEATH PENALY IN JAMAICA

Amnesty International, London *

1. Preface

Amnesty International opposes the death penalty in all cases without reservation on the grounds that it is a violation of the right to life and the right not to be subjected to cruel, inhuman or degrading treatment or punishment as proclaimed in the Universal Declaration of Human Rights and other international human rights instruments. Amnesty International appeals for clemency for prisoners in danger of execution and works for the abolition of the death penalty throughout the

* Amnesty International opposes the death penalty

world. In pursuance of these objectives it sent a mission to Jamaica in November 1983. The purposes of this mission were to convey Amnesty International's concern about the death penalty to government officials and to gather information and views on its abolition.

The mission comprised Dr Ezzat A. Fattah, Professor of Criminology, Simon Fraser University, Vancouver, Canada, and Martin Ennals, former Secretary General of Amnesty International, London, England.

The mission met His Excellency, The Most Honourable Florizel Glasspole, Governor-General of Jamaica, The Honourable Edward Seaga, Prime Minister of Jamaica, and The Honourable Winston Spalding, Minister of National Security and Justice. The mission also met Dennis Daly, President of the Jamaica Council for Human Rights and others.

Amnesty International's major concern in sending the mission was an increase in executions after 1980. This followed a period of more than four years (April 1976/August 1980) in which no executions had been carried out. During this period, parliament had set up a committee to consider whether or not the death penalty should be abolished. In January 1979 the House of Representatives voted by a narrow majority to retain capital punishment but recommended unanimously that all outstanding death sentences be reviewed. In February 1979 the Senate passed a resolution recommending that capital punishment be suspended for a further 18 months while another committee sat to examine the issue in greater depth. Although this second committee (The Fraser Committee on Capital Punishment and Penal Reform), referred to hereafter as the Fraser Committee) sat from June 1979 until March 1981, executions resumed in August 1980.

Twenty-four prisoners were executed between August 1980 and July 1984. Nearly all those executed had been sentenced to death either before or during the period in which executions were held in abeyance while parliament considered the issue. Most had spent long periods - of up to nine years - on death row.1 The executions were carried out despite a recommendation of the Fraser Committee in December 1981 that all death sentences passed before 31 March 1981 be commuted to life imprisonment.

At the time of the mission there were more than 150 prisoners under sentence of death in Jamaica.

The last execution as of 23 July 1984 was on 3 July 1984.

The Jamaican Government expressed the view to Amnesty International's delegates that public opinion and the high rate of violent crime in Jamaica made total abolition of the death penalty impossible at the present time, but it expressed a willingness to consider moves toward limiting the offences for which the death penalty could be imposed. There are a number of factors regarding the death penalty in Jamaica which Amnesty International hopes the government will take into consideration in moving towards the abolition of the death penalty. These are described in this report, which was submitted to the Jamaican Government on 24 July 1984.

2. General background, The death penalty in Jamaican law

The death penalty in Jamaica is mandatory on conviction of murder. This is provided under Section 3(l) of the Offences against the Person Act, 1864, with amendments enacted in 1953 and 1958.

The death sentence may not be passed on a pregnant woman or on any person under 18 years of age at the time of the commission of the offence. These provisions are in keeping with Jamaica's obligations under the International Convention on Civil and Political Rights and the American Convention on Human Rights.

After a death sentence has been passed by the trial court (which sits with a judge and jury) the accused may apply within one month for leave to appeal to the Jamaica Court of Appeals. If the sentence is upheld, the prisoner may appeal to the Jamaica Supreme Court. The final court to which a prisoner may appeal is the Judicial Committee

of the Privy Council in England.2 Sections 90 and 91 of the Jamaica Constitution of 1962 provide for the prerogative of mercy to be exercised by the Governor-General, acting on the recommendation of the Privy Council of Jamaica.3

The Privy Council usually reviews a case after the sentence has been upheld by the Jamaica Court of Appeals, although a decision will be deferred pending any further appeals. In cases where clemency is not granted, warrants for execution are issued by the Governor ¬General, 15 days before the date set for execution.

Execution in Jamaica is by hanging.

3. Conditions under which prisoners under sentence of death are held.

All prisoners sentenced to death are immediately placed on conviction and sentencing in a special unit of St Catherine District Prison known as "death row". Unless their sentence is overturned on appeal, or commuted to a lesser sentence, prisoners under sentence of death are held on death row until their execution. Once a date for execution has been set, the prisoner is taken to a special cell on death row used exclusively by men whose execution is imminent. A number of prisoners have spent several days in this cell before receiving a stay of execution shortly before the date set for their hanging.

In 1975 a commission of inquiry (the Barnett Commission) strongly criticized conditions on death row, citing among other things the lack of provision for work, recreation or regular exercise for prisoners under sentence of death. Five years later, the Fraser Committee recommended that a work project involving men on death row be introduced as an experiment to see if this could have a rehabilitative influence. However, the Department of Corrections reportedly refused to agree to such a project. (In its report to the government in 1981 the Fraser Committee said it was "of the opinion that the policy whereby the men in the condemned cells are prohibited from doing any kind of work whatsoever, whether voluntary or otherwise, is wasteful of human resources.") Although some craft activities are available to prisoners under sentence of death, Amnesty International has been told that they spend long periods confined to their cells and, unlike most other prisoners, have no provision for regular work and few facilities for recreation, education or other rehabilitative programs. Although other prisoners in maximum security units are held in similar conditions in Jamaica, such facilities are denied to death row prisoners solely by virtue of their being under sentence of death.

4. Studies and debates on the death penalty in Jamaica

During the 30 years following the end of the Second World War until 1976 there were, on average, five executions annually in Jamaica. There then followed a period of more than four years - from April 1976 until August 1980 - in which no executions were carried out, although death sentences continued to be passed in murder trials. During the greater part of this period, until early 1979, executions were suspended while the question of capital punishment was under consideration by parliament.

Although executions were not formally suspended by act of parliament or government directive, the government has told Amnesty International that the Privy Council of Jamaica “suspended taking a decision as to whether or not the law should take its course”4 while the matter of capital punishment was before a parliamentary committee established in 1977. The committee submitted its final report to parliament in October 1979, and the suspension of executions continued until parliament had debated the matter in January 1979. It appears that, in effect, executions were held in abeyance from the time of the last execution in April 1976, possibly in anticipation of the government's intention at that stage to put the matter before parliament. The Judicial Committee of the Privy Council in England, in a decision given in June 1982 on the case of a number of prisoners sentenced to death in the 1970s in Jamaica, stated that "political factors in Jamaica led to the execution of sentences of death being held in abeyance from April 1976 until early 1979 during a period of acute controversy over capital punishment".

The result of this de facto suspension of executions was that a number of prisoners under sentence of death whose appeals were dismissed by the

Jamaica Court of Appeals were not immediately issued with warrants for execution as would otherwise have been the case.

5. The Barnett Commission of Inquiry, 1975

Capital punishment in Jamaica had, indirectly, been the subject of an inquiry as early as 1975. The Barnett Commission (chaired by Dr Lloyd Barnett) was established on 31 December 1974 to examine the causes and circumstances surrounding incidents that occurred on 27 December 1974 in the high security wing of St Catherine District Prison, where death row inmates are held. The disturbances were described by the prison authorities as an "attempted mass break-out" and involved the taking hostage of a warder by a group of death row prisoners. The commission was assisted by a team of two psychiatrists, a psychologist and two social workers, who interviewed the 36 prisoners under sentence of death at that time.

The commission's report, which was submitted to the government in June 1975, described the very poor conditions prevailing in the institution at that time, particularly on death row. Prisoners on death row slept on the floor with only a mattress and a blanket and lived in generally unhygienic conditions, had little or no provision for work, healthy recreation or regular exercise, and were housed in a unit which was poorly ventilated and inadequately lit. There was no regular system for medical examination in the prison and no suitable provision for the treatment of the mentally ill. The commission found that two-thirds of the prisoners on death row were first offenders, and that 83 per cent came from poor socioeconomic backgrounds and had parental or other family problems. They also noted the inadequacy of legal representation in most of the cases and the lengthy delays in the legal process, expressing the view that "the long interval which separates imposition of sentence from execution imposes a severe strain on the condemned men, and is a major factor for tension in the prison". They also expressed the view that "the long delay in the execution of the death penalty after it has been pronounced constitutes cruel and inhumane punishment". The commission found that the conditions of their confinement and the "apprehensions that troubled the minds of the condemned men as to the manner of the execution of the death penalty" created a state of anxiety among death row inmates that was a major cause of the disturbances of December 1974. As well as being "in terror of the prospect of hanging" many of the prisoners told the commissioners that they believed they would be assaulted or even beaten to death on the way to the gallows. The commission found that "Fantasy is given credence, and the men's fears are reinforced and magnified by the physical beatings, taunts and threats they regularly receive from the warders."

The commission made a number of recommendations for speeding up the legal process and improving conditions on death row. It also stated in its report.

"This team questions fundamentally the use of hanging as a deterrent against murder, or a deterrent against violent crime. We feel that most men who commit the crime of murder can be adequately rehabilitated to lead normal productive lives. It is felt by this team that hanging as a punishment is regarded by most people as a revenge and does not serve the purpose for which it was devised."

Amnesty International does not know what measures have been taken to improve conditions on death row since the Barnett Commission's report was submitted to the government. In its report, the commission had noted that severe overcrowding was a major problem in the prison. Amnesty International does not know whether extra facilities have been made available to death row prisoners, whose number had grown from 36 at the time of the Barnett inquiry to more than 150 in July 1984.

6. Parliamentary debates on the death penalty

A House of Representatives Select Committee on National Security was formed in May 1977 to consider the question of capital punishment in the context of the general security of the country, with a view to recommending retention or abolition of the penalty. The committee reportedly decided without discussion in November 1977 that the law governing capital punishment should not be changed at that time. Opposition members of the Jamaica Labour Party (JLP) on the committee reportedly opposed this decision on the grounds that further study was needed. The cabinet decided to re-commit the issue to the committee in early 1978. A majority of the select committee, which reported to the House of Representatives in October 1978, again recommended retention of the death penalty in view of the serious problem of violent crime in Jamaica. However, the committee noted that it had not had the resources or expertise to carry out a thorough study of its effect as a deterrent to major crime, and that the expert assistance it had requested had not been provided.

The Minister of Justice, the Honourable Carl Rattray, submitted a minority report in which he called for a period of further suspension of the penalty, pending a detailed study of the causes of violence and the effects of the death penalty on Jamaican society.

The report of the Select Committee led to a motion to retain the death penalty, which was introduced into the House of Representatives in January 1979. An amendment to the motion was presented by Dr Mavis Gilmour (a member of the opposition JLP) calling for a suspension of the death penalty pending a further study. The Prime Minister, Michael Manley, was among the 13 government members who supported this amendment, together with seven opposition members who were present for the vote. The amendment was defeated by a narrow majority of 23 to 20, with one abstention. The House of Representatives also voted by a majority of 24 to 19 to retain capital punishment. The vote was according to conscience, not party allegiance, and there were members from both parties who voted for abolition.

The House of Representatives then voted unanimously for a second motion recommending that the Governor-General and the Jamaica Privy Council review the cases of all 79 prisoners then on death row. It appears from reports of the debates that this resolution reflected a widespread concern in parliament at the length of time many prisoners had by then spent on death row.

Shortly after the debate in the House of Representatives, the Senate passed a resolution by a majority of 10 to 5 recommending that "capital punishment be suspended for a period of 18 months pending a detailed study and assessment ... of the sociological and psychological effect of capital punishment in Jamaican society". This resolution was identical to the amendment proposed by Dr Mavis Gilmour in the House of Representatives and was similarly based on the Minister of Justice's minority report to the Select Committee.

In opening the debate in the Senate, the Minister of Justice stated that he had received a petition signed by some 2,000 individuals calling on the government to set up a committee to examine the justification for retaining capital punishment He stated that,

“Whatever action Parliament takes should be action supported by research and not action taken by emotionalism and not action of people floundering in the dark ... What we as Parliamentarians can do is to ask that capital punishment be suspended and a committee set up by persons who will dedicate themselves to find out what the true facts on this matter are so that Parliament can move from a platform to see whether capital punishment should still be allowed in the jurisprudence of the nation."

Although the Senate resolution had no binding effect on whether executions would continue to be carried out, the Minister of Justice was quoted as saying that he hoped the motion would have an effect on the Governor-General and the Privy Council in exercising the prerogative of mercy in the cases of the prisoners then on death row.

Following the passage of the above resolution, the Minister of Justice appointed a non-parliamentary Committee on Capital Punishment and Penal Reform with the following terms of reference,

"To consider and report within a period of 18 months whether liability under the criminal law in Jamaica to suffer death as a penalty for murder should be abolished, limited or modified and if so, to what extent, by what means and for how long and under what conditions persons who would otherwise have been made to suffer capital punishment should be detained and what changes in the existing law and the penal system would be required."

The committee, which was chaired by Sir Aubrey Fraser, a former appeal court judge, sat from June 1979 until early 1981. By this time there had been a change of government in Jamaica and the Honourable Carl Rattray was no longer Minister of Justice.[5]

The findings and recommendations of the Fraser Committee are discussed in Chapter 4 of this report. Meanwhile, warrants for execution were issued in the cases of a number of prisoners who had been sentenced to death before or during the period in which the death penalty was under consideration by parliament.

7. Executions in Jamaica 1979 / 1984

During the period in which executions were held in abeyance the number of prisoners on death row more than doubled, from 36 at the time of the Barnett Commission, to 79 in January 1979.

After the House of Representatives voted to retain capital punishment the Jamaica Privy Council met and decided to issue warrants for execution in a number of cases on which it had previously deferred taking a decision. In May and June 1979 warrants for execution were issued in the cases of Noel Riley, Anthony Forbes, Clifton Irving, Elijah

Beckford and Errol Miller, who had been sentenced to death between March 1975 and March 1976; their appeals had been dismissed by the Jamaica Court of Appeals between late 1975 and early 1977. The five prisoners immediately lodged an appeal to the Jamaica Supreme Court on the ground that their execution in 1979 would amount to inhuman or degrading punishment in violation of Section 17 of the Jamaica Constitution by reason both of the length and circumstances of the delay since being sentenced. Their appeals were turned down in March 1980, but they were subsequently granted leave to appeal to the Judicial Committee of the Privy Council in England. The Judicial Committee did not issue a decision in the cases until June 1982.

The appeal lodged on constitutional grounds in the above cases caused a further delay in the execution of these prisoners. It also directly affected the cases, of a number of other prisoners on death row sentenced to death during the same period, for whom warrants for execution would not have been issued pending a decision by the Judicial Committee in Riley et al.

Meanwhile, on 27 August 1980, Conrad Dwyer became the first prisoner to be hanged since April 1976. He had been sentenced to death in 1977.

The execution of Conrad Dwyer caused considerable concern among members of the Fraser Committee, which was still sitting to consider whether there should be any change in the laws providing for the death penalty. Sir Aubrey Fraser, Chairperson of the committee, wrote to the Jamaica Privy Council on 10 October 1980, expressing "the profound concern shared unanimously by the Committee" with respect to the hanging of Conrad Dwyer. He stated in the letter that "At the time of its nomination, the Committee did not expect that any hangings would take place during the period prescribed in the terms of reference." Although noting that the Minister of Justice had not expressly stated that this would be the case, Sir Aubrey pointed out that " . . . it seemed to my colleagues and to me that this was a fair assumption to make having regard to the subject matter under consideration." The letter went on to request that "consideration be given to granting a stay with respect to all other executions" while the committee completed its work. The date for completion of the committee's report was subsequently extended from 31 December 1980 to 31 March 1981.

No executions were, in fact, carried out between the date of the above letter and 31 March 1981. Amnesty International does not know if this was as a consequence of the Fraser Committee's request that stays of execution be granted during this period. The Committee subsequently included among its recommendations to the government a provision that all sentences of death passed prior to 31 March 1981 be statutorily commuted to life imprisonment.

This recommendation had no effect on the cases of prisoners sentenced to death, however, and the following five prisoners were hanged between May 1981 and June 1982: Lloyd Collins, executed on 12 May 1981; Joseph Baker, executed on 17 November 1981; Sydney Campbell and Anthony Needham, executed on 16 March 1982, and Rudolf Smith, executed on 15 June 1982. All five prisoners had been sentenced to death before or during the period in which the Fraser Committee sat and there was a delay of from two-and-a-half to more than five years between sentence and execution.

8. Decision of the Judicial Committee of the Privy Council in England in the cases of Noel Riley and others

The applicants sought a ruling from the Judicial Committee of the Privy Council in England that "to execute the sentences of death passed upon them in 1975 and 1976 would now be, and indeed would have been at any time after the issue of the warrants in 1979, by reason both of the length and circumstances of the delay between sentence and execution, "inhuman or degrading punishment or other treatment", in violation of the Jamaica Constitution. Section 17 of the Constitution provides that:

(1) No person shall be subjected to torture or to inhuman or degrading punishment or other treatment.

(2) Nothing contained in or done under the authority of any law shall be held to be inconsistent with or in contravention of this section to the extent that the law in question authorize the infliction of any description of punishment which was lawful in Jamaica immediately before the appointed day.

The appeal was denied by a narrow majority of three to two, in a judgment delivered on 28 June 1992.

The majority opinion6 reviewed the history of the five cases and acknowledged that

"Apart from the delays necessarily occasioned by the appellate procedures pursued by the applicants (of which it could hardly lie in any appellants mouth to complain) it is also a fact that political factors in Jamaica led to the execution of sentences to be held in abeyance from April 1976 until early 1979 during a period of acute controversy over capital punishment." It also stated that "Their Lordships fully accept that long delay in the execution of a death sentence, especially delay for which the condemned man himself is in no way responsible, must be an important factor to be taken into account in deciding whether to exercise the prerogative of mercy. But it is not for this Board to usurp the function allocated by Section 90 of the Constitution to the Governor-General acting on the recommendation of the Privy Council of Jamaica. The sole question for their Lordships' decision is whether the execution of sentence of death upon any of the appellants would contravene Section 17 of the Constitution."

The majority judgment based its rejection of the appeal on the provision contained under Section 17(2) of the Constitution - that nothing should be deemed to contravene the section to the extent that such punishment was already lawful in Jamaica at the time the constitution entered into effect. The majority judges found that because the sentence of death was mandatory under pre-existing law in Jamaica, and provided lawful authority for the detention of the condemned man in prison until such time as sentence was executed, then a delay in execution was per se lawful, and the length of the delay did not render the punishment less lawful. Thus, rather than considering whether such a delay of execution of a death sentence could in fact amount to cruel and inhuman treatment, the judges found that Section 17(2) automatically negated such a claim.

The two dissenting judges - Lords Scarman and Brightman found that the majority opinion was based on an interpretation of 17(2) that amounted to an "austere legalism" which they believed had been erroneously applied to these cases. The error, in their opinion, lay in the majority judges failure to recognize that the act of the state which was challenged in the proceedings was not the sentence of the court, but its execution after a prolonged delay. They noted that the primary purpose of Chapter III of the Constitution (containing the Jamaican charter of fundamental rights and freedoms) "is the protection of the individual against abuse of power by act of the State, whether the act be legislative, judicial or executive." They went on to state "It follows that the fact that in these five cases the death sentence when passed was in accordance with the law cannot be determinative of the appeals. The challenge is not to the judicial sentence but to the decision of the executive to carry it out at the time fixed and in the circumstances which had arisen."

The dissenting judges pointed out that the delay in execution of the appellants' sentences arose from the exercise of an executive power (by which the Governor-General, acting on the rule of the Jamaica Privy Council, reviewed death sentences with a view to deciding on clemency) conferred not by a pre-existing law, but by the Constitution. They stated "Clearly, it would be an improper exercise of the power conferred by Sections 90 and 91 of the Constitution if it should result in subjecting a condemned man to inhuman or degrading punishment or treatment. Indeed, it would be a travesty of the law if powers intended to enable mercy to be shown in appropriate cases were so used." The only remedy against an abuse of power conferred by the Constitution, if found, law in the protective powers of Chapter III of the Constitution: in this case Section 17.

The dissenting judges found that the appellants had, in their opinion, "proved that they had been subjected to a cruel and dehumanizing experience" and that "the execution of the respective death sentences in May and June 1979, against the background of the lapse of time since conviction, would have been 'inhuman treatment' within the meaning of subsection (1) of Section 17 and would not have been saved from being unconstitutional or illegal by subsection (2)."

Their Lordships further stated that "a period of anguish and suffering is an inevitable consequence of sentence of death. But a prolongation of it beyond the time necessary for appeal and consideration of reprieve is not. And it is no answer to say that the man will struggle to stay alive. In truth, it is this ineradicable human which makes prolongation inhuman and degrading. The anguish of alternating hope and despair, the agony of uncertainty, the consequences of such suffering on the mental, emotional and physical integrity and health of the individual are vividly described in the evidence of the effect of the delay in the circumstances of these five cases . .
In arriving at the above opinion , the dissenting judges reviewed not only the appellants' actual circumstances, but also decisions in a number of other countries in which the courts had "recognized the inhumanity and degradation a delayed death penalty can cause".7 The judges also referred to a case previously reviewed by the Judicial Committee of the Privy Council in England (Abbott vs. the Attorney General of Trinidad and Tobago, 1979) in which the Judicial

Committee recognized that inordinate delay might mean that the taking of a condemned man's life would not be "by due process of law".

They concluded that:

"It is no exaggeration, therefore, to say that the jurisprudence of the civilized world, much of which is derived from common law principles and the prohibition against cruel and unusual punishments in the English Bill of Rights, has recognized and acknowledged that prolonged delay in executing a sentence of death can make the punishment when it comes inhuman and degrading."

The dissenting judges summed up their opinion with the following paragraph:

"We answer, therefore, the question as to the meaning and effect of Section 17(l) as follows. Prolonged delay when it arises from factors outside the control of the condemned man can render a decision to carry out the sentence of death an inhuman and degrading punishment It is, of course, for the appellant for constitutional protection to show that the delay was inordinate, arose from no act of his, and was likely to cause such acute suffering that the infliction of the death penalty would be in the circumstances which had arisen inhuman or degrading. Such a case has been established, in our view, by these appellants. Accordingly in our opinion these appeals should be allowed."

Amnesty International has considered it worth summarizing some of the arguments in what was a detailed and complex judgment, particularly the minority opinion of Lords Scarman and Brightman, who addressed the issue in far greater depth than did the majority Lords. As shown, the appeal was lost by the narrowest of margins and the vigor of the dissent reveals the controversial nature of the issue. It is also noteworthy that the majority decision, while rejecting the appeal on what amounted to a technicality, found that a long delay in the execution of a death sentence for which the condemned man was in no way responsible, must be an important factor in the exercise of the prerogative of mercy.

Shortly after this decision a British barrister, Geoffrey Robertson, wrote in the Guardian newspaper in the United Kingdom on 4 September 1982 that there had been an established practice in Great Britain of commuting the death sentence in the event of any judicial disagreement. He went on to state that this convention was expressly accepted by the British Home Secretary in a leading case involving a disputed judgment in

1960, and that the Jamaican authorities had also followed this practice in the cases of a divided Privy Council decision in 1974.

Nevertheless, clemency was not granted in the cases of Noel Riley and the other appellants in the above case.

9. Executions after June 1982

The five appellants in the above case - Noel Riley, Anthony Forbes, Clifton Irving, Elijah Beckford and Errol Miller- were executed on 7, 9 and 16 September 1982, after spending more than six years on death row. Two other prisoners, Vincent O'Sullivan and Enos Henry, were also executed on 19 September 1982. These last two prisoners had been sentenced to death in 1976 and had lost their appeals to the Jamaica Court of Appeals in early 1977, that is, in the early part of the period in which executions were suspended.

Eight prisoners were executed in 1983: Lloyd Aitken and Anthony Hewitt, executed in May 19 83; Junior Whyte and Stafford Pyne, executed in June 1983; Clive Hayles and Ransford Thomas, executed in July 1983 and George McLeish and Fernando Marks, executed in August 1983. As with the other prisoners named above, all had been sentenced to death and/or had exhausted their normal appeals during the period in which executions had been held in abeyance (Ransford Thomas was sentenced to death in 1974, the others between 1975 and 1978).

Two prisoners - Allen McKenzie and Nathaniel Lewis - were executed on 21 February 1984. They had been sentenced to death in November 1980 and March 1981- respectively. Derrick Wallace, convicted of murder in June 1981, was executed on 3 July 1984.

A total of 24 prisoners have been hanged in Jamaica since executions resumed in August 1980. The rate of executions between September 1982 and July 1994 (when 18 prisoners were hanged) is far higher than in any similar period in Jamaica since the war.

The executions were carried out despite a recommendation in December 1981 made by

the Fraser Committee (established by the former Minister of Justice in 1979) that all death

sentences passed before 31 March 1981 - the date to which the Committee sat – be statutorily commuted.

As of 23 July 1984 there were more than 150

prisoners under sentence of death in Jamaica, of whom some 60 were sentenced prior to March 1981.

10. Some further information on four prisoners executed between 1981 and 1983

i) The case of Stafford Pyne.

Amnesty International had appealed for clemency in the cases of all those executed after August 1990. In the case of Stafford Pyne, Amnesty International also referred to a psychiatric report in which the prisoner was said to be suffering from mental illness at the time of his execution.

Stafford Pyne was convicted of murder in May 1977 and his appeal was denied in November 1977. He was examined by a psychiatrist on 25 June 1983, shortly before his execution after six years on death row. In his report, the psychiatrist made reference to a number of previous medical reports both before and during his imprisonment, in which Pyne had been found to be suffering from symptoms of schizophrenic illness. Stafford Pyne had, in fact, been treated in the Bellevue mental hospital as early as the age of 14. He told the psychiatrist that, while awaiting trial in 1977, he had also been taken to Bellevue hospital for treatment. During the1983 examination, the psychiatrist noticed features of anxiety and depression in keeping with the approaching execution. However,

he also found evidence of schizophrenic disturbance in the form of thought disorder and paranoid thinking. He concluded that "It is my opinion, based on the foregoing, that at the time of my examination on 25 June, Stafford Pyne was suffering from severe psychiatric disturbance, namely schizophrenic illness. A review of his history suggests

he had a basic liability to suffer from schizophrenic disturbance in response to appropriate stresses."

In discussing mental illness in relation to the death penalty, several United Nations (UN) surveys have pointed to the widespread recognition of mental illness or insanity as a ground for exclusion from imposition or execution of a death sentence. In a series of "safeguards guaranteeing protection of the rights of those facing the death penalty", adopted by the UN Economic and Social Council in May 1984, there is included a provision that the death sentence shall not be carried out "on persons who have become insane" (ECOSOC Resolution 1984/50 of 25 May 1984).

Although Stafford Pyne had an early history of mental illness, and was reportedly found to be suffering from symptoms of mental illness shortly after his arrest, Amnesty International does not know whether this was a factor that was introduced at his trial.

ii) A letter to Amnesty International from a prisoner on death row dated August 1979. Fernando Marks was executed in August 1983.

"My Dear Sir,

My greetings and best wishes to you and all the other members of your organization. I would like also to congratulate you all for what you are doing and what you have done so well.

The significance of my missive to you is that, I am an inmate presently on death row, for the murder of Alex Parker, and one who has lost my first appeal, and now pending the decision of the Jamaica Privy Council. I hereby request that as a humanitarian, noble and highly recognizable organization, you write to the Jamaica Governor-General and Privy Council asking that my death sentence be commuted to life & etc. I hereby promise that you will hear of my deeds in the fields of rehabilitation, with the launching of my poems, paintings, and craft, and in future send you some. I was before a printers' proof reader and compositor. Presently I am hoping to have two songs released by 5 Star Music Masters, Boston, Massachusetts, USA.

I pray your help will be successful on my behalf. And may God bless and guide you all.

Yours truly,
Fernando Marks."

iii) Extract from a news release issued by the Jamaica Council for

Human Rights on 11 May 1981, shortly before the execution of Lloyd

Collins. (Lloyd Collins was hanged on 12 May 1981).

"Lloyd Collins, 26 years old, formerly resident in Bull Bay, father of three children, will face the hangman tomorrow morning at the St Catherine District Prison.

Collins will hang although there is significant doubt about his guilt. The sole witness whose evidence linked Collins to the scene of the crime, was only able to claim that the voice of one of the men he saw, sounded like Collins. The way in which Collins' trial was conducted gave rise to sufficient doubt among the three judges hearing his appeal, to cause one of them to disagree with the final judgment that his conviction should be upheld.

Petitions were made on Collins' behalf to the Privy Council, asking them to exercise the prerogative of mercy, in light of the questionable nature of the evidence which convicted him. They also pointed out that the Ministerial Committee on Capital Punishment is in the final stages of preparing its report. They stated that in many countries, capital punishment is suspended during such investigations.

The Privy Council, however ... have instructed that the law should take Its course.

So Lloyd Collins, a mason by trade; a young man to whom more than one hundred citizens from Bull Bay asked that mercy be shown; a young man who taught himself woodcarving during the over four years of his imprisonment, will pay the ultimate price for the first offence he ever committed."

iv) Extract from a news release issued by the

Jamaica Council for Human Rights dated 15 March 1982 on the case of Anthony Needham, who was executed on 16 March 1982.

"Anthony Needham earned a Scholarship to attend Kingston College in 1969. In 1973 he was forced to leave school due to financial difficulties being experienced by his parents.

Despite leaving school prematurely, Needham did his National Youth Service in 1974. His behavior was such that his supervisor has also petitioned the Governor-General and the Privy Council for Mercy.

Charged with the killing of his girlfriend in 1976, Needham was granted bail until the end of his trial in 1977, during which time he was faithful to the terms of his bail and received instructions in welding in his quest for knowledge and the means of economic independence.

Evidence at the time disclosed that the deceased was unfaithful to Needham, he had been the subject of ridicule by his associates, all of which contributed to his extreme action, and the chief witness was the person with whom the deceased had been unfaithful.

Needham had never previously been in conflict with the Law. He was 18 years and one month old at the time of the offence. Had he been less than two months younger the sentence of death could not have been passed.

The Council was therefore of the view that based on the above considerations, this was a fitting case in which to demonstrate the magnanimity of the State.

The infliction of the death penalty cannot in this case serve as a deterrent or otherwise further the cause of justice."

11. The Fraser Committee on Capital Punishment and Penal Reform

The Fraser Committee on Capital Punishment and Penal Reform which was established by the Minister of Justice in June 1979, was mandated:

"To consider and report within a period of eighteen months whether liability under the criminal law in Jamaica to suffer death as a penalty for murder should be abolished, limited or modified and if so, to what extent, by what means and for how long, and under what conditions persons who would otherwise have been made to suffer capital punishment should be detained and what changes in the existing law and the penal system would be required."

The committee was chaired by H. Aubrey Fraser, Director of Legal Education at the Norman Manley Law School and a former judge of the Trinidad and Tobago Supreme Court. The six other members of the committee were an attorney-at-law, a psychologist, a social educator, a Methodist priest, a journal editor and a psychiatrist (the latter resigned from the Committee in June 1980). The committee appointed a research team, headed by Delroy Chuck, a lecturer in law and criminology at the University of the West Indies.

The committee considered data from three sources: research carried out by the research team; submissions made during public and private sittings; and an extensive body of individually submitted or published material. The committee also visited death row in St Catherine Prison, inspected the facilities and spoke with prisoners under sentence of death.

The committee stated in its report that it was "...of the opinion that death as a penalty for murder should be abolished". However, it concluded that "... a proposal to wholly abolish capital punishment would not now be generally accepted by the Jamaican public, having regard especially to the state of violent crime in the society". It recommended that moves toward abolition of the death penalty be undertaken "as a part of a comprehensive system of penal reform which should commence without delay".

The committee went on to recommend as an immediate first step that:

"All sentences of death imposed prior to December 31, 1980, which was the date originally prescribed for submitting the Committee's report, or alternatively, prior to March 31, 1981, to which time it was extended, should be statutorily commuted to sentences of life imprisonment"

The committee noted that as of 31 March 1981 there were 97 men on death row, of whom 54 had been sentenced to death during the period 1973/1978 and the others during the period in which the committee sat.

The committee also recommended that the present application of the death penalty be modified to restrict it to a limited class of homicide. It recommended that, for an interim period of five years, capital punishment should be retained as a penalty for murder only with respect to murder committed by use of a firearm or explosive. As a guideline in this respect, it recommended that the death sentence be imposed only on the person or persons found guilty of having actually used or possessed the firearm or explosive - or the principal in the first degree - and should not be imposed on unarmed accomplices. The committee further recommended that prisoners committed to prison for the offence of murder be required to undertake productive and rehabilitative work, part of the proceeds of which should go toward compensation for the dependents of the victims of murder.

12. Findings of the research team

It is worth summarizing some of the findings of the research team which assisted the Fraser Committee. As the team itself acknowledged, some of its research was limited by a lack of comprehensive data on the murder cases or homicide statistics studied. Also, its observations regarding prisoners on death row were based to a large extent on the prisoners' own subjective accounts of the various factors involved in their crimes, although the team was able to cross-check much of this information from court records of their cases. Despite such limitations, their report gives a valuable insight into the types of killings from which murder prosecutions have resulted and how the criminal justice system has dealt with such cases.

The team interviewed 40 of the 81 prisoners on death row in August and September 1979.8 They studied the socioeconomic background of the prisoners and, from court records of their cases, listed the types of crimes for which they had been sentenced to death.

The team also made a survey of the patterns of murder in Jamaica during the previous 20 years by studying inter alia the cases of recorded killings, prosecutions for murder and conviction rates.

13. Types of murder and weapons used in cases of 40 men on death row in 1979

The research team found that in 12 cases (30 per cent of the sample) the condemned prisoners were convicted of murder committed during the course of a robbery; these were also the cases in which guns were most often used in the commission of the murder, and accounted for 10 of the 12 cases. However, in nine of the 10 robberies in which guns were used, the prisoners on death row had been charged as accomplices only in the murder and had not discharged the firearm that killed the victim. They were convicted on the same basis as the principal perpetrator of the murder. The statistics do not show how many of the condemned prisoners were also carrying firearms during the commission of the robbery.

The second most common type of crime was murder committed during or after a fight, quarrel or dispute. These accounted for 11 of the 40 cases (or just under 30 per cent of the sample). The fatal injuries in these cases were inflicted with what the research team called "traditional instruments of murder": knives, batons, cutlasses and, in one case, a bottle. One of the prisoners falling within this category was convicted as an accomplice in a Fight. The team reported that "Some of these cases are consistent with slight provocation by the victims, interference with the offenders' personal property by the victims and other contributing activities by the victims which caused the offender to react in the manner which caused death." (Amnesty International does not know how far this statement was based on the prisoners' own accounts or from information gained from court records of the trials.)

In a further six cases, the circumstances in which the murder was committed were classified by the team as being due to "emotional factors". The exact circumstances in which this type of crime was committed were not revealed in the report. However, it was recorded that, of the total sample of 40 cases, seven of the murder victims were the wives or girlfriends of the offender. Amnesty International assumes that some of these victims fell either under this category or under the above category of murder committed during a quarrel or dispute.

Four of the 40 cases (10 per cent of the sample) involved killings during gang warfare or political conflicts, the latter also usually between rival gangs. Guns were used in three of these four cases.

In the remaining seven cases, either the type of crime or the murder weapon was unknown.

From the above statistics, the research team distinguished two broad categories or types of murder. They found that the majority of gun murders - those committed during the course of a robbery, and the smaller sample of rival gang/political conflicts - were carried out by persons operating in a group (this was borne out by the large number of accomplices among the condemned men in the sample). The team noted that the offenders in this type of crime "are very often members of juvenile gangs, or members of a clique associated with committing crimes for a specific purpose . . . " and that they "prove themselves by engaging in crimes which bring them status and recognition by the peer groups".

The team noted that this type of offender rarely acted alone and that " . . . as sociologists and psychologists have pointed out, these offenders would rarely pursue this form of career without direct or indirect cooperation of others." Many of the crimes falling under this category were planned rather than spontaneous.

The second broad category of murder defined by the team, comprised most of the killings committed during a quarrel or fight (as distinguished from gang/political conflicts) and those due to “emotional factors”; these were what the research team described as "individual crimes". They found that most of the offenders in this category were influenced by personal and emotional factors, and the crimes were usually committed on impulse. The type of weapons used in this category of murder were usually those most readily available. (Elsewhere in their report, the team remarked that a restriction in the widespread practice of carrying knives might reduce this type of killing.) These crimes also accounted for most of the cases in which the victim was known to the offender (of the total sample of 40 cases, 17 of the murder victims were known to the murderer). Taken together, murders arising from disputes, quarrels or fights, and those attributed to "emotional factors", accounted for just over half of the crimes for which the prisoners in the sample had been sentenced to death.

14. Patterns of murder in Jamaica since 1964

From a study of prosecutions for murder taken at four-year intervals between 1964 and 1976,9 the research team found that there had been an increase in the number of prosecutions for murder committed with guns. However, they did not find that an overwhelming number of gun murderers were prosecuted. On the contrary, they found that the increased rate of prosecutions for gun murders did not match the very high increase in the incidence of this type of crime during the 1970s (when there was a dramatic increase in both armed robberies and political/gang killings). In fact, their statistics showed a particularly low rate of apprehension and prosecution for this type of killing. This, they found, was partly accounted for by the fact that many of the perpetrators were themselves killed in gun battles between gangs or in shoot-outs with the police. There was also evidence of silence and intimidation at the local level, which inhibited efforts to bring to justice those responsible for political killings in particular. The fact that some of these crimes were planned with precision might also have made apprehension more difficult.

Taking the period as a whole, the team found that the overwhelming number of murders which resulted in prosecutions were those arising from quarrels or rights between friends, neighbours or associates; private domestic quarrels or business disputes. Together, these accounted for some 60 per cent of all murder cases prosecuted during the period reviewed. The team found that these killings arose largely from spontaneous reactions to a situation in which emotions were aroused and the killers acted on impulse. The team observed that "it is unlikely that any penalty will deter these actions . . .. They are situational offences which occur because of the impulsive reaction of the offender". Their observations appeared to be confirmed by the victims of murder: they found that acquaintances, friends, associates and colleagues were the main victims of murder, closely followed by wives, common-law spouses, girlfriends and close relations. In cases prosecuted, knives remained the most common murder weapon throughout the period covered. The team commented that the detection rate tended to be higher with this sort of crime, precisely because of its spontaneous nature and the fact that the murderer was known to the victim.

The team noted that the above statistics were taken only from a record of cases prosecuted, and that the acquittal rate was probably higher in cases involving fights or disputes with associates or relatives. Nevertheless, a significant proportion of prisoners on death row had been convicted of this type of crime, according to the research team's findings.

The team went on to look at the statistics for criminal homicide cases recorded by the police from the years 1962/1978. They noted that these figures did not give a true picture of the actual murder rate in Jamaica at the time, since not all killings could be classified as murder in the legal sense.10 They thus compared the number of cases reported to the police with, first, the "clear-up" rate (also taken from police records) and, secondly, the number of prosecutions for murder(taken from the Director of Public Prosecutions' office) over the same period. They found that there had been a progressive decline in the percentage of all cases cleared-up or prosecuted, although the number of reported killings of all types had increased greatly over the period covered. For example, the clearance rate had dropped from 90 per cent in 1962/1966 to 60 per cent in 1973/1978, whereas the number of killings had risen from 341 cases in the earlier period to 1,845 in 1973/1978. The prosecution rate had also dropped from 71.6 per cent (1964/1968) to 32.2 per cent (1974/1978).

The research team stated that "The impact of the cleared-up figure is of extreme importance. Criminologists now recognize that the most important factor in deterring crime is the surety of being caught"

The team also looked at figures giving the outcome of murder cases prosecuted. They found that convictions for murder averaged only about 25 percent throughout the period reviewed(from 1964). A number of these prosecutions resulted in convictions for a lesser offence, such as manslaughter. There was also a high acquittal rate of 38.4 per cent in murder trials from 1974/1978.

They further found that 30 per cent or less of convicted murderers were actually hanged. Some had their sentences overturned on appeal, others were granted clemency and had their sentences commuted to life imprisonment by the Governor-General and the Jamaica Privy Council.

The team suggested that a number of factors apart from the severity of crime and degree of guilt of the offender could have affected the outcome of the trial, including the socio-economic background of the defendant and the quality of his defense. They quoted a passage from material submitted by Amnesty International to the Fraser Committee which, while not referring specifically to Jamaica, made the following general comment:

"When the ability to obtain good legal representation becomes one of the most important factors in determining the outcome of a trial, questions of race, class and poverty can have a considerable effect upon the administration of justice. The wealthy, the politically well-connected and members of dominant racial and religious groups are far less likely to be executed for offences of comparable severity than are the poor, supporters of the political opposition and members of unpopular racial and religious groups."[11]

They also cited the findings of statistics into types of offender that had received the death penalty in California, United States, during the 1950s and 1960s, according to which 42 per cent of blue collar workers charged with first degree murder were sentenced to death whereas only five per cent of white collar workers so charged received the death penalty.

The team found that their own assessment of the background of the 40 men on death row in August and September 1979 appeared to show similar results, noting that "They were men from low socio-¬economic backgrounds, low job stability, and. mainly men who wore dreadlocks at the trial. The effect of these extraneous factors on the juries' perception of the culpability of the murder charge, cannot be underestimated."

15. Characteristics of men on death row in August and September 1979

From their interviews with 40 men on death row in August and September 1979, the research team noted the following:[12]

a) In accord with the findings of the Barnett Commission, the research team found that men on death row were mainly from the lower socio-economic strata. They grew up in neighbourhoods characterized by frequent violence, gang warfare, and political conflicts. The dominant faith among the condemned men was found to be the Rastafarian religion. They wore their dreadlocks throughout the court procedures until they were shaved on entering prison. Many of them believed that their appearance caused the judge and jury to be biased against them. They were convinced that their failure to get proper justice was due to their way of life, their style of dress, their manner of speech, etc., to the fact that they were different from the men in the jury box or others who participated in the trial. Many of them expressed the belief that the police had framed them, and several claimed that they had been wrongly identified.

Of the 40 men interviewed, four were completely illiterate and 21 were semi-illiterate who dropped out before finishing primary school and were barely able to read and write. Thirty-one were characterized by the team as unskilled and only nine were deemed skilled or semi-skilled.

Only 10 of the men had previous criminal convictions recorded against them. Four of the 10 had only single convictions prior to their death sentence.

b) Thirty-three of those interviewed were represented by legal aid lawyers. Only four retained private lawyers while the information was not available on the remaining three. The team found that many legal aid lawyers appointed in murder cases spent very little time investigating their clients' defense and many never, discussed the case with their client in any great detail; witnesses for the defense often did not turn up to give evidence, frequently because they were not notified".13

The research team also observed that many of the death row inmates inter-viewed displayed scars, bruises and other signs of injury, which they alleged had been inflicted by police officers. A number of the prisoners alleged that they had been beaten in order to elicit confessions.

The team also cited the assertions of innocence made by all of the prisoners it interviewed, and pointed to the possibility that at least some of these assertions might be true.

16. The Prerogative of mercy

Although executive clemency cannot eradicate all defects in the administration of the death penalty, and is no substitute for justice at the judicial level, it can play a crucial role in mitigating the rigidity of a death sentence, particularly mandatory sentences.

The power of executive clemency in Jamaica is vested in the Governor-General, acting on the recommendation of the Privy Council. Section 91 of the Jamaica Constitution provides that:

1. Where any person has been sentenced to death for an offence against the law of Jamaica, the Governor-General shall cause a written report of the case from the trial judge, together with such

other information derived from the record of the case or elsewhere as the Governor-General may require, to be forwarded to the Privy Council so that the Privy Council may advise him in accordance with the provisions of section 90 of this constitution.

2. The power of requiring information conferred on the Governor General by sub-section (1) of this section shall be exercised by him on the recommendation of the Privy Council or, in any case in which in his judgment the matter is too urgent to admit of such recommendation being obtained by the time within which it may be necessary for him to act, in his discretion.

Section 90 of the Constitution provides that .

1. The Governor-General may, in Her Majesty's name and on Her Majesty's behalf -

a) grant to any person convicted of any offence against the law of Jamaica a pardon, either free or subject to lawful conditions;

b) grant to any person a respite, either indefinite or for a specified period, from the execution of any punishment imposed on that person for such an offence;

c) substitute a less severe form of punishment

for that imposed on any person for such an offence; or

d) remit the whole or part of any punishment imposed on any person for such an offence or any penalty or forfeiture otherwise due to the Crown on account of such an offence.

2. In the exercise of the powers conferred on him by his section the Governor-General shall act on the recommendation of the Privy Council.

17. Wordings of the Privy Council

After a death sentence has been upheld on appeal, the case is reviewed by the six members of the Jamaica Privy Council. Each member receives a file on the case, with notes of the evidence, report of the trial and appeal, and a separate report from the judge who passes sentence. There is some delay in preparing a case for the Privy Council. As the list of prisoners in Appendix I shows, appeals to the Jamaica Court of Appeals are usually disposed of within about one year after sentencing but, even if no further appeals are lodged, the case may not be reviewed by the Jamaica Privy Council for some time after this. Once the privy councillors have looked at a case, the council meets and discusses the matter. The

Governor-General takes part in these discussions, but is only called upon to vote in the event of a tie. In keeping with the entirely discretionary nature of executive review, all the deliberations are in private and no reasons are given for the decisions taken. If the Privy Council gives a negative decision in the case, a warrant for execution is issued. If the prisoner then indicates that he intends to lodge a further appeal - for example to the Judicial Committee of the Privy Council in England - a stay of execution will be granted.

18. Reasons for Granting Clemency

Amnesty International tried to discover what criteria, if any, were used by the Privy Council in deciding whether or not to recommend clemency in death penalty cases. It found that the Privy Council does not have a clear set of written guidelines for the exercise of clemency in such cases.

His Excellency the Governor-General told Amnesty International that clemency would always be granted in the case of a woman sentenced to death, and in cases where there was doubt about the prisoner's guilt. His Excellency also indicated that murders arising out of domestic jealousy and those where there was evidence of mental illness were cases in which clemency would usually be granted. The Governor-General also stated that the Privy Council did take account of lengthy periods spent on death row but would be disposed to take this as grounds for granting clemency only if the delay as not provoked by the prisoner's own lawyer in lodging appeals for the purpose of prolonging the prisoner's life.

In Amnesty International's view, it would certainly be perverse to penalize a prisoner on this last ground: indeed, a lawyer would be liable to an accusation of gross negligence if he or she did not pursue all legal avenues available to the prisoner which might prevent his execution, and the granting of leave to appeal in a case indicates at least prima facie grounds for judicial challenge to the sentence; some delays might also have been occasioned by inadequacy of defense counsel, at the trial or at a later stage of the appeal procedure.

Amnesty International does not know why clemency was not granted in the case of Stafford Pyne (where there was evidence of mental illness, even before his trial) or in the cases of Noel Riley and five others (executed in June 1982 after six to seven years under sentence of death, a crucial part of which time was caused by the de facto suspension of executions). These executions would appear to be at variance with some of the criteria reportedly considered by the Privy Council in recommending clemency.

In the case of Riley and others, Amnesty International finds it disturbing that clemency was not granted both in view of the narrowly divided judgment of the Judicial Committee of the Privy Council in England and the majority opinion that a long delay for which the condemned man is in no way responsible must be an important factor in exercising the prerogative of mercy. Amnesty International finds that particularly regrettable, in view of the fact that the appeal itself had occasioned a further prolongation of the period spent under sentence of death, not only in the cases of the five appellants, but also in the cases of most of the 10 other prisoners executed between September 1982 and August 1983, who had been sentenced to death during a similar period. Since the appeal in the case of Noel Riley and others concerned a matter of constitutional law of crucial and direct relevance to these cases also, the prisoners themselves could hardly be held responsible for the further delay (from 1979 to 1982) in the execution of their sentences pending this appeal.

The Governor-General told Amnesty

International's delegates that he views his role and that of the Jamaica Privy Council as "applying the law of murder as it stands unless there are exceptional extenuating circumstances" and believes that, otherwise, the law should take its course. As stated above, the Privy Council in Jamaica does not have a clear set of written guidelines for exercising clemency, and decisions appear to be taken largely on an ad hoc basis.

It is worth noting that some other countries have laid down clear criteria for the consideration of clemency in death penalty cases. Those used by the British Home Secretary prior to abolition are cited in the following extract from the Report of the Royal Commission on Capital Punishment in the United Kingdom (1953). It is possible that some of these factors may have been present in cases in which clemency has been denied in Jamaica:

"Apart from three classes of case we have mentioned in which it has long been the established practice to recommend the commutation of the death penalty,14 certain types of murder are recognized as needing specially close scrutiny to see whether there are such extenuating circumstances as would justify a reprieve. Among such cases are unpremeditated murders committed in some sudden excess of frenzy, where the murderer has previously had no evil animus towards his victim, especially if he is weak-minded or emotionally unstable to an abnormal degree; murders committed under provocation which, though insufficient to reduce the crime to manslaughter, may be a strongly mitigating circumstance; murders committed without intent to kill, especially where they take place in the course of a quarrel; murders committed in a state of drunkenness falling short of a legal defense, especially if the murderer is a man of hitherto good character, and murders committed by two or more people with differing degrees of responsibility.

Finally there are three rare classes of case in which reprieves may be granted. One is where the Home Secretary feels that despite the verdict of the jury there is a "scintilla of doubt" about the prisoner's guilt. Secondly ... it has occasionally been felt right to commute the sentence in deference to a widely spread or strong local expression of public opinion, on the ground that it would do more harm than good to carry out the sentence if the result was to arouse sympathy for the offender and hostility for the law. Lastly, it is occasionally, though very rarely, necessary to commute the sentence if the physical condition of the prisoner is such as to give ground for thinking that it could not be carried out expeditiously and humanely."

19. Statutory commutation of death sentences

Both the Prime Minister and the Minister of Justice were clearly concerned by the length of time many prisoners had spent on death row. However the Minister of Justice stated that the recommendation by the Fraser Committee that death sentences passed prior to March 1981 be statutorily commuted would be unconstitutional, since the prerogative of mercy was vested exclusively in the office of the Governor-General and the Jamaica Privy Council. However, the Governor-General himself expressed the view to Amnesty International that Parliament was sovereign in all matters regarding prisoners and that, although executive clemency rested in the hands of the Governor-General, there would be nothing unconstitutional in Parliament passing a bill either to restrict application of the death penalty or to commute existing sentences.

Following its mission to Jamaica Amnesty International wrote to the Minister of Justice on 5 November and stated inter alia:

"In the light of our conversation with the Governor-General, we are convinced that Parliament is sovereign in all of these areas under discussion. It follows, therefore, that any decision taken by Parliament with regard to the commutation of sentences of those awaiting execution, or limiting the crimes for which the penalty of death is applicable, would be constitutional. . . ".

Amnesty International also stated in its letter that:

"...a decision by the Cabinet to restrict the offences for which death is the penalty would be influential in the deliberations of the Privy Council without impinging upon their integrity and independence."

20. Some general considerations on the death penalty. The death penalty as a deterrent to crime

One of the most common arguments for retaining the death penalty is that it acts as a deterrent to murder. The state of violent crime in Jamaica was one of the main reasons given by the House Select Committee for recommending retention of the death penalty in 1978. The high incidence of gun murders was a factor which influenced the

Fraser Committee in avoiding a recommendation to abolish the death penalty completely for the present time. The high rate of crime in Jamaica and strong public support for capital punishment were reasons given by the Jamaican Government, in discussions with Amnesty International's delegates, for retaining the death penalty.

Figures for reported murders from 1976 to 1982 (given in Appendix II)15 suggest that neither the suspension nor the resumption of executions in Jamaica had any significant effect on the criminal homicide rate, which remained high throughout the period. The marked increase in gun killings in the year 1980 is believed to have been due to violence between rival political gangs claiming to support one or other of the two main political parties before and during the October 1980 general election. In 1981 and 1982 there was a decrease in gun murders; this is believed to have been due to the decline in political violence after the elections, a factor unrelated to the death penalty. Were the death penalty to have a unique deterrent effect, the resumption of executions in 1980 after more than four years might have been expected to produce a drop in other types of murder, which was not the case. In fact, the overall criminal homicide rate in 1982 did not differ greatly from that in 1976. Figures for the earlier period show that the murder rate rose progressively from the mid-1960s to 1966/67, despite the regular use of capital punishment during most of this period.

Despite careful research in a number of other countries, the death penalty has never been shown to act as a unique deterrent to violent crime: this conclusion is borne out by the experience of Jamaica. As described in Chapter 4 of this report, the Fraser Committee's research team found that many murders in Jamaica were unplanned and committed in circumstances in which it is doubtful that the death penalty would act as a deterrent. Such murders were among those in which the perpetrator was most likely to be apprehended. The team also found that the low clearance rate for murders generally, and especially for the case of gun killings, lessened the deterrent effect of any penalty. Research into criminal homicide in Jamaica suggests that - as in many other countries - the murder rate is affected less by the death-penalty than by social and other factors.

Dr. Carl Stone, a Jamaican journalist who has carried out research into the death penalty, made the following observations in an article which was published in the Daily Gleaner on 4 October 1982. The Figures he quotes are similar to those given by the Fraser Committee's research team.

"The suggestion that hanging deters murder and violence has no basis in fact. Most murderers are not caught and the probability of being caught is so low that hanging in our society is not an effective deterrent.

Over the 1970-71 to 1978-79 period murder convictions represented only 20% or about one-fifth of the murders reported. Over the period only 58% of the reported murders had in fact led to arrests: and there was a high rate of acquittals. Over the period more persons were acquitted of murder than the number found guilty. Between 1970-71 and 1976-77 when the last executions took place in the 1970s only about 14% of the murders committed resulted in execution sentences ...".

21. Public opinion and the death penalty

Polls indicate that public opinion in Jamaica favours the retention of capital punishment. One such poll, conducted in October 1982, found that 86 per cent of people polled were in favour of hanging convicted murderers, with 13 percent against.

However, a significant body of informed opinion is opposed to the death penalty in Jamaica. As described above, there was strong support for abolition among members of both houses of Parliament and from both major political parties during the 1970s. A number of other organizations and individuals have also spoken in favour of abolition. Seventy-seven lawyers signed a petition prepared by the Jamaica Council for Human Rights in 1973, calling for an end to capital punishment on the ground that the "cold and deliberate execution", or infliction by the state of severe and painful injury upon a captive victim, was inconsistent with a civilized and humane penal system. The Jamaica Council for Human Rights since 1979 has repeatedly urged the government to reintroduce a parliamentary motion to abolish the death penalty. The Jamaica Council of Churches protested against a resumption of hangings when warrants for execution were issued in the cases of Noel Riley and others in 1979. The Jamaican branch of the American Association of Jurists called for suspension of capital punishment in 1982, while the findings of the Fraser Committee were considered. In November 1982 the Ombudsman for Jamaica, while decrying the increase in violent crime, called for an end to tile death penalty.16

Public opinion, while showing support for capital punishment may often not be well informed about the ways in which the criminal justice system works in practice; of the effectiveness or fairness of the penalty, or of the types of persons who are executed. The Jamaican public is probably far more likely to be influenced by the frequent press reports of gun killings than by informed opinion on the actual use of the death penalty.

It is relevant here to quote the following passage from the Ceylon Commission of Inquiry on Capital Punishment, 1959:

"Even if public opinion is assumed to be in favour of capital punishment, this would not be a conclusive argument in favour of the reintroduction of this punishment. Unless public opinion is itself based on rational and informed grounds (and this our experience has shown to be unlikely), the existence of a public opinion strongly favouring capital punishment may be a reason, from the standpoint of practical politics, why that punishment is retained, but it cannot be a rational justification for retention .... Where public opinion is neither informed nor clearly ascertained, the social wisdom of a suggested legislative step must be determined by reference to considerations other than the belief of the public in the wisdom of that step."

22. Mandatory death sentences

Jamaican law provides for a mandatory death sentence on conviction of murder. The question of mandatory death sentences has been addressed in a number of countries, in view of the irrevocable nature of the punishment. The US Supreme Court has ruled, for example, that mandatory death sentences (imposed regardless of mitigating or aggravating circumstances of the individual offence) are per se a denial of due process of law".17

It is widely acknowledged that executive clemency, while mitigating the rigid application of the death penalty in certain cases, does not provide an adequate substitute for safeguards at the judicial stage of the proceedings. It has also been recognized that mandatory death sentences can exercise an inhibitory effect on judges and juries. A jury's belief that a death sentence may not be deserved or appropriate in a particular case can interfere with their assessment of the guilt or innocence of the accused leading to an artificially high rate of acquittal in such cases.

The Minister of Justice expressed concern about mandatory death sentences in Jamaica and told Amnesty International that he was seeking advice on how this could be changed.

23. Other considerations

In the course of its work for abolition of the death penalty, Amnesty International monitors the use of it throughout the world. Its conclusions include the following:

- The death penalty violates the right to life. Concern for the victims of crime must not be used to justify the state deliberately taking the life of a prisoner.

-The death penalty is the ultimate cruel, inhuman and degrading punishment. Those sentenced to death often suffer acute anguish, both physical and mental, before execution. There is no means by which a person can be executed "humanely". Many means, including hanging, may not kill instantly.

-The death penalty is irrevocable and can be inflicted on the innocent, despite tile most stringent judicial safeguards.

-No means of limiting the death penalty can prevent its being imposed arbitrarily or unfairly.

The impossibility of drafting legislation which would distinguish fairly between those offences which are punishable by death and those which are not was expressed most recently in the parliamentary debates on a motion to reintroduce the death penalty in the United Kingdom in July 1983.18 During this debate, a number of members of Parliament pointed to the problems created by the Homicide Act of 1957, which had attempted to restrict the death penalty in Britain to a limited class of "capital" murders. The Act created anomalies which were followed by the suspension and later the abolition of the death penalty in Britain for all categories of murder. As the British Home Secretary commented in the 1983 parliamentary debate:

"Although attempts can be made to single out from other crimes murders that are specially prevalent, or that are believed to be deferrable by the death penalty, the problem remains that any such differentiation, when put into practice, is likely to lead fairly quickly to growing feelings of injustice. There will soon be cases outside, whatever criteria is used, that are felt to be more grave than those within them."

A former Prime Minister said in the same debate that the 1957 Homicide Act had:

"failed because the general public was not prepared to support an Act - nor was tile judiciary for that matter ¬which said that one kind of murderer was worthy of the death penalty and another was not."

The problem of distinguishing fairly between capital and non-capital offences applies to other countries as well. The giving of unguided discretion to a jury to decide whether or not to impose a death sentence was ruled unconstitutional by the US Supreme Court (in Furman v. Georgia, 1972) on the ground that this had led to arbitrary and capricious sentencing. Such a system has also been criticized on the grounds that this could lead to discrimination against an offender on the grounds of race, class or other factors. An alternative judicial process of "guided discretion" (used in the United States and elsewhere) through an assessment of predefined "aggravating" or "mitigating" circumstances does not resolve the problem, since it is impossible to specify in advance all the characteristics of a given crime and weigh their relative importance. As Amnesty International stated in its Report on the Death Penalty, (1979), "No legal provision can classify fairly the emotional, social and other factors which may have a bearing upon the commission of a capital offence". Such a process does not exclude discrimination on extraneous grounds such as race, and may work for the further disadvantage of those with less adequate legal counsel.

There are many ways in which the death penalty is unfairly applied. The distinction between one prisoner who is executed and another who is not depends not only on the crime but also on a series of recommendations and decisions made by the prosecutor, the defending lawyer, the judges and/or jurors and those who exercise clemency. It is impossible to rule out the possibility that, somewhere along this chain of decision, a step will be taken leading to one person being executed while another, having committed a similar crime in similar circumstances, is not. Along this chain of decision, it is also possible that - intentionally or not - the death penalty will inconsistently be inflicted in a way that discriminates by race, economic or educational or other social factors.

24. The death penalty and international human rights standards

The right to life and the right not to be subjected to cruel, inhuman or degrading treatment or punishment are enshrined in the Universal Declaration of Human Rights and other international human rights documents. There is growing international consensus that the death penalty is incompatible with those standards. In December 1971 the UN General Assembly adopted resolution 2857 (XXVI) in which it affirmed that:

" . . . in order fully to guarantee the right to life, provided for in Article 3 of the Universal Declaration of Human Rights, the main objective to be pursued is that of progressively restricting the number of offences for which capital punishment may be imposed, with a view to the desirability of abolishing this punishment in all countries".

This decision was re-affirmed by the General Assembly in Resolution 32/61 of 8 December 1977. The UN Secretariat has further stated that the death penalty constitutes "cruel, inhuman or degrading punishment" and the UN Secretary-General stated in 1980 that the death penalty "clearly violates the right to life".19

The American Convention on Human Rights lays down standards for the application of the death penalty in countries that have not abolished it and also provides, under article

4(3), that "the death penalty shall not be reestablished in states that have abolished it". The Inter-American Commission on Human Rights, whose principal function is to promote tile observance and protection of human rights the Americas region, recommended in its Annual Report of 1981-¬1982 that "the Government of Jamaica suspend the execution of those persons sentenced to death and consider the abolition of the death penalty".

Today 26 states have abolished the death penalty for all offences and 18 have abolished it for ordinary offences, but retain it for exceptional offences such as crimes in wartime. Information gathered by Amnesty International indicates that, in recent years, at least one country a year abolishes the death penalty or, having done so for ordinary offences, goes on to abolish it for all offences. The trend in other countries in the Caribbean shows a decline in the use of the death penalty. In the Dominican Republic use of the death penalty is prohibited under the 1966 Constitution. The practice in Guyana for the past decade has been to commute all sentences of death passed in the courts to life imprisonment. No executions have been carried out for more than five years in Dominica, Grenada and Trinidad and Tobago.

Jamaica has ratified both the International Covenant on Civil and Political Rights and the American Convention on Human Rights, and has generally been prominent in promoting human rights standards in the region. The resumption and increase in the rate of hangings in the 1980s in Jamaica would appear to be incompatible with internationally recognized objectives to restrict the use of the death penalty, with a view to its ultimate abolition. Any further moves towards abolition in Jamaica - such as appeared to take place during the 1970s - would clearly be in keeping with these objectives.

25. Conclusions and Recommendations
Summary and Conclusions

The death penalty has been the subject of acute debate in Jamaica in recent years. A significant body of informed opinion there including penologists, criminologists, lawyers and politicians, have expressed support for the abolition of the death penalty.

From April 1976 until January 1979 executions in Jamaica were held in abeyance while a parliamentary committee considered whether or not the death penalty should be abolished. In January 1979 the House of Representatives voted by a narrow majority to retain the death penalty, but recommended unanimously that all existing death sentences be reviewed.

Two extra-parliamentary official committees have considered the death penalty in Jamaica, both of which were critical of its current application. In 1975 the Barnett Commission questioned the effectiveness of hanging as a deterrent to violent crime and criticized conditions under which prisoners under sentence of death were held. The Fraser Committee, which submitted its report to the government in December 1981, expressed the view that "death as a penalty for murder should be abolished" and recommended, as a first step toward abolition, restrictions in the circumstances in which it should be imposed. The committee also recommended that all death sentences passed prior to 31 March 1981 (the period to which it sat) be commuted to life imprisonment.

Despite the recommendation made in 1981 that the death penalty be modified, Jamaica retains a mandatory death penalty on conviction of murder.

Hangings resumed in August 1980. Twenty-four prisoners were hanged between August 1980 and July 1984. Nearly all those executed had been sentenced to death before or during the early part of the period in which executions were field in abeyance. Most had spent long periods - of up to nine years - on death row. The executions were carried out despite recommendations that their sentences be reviewed or commuted.

There are currently more than 150 prisoners under sentence of death in Jamaica, of whom some 60 were sentenced before 31 March 1981.

An opinion given in June 1982 by the Judicial Committee of the Privy Council in England reflects the concern expressed by politicians and others at the length of time prisoners had spent under sentence of death while the penalty was under review. The Judicial Committee considered final appeals in the cases of five prisoners who had been sentenced to death in Jamaica between March 1975 and early 1977. Although the prisoners' appeals were rejected on technical grounds (by a majority of 3-2), the majority opinion stated that " long delay in the execution of a death sentence, especially delay for which the condemned man is himself in no way responsible, must be an important factor to be taken into account in deciding whether to exercise the prerogative of mercy." Despite this opinion, clemency was not granted in these cases.

Studies of prisoners sentenced to death in Jamaica have shown that such prisoners have come overwhelmingly from the lower socio-¬economic sectors of society; a majority had received little or no education; most were first offenders; many may not have had the benefit of adequate legal counsel.

There is no evidence that the death penalty deters crime more effectively than other punishments. Research carried out in Jamaica suggests that many murders arise from quarrels or fights between relatives or associates, and are committed on impulse, in circumstances in which the perpetrator is therefore unlikely to be deterred by the legal consequences. Statistics on criminal homicide also show a low rate both of conviction and apprehension in murder cases in Jamaica which inevitably lessens the deterrent effect of any penalty. The low apprehension rate applies particularly to cases of gun killings, which have accounted for a large proportion of the murders committed in recent years.

The executive, in applying the prerogative of mercy in Jamaica, takes the view that the law should take its course unless there are exceptional circumstances, such as doubt about the guilt of the offender. The Jamaica Privy Council has no set of written guidelines for exercising clemency in death penalty cases. Some prisoners have been denied clemency in the presence of factors which would seem to constitute especially strong grounds for exercising mercy.

The Jamaican government has expressed the view that total abolition of the death penalty cannot be introduced in Jamaica in view of the high rate of violent crime and apparent public support for capital punishment. However, the Minister of Justice was concerned to seek ways in which the present laws may be modified.

26. Recommendations

On the basis of the visit of its representatives to Jamaica, Amnesty International recognizes that there are deeply rooted convictions held by all concerned with the issue of the death penalty and that, despite continued division in public opinion, a significant proportion of informed opinion supports the cause of abolition or the need for radical changes in the current laws governing the death penalty. The organization believes that changes in legislation falling short of total abolition of the death penalty, as have been introduced in some other countries, have served neither to eliminate the inherent unfairness in its application nor reduce controversy on the issue. Amnesty International therefore respectfully submits the following recommendations to the Jamaican Government:

1. All executions should cease, permanently. Amnesty International believes that this could be achieved by the introduction by the government of an appropriate parliamentary resolution which would stop the execution of those already under sentence of death and suspend all future executions, pending changes in the laws providing

for the death penalty. Such a resolution might, for example, call upon the Jamaica Privy Council and the Governor-General to commute all death sentences coming before them, or to suspend the issuing of warrants for execution, pending legislative changes. All sentences that are suspended in this way should be commuted ex post facto upon the introduction of changes to the law.

An alternative measure, which Amnesty International believes would be constitutionally acceptable, would be the introduction of a bill to statutorily commute all existing and future death sentences, pending the introduction of changes to the law.20

2. The death penalty should be abolished for all offences. Legislation should be prepared for submission to Parliament whereby alternative penalties be established for crimes of murder or other offences which presently warrant the death penalty.

As one means to this end, Amnesty International suggests that a detailed study be commissioned with full governmental support which would examine all aspects of the death penalty as currently applied in Jamaica. Such a study should include an examination of the social and economic background and circumstances of all those accused of crimes for which death is the penalty; those who have been sentenced to death and those who have been executed in recent years, to assess whether the death penalty is a punishment which affects principally the poor, the underprivileged and the uneducated from which those with resources can escape. The study should examine the relevance of the death penalty to the level of crimes of violence and alternative measures by which such crimes may be dealt with effectively.

3. In preparation for abolition of the death penalty, the government should inform the public about criminological and penal issues related to the death penalty, including its lack of special proven deterrent effect. This is in line with a recommendation of the UN that "It ... seems to be an important task of governments, the academic community, the mass media and other publicly minded organizations ... to educate the public as to the uncertainty of the deterrent effect of capital punishment".21

4. Pending the introduction of measures to suspend or commute the sentences of those currently under sentence of death, the Minister of Justice should review arrangements for the treatment and custody of such prisoners, to ensure

that they do not exacerbate the already cruel, inhuman and degrading experience of being under sentence of death.

Editor's Note: The death penalty in Jamaica continues to exist.

Editor's Note:

The death penalty in Jamaica continues to exist.

NOTES

1. A separate part of the prison where prisoners under sentence of death are held until their execution.

2. The Judicial Committee of the Privy Council serves as a final court of appeal in a number of Commonwealth countries, including Jamaica. It is composed of five judges from the House of Lords (part of the United Kingdom Parliament). The Judicial Committee represents Her Majesty Queen Elizabeth II, in her capacity as Head of State of the Commonwealth country concerned.

3. The Jamaica Privy Council consists of six members appointed by the Governor General. The Privy Council's function is inter alia to advise the

Governor-General on the exercise of the Royal Prerogative of Mercy.

4. In a letter from the Minister of Justice dated 29 March 1984.

5. The People's National Party, led by Michael Manley, was defeated in the general elections in October 1980, when the Jamaica Labour Party came to power.

6. Given by the Lord Chancellor (Lord Hailsham of Marylebone). Lord Diplock. And Lord Bridge of Harwich.

7. Citing cases from the US Supreme Court; the California Supreme Court; the Indian Supreme Court and a case before the European Commission on Human Rights (Tyrer v. UK).

8. The team's original proposal was to collect information on all the men on death row, but their visits to the prison were curtailed due to bad weather and they were unable to complete the interviews. Thus, the sample cannot strictly be said to be selected "at random" although the team expressed the view that the 40 men interviewed (nearly 50 per cent) constituted a reasonable sample.

9. The research team examined a sample of 40 cases each from the years 1972 and 1976, taken at random from the Director of Public Prosecutions' office ¬records of prosecution only. The outcome of trials was not known in many cases.

10. It was also not clear from these statistics whether the "case" recorded by the police included some multiple killings under one case, or whether each one homicide was recorded separately.

11. Amnesty International and the Death Penalty, a booklet published in June 1979.

12. The team pointed out that, while the data was based almost solely on the interviews, the prisoners antecedents were available to the team in most cases, and that the court records of the preliminary inquiry and trial tended to corroborate their stories, although placing a different emphasis on some of the accounts.

13. Delroy Chuck, the leader of the research team, was so concerned by his findings regarding the quality of legal representation in most of the cases examined, that he wrote to the general Legal Counsel and Bar Association on 25 October 1979. In his letter he stated inter alia that " . . . my research revealed that many defense counsel appointed by legal aid spend very little time

investigating the cases assigned to them. Many, it seems, never discuss the case with their clients in any great detail. There are many areas of discrepancies, inconsistencies and flaws in a trial which defense counsel never see because they know very little about the case they are actually defending. It is crystal clear that in some trials the case for the defense is a half-hearted effort. When such a state of affairs exists in the legal profession, justice is rarely done, and the profession is brought into disrepute. Your urgent attention to this problem is sought."

14. These were given in the commission's report as being mercy killings; survivors of genuine "suicide pacts" and certain cases of infanticide.

15. The statistics up to 1978 are those for murders reported to the police, compiled from police records by the Fraser Committee's research teams. Amnesty International's delegates were unable to obtain official statistics for the period 1979/82: these latter figures were taken from a report published in the Daily Gleaner on 16 March 1983, which gave a breakdown of murders into killings by gunmen, killings other than by the gun and killings of members of the security forces (many of which may also have been carried out by the use of guns).

16. In an address to an award dinner of the Shell Company (West Indies).

17. This ruling was given in a number of different decisions. In Gregg v. Georgia. 1976, the US Supreme Court ruled that mandatory death sentences for a broad category of homicide constituted "cruel and unusual" punishment and were unconstitutional. In later rulings (Woodson v. North Carolina, 1976; Roberts (Stanislaus) v. Louisiana, 1976, and Roberts v. Louisiana, 1977) the Court ruled that mandatory death sentences, even when applying to a more restricted category of homicide, were a denial of due process of law.

18. The Motion was defeated by a large majority.

19. From a statement by Secretary-General Kurt Waldheim at the opening of the Sixth

UN Congress on the Prevention of crime and the Treatment of Offenders, 25 August 1980.

20. These options, including the latter, are discussed in Chapter 5 of this report, and were

also raised in a letter from Amnesty International to the Jamaican Government, attached in Appendix III to this report.

21. Capital Punishment: Working Paper

Prepared by the United Nations Secretariat for the Sixth United Nations Congress on the Prevention of Crime and the Treatment of Offenders, Caracas, Venezuela, 25 August - 5 September 1980 A/CONF 87/9.

CHAPTER 8

POLITICAL CRISIS AND THE DEALTH PENALTY IN UGANDA

Akena Adoko *

The history of death penalty in Uganda is very instructive. But, it is yet to be told by persons whose judgements have not been perverted by partiality. I have myself examined very temperately the reasons our people have given for and against the retention of capital punishment in the country. My conclusion was that many of them were obscured and distorted by prejudices and passion. After some time however, I discovered that I too had acquired feelings on the subject which were hardly compatible with an objective academic analysis. The existence of capital punishment in our statute books up to now has indeed aroused much anger in some of us. Our number is indeed small but many of us are eminently learned and fairly articulate. We have thus made it clear that the retention of capital punishment in our penal code is seen by us as a monument that even now, at the close of the twentieth century, our rules still believe in the official taking of human lives. There are no other explanations as to why capital punishment has remained the sole sentence for any murder and for some treasonable offences such as the attempted murder of the head of state.

It is certainly a signal example of human unteachability that many of us in Uganda should have, for so long, regard capital punishment as an effective deterrent for murders. It is difficult to see how we could so believe when it is common knowledge that in spite of its retention, murders and political assassinations and massacres have been increasing unabated! There is now hardly a place in the whole wide world where human life has become as cheap as in Uganda. We have become like the chickens. When you slaughter a chicken the other chickens fight for its entrails. When you murder a Ugandan, the relatives fight to inherit his properties!

* Akena Adoko is a Ugandan lawyer and at the time of writing this paper, was based in the U.K.

But, although their belief in capital punishment as a deterrence is contrary to their knowledge, it would be wrong to accuse the advocates of hanging in Uganda of dishonesty. They are not. On the contrary, their faith in hanging is strong even to the extent of martyrdom. Many of them are men of integrity. Indeed, they would never have succeeded to deceive so many people had they not begun by deceiving themselves. They sincerely hold and maintain that capital punishment is still a necessary and an effective deterrent to murders.

To them life imprisonment for murderers is dangerous because it exposes prison staff and other prisoners to murderers and in due course, the society itself becomes exposed to the same risks as those faced by prison staff and other prisoners when the murderers get released. They thus hold that capital punishment is certainly a solution to crimes likely to be committed by the convicted murderers. They held that it is an effective deterrent for murderers.

Besides, they do not look upon hanging as savage. On the contrary they claim it to be relatively painless and that if done properly, it takes only a couple of seconds. They point out that capital punishment has been around for so long and is too deep rooted to be abolished without adverse ripples in the society. They thus conclude that it is unworthy of the time of the legal profession to make so much fuss about capital punishment which is so much accepted by the population that its very existence is taken for granted like breathing in and breathing out.

This argument, as some of us see it, is a mere bugbear with which the advocates of capital punishment frighten the others. It is a mere nursery tale which cannot scare an adult.

The way we see it, the task of capital punishment abolitionists should be an easy one. We have good grounds with which to support our case. We have, on our side, those countries which have already abolished capital punishment. We also have illustrious authorities supporting our case. On the other hand, we have opposed to us mainly traditions and prejudices. Let us explain. The Mosaic Law of an eye for an eye and a tooth for a tooth is based on the then generally held view that the offender ought to suffer as much as he made his victim suffer. The doctrine of tit for tat implies that an evil which is wrong for a member of the society to inflict on others is right for the society to inflict on him! It goes without saying that very few people can argue that such an archaic doctrine should have a place in our modern legal system. It is, for instance, universally admitted that a criminal who blinds another should not have his eyes plucked out. Nor does a criminal who causes another to lose a tooth now has his tooth extracted by the order of the courts.

The society in effect tells the convict: You are a savage. You have blinded a fellow citizen. In the olden days we would have plucked out your eyes as a punishment. But we are no longer savages. We are now more civilized than you are. We will not therefore blind you. But, we will instead deprive you of your liberty and or fine you so as to stigmatize you as a convict and to punish and reform you on the one hand, and, on the other hand, deter others from following your footsteps.

We fear that a society which gives itself the right to cut short the life of one man, may end up by us usurping the right to cut down the lives of several thousands of men. That, indeed, is the story of Uganda.

At the time when the tit for tat law ruled supreme, the life of all was everything and the life of one was nothing. Yet, it would have been clear even then

that all is but a totality of several ones. Hence if one is treated as nothing, all will end up in the same way. It is thus not surprising that even in this twentieth century a government of one of the most civilized nations adopted a policy of mass murders as the final solution.

A sage has therefore taught us to treat one as everything and all as nothing. In the parable of the Lost Sheep and the lost coin we are taught that when a good shepherd loses one of his hundred sheep or a conscientious man loses one of his hundred coins, he will leave the remaining ninety-nine and look for the lost one until he finds it! The old saying that we should look after the penny and the pound will take care of itself sums it well. Let us save the life of the individual and the lives in the society will be secured.

Those of us who are the product of Christian Missionary Schools cannot help noticing the marked difference between the Canon Law and the Mosaic Law. We are instructed by the Holy Writ not merely to love one another but to do unto others as we would have them do unto us. The Mosaic Law, on the contrary, provides that we do unto others as they have done unto us. The former law is thus based on love and forgiveness whereas the later is based on hatred and revenge. The Canon Law specifically provides that we do not kill. It allows no exception. It does not state, "Do not kill except as a government."

The Bible commands man to go and multiply; it commands man to produce; not to kill. Execution of convicts is thus a breach of this Canon Law. Besides, it has ramifications with extremely serious psychological consequences. By ordering a hangman to execute a convict, the government proves to members of the society that a human life can actually be cut short by another man with immunity! That neither nature nor man would take the trouble to avenge the sacrilege! It is a lesson which goes against the grain. It is a lesson more likely to spread the seed of murder.

A feeble-minded youth whom I successfully defended in a murder case but whose elder brother was convicted of the murder once said to me, "Mr. Adoko, you are an advocate. You know all about the law. Tell me about it. The judge has said that my brother must hang to deter other men from committing murder. But my brother committed murder in order to eliminate a man planning to kill him. Surely if deterrence is a defense for the government, it should also be a defense for my brother."

Then there are cases where errors of judgement have resulted in the conviction and executions of persons subsequently found to have been innocent of the offences with which they were charged. The taking of life as a mode of punishment thus sometimes involves irretrievable miscarriages of justice. Because of this fear of hanging an innocent man some presidents of Uganda have been unwilling to sign authority for execution. President Milton Obote always locked himself up in his office for hours to consider pleas for mercy for convicted murderers and to sign authority for execution. In about ten years of his rule he never brought himself to sign even one warrant authorizing an execution.

On the same principle, it has always been the policy of the directorate of public prosecution in Uganda not to charge an accused person of murder if there was the slightest excuse for reducing the charge to manslaughter. When I was a crown prosecutor all homicides effected in drinking places or after some drink however small, or during the course of a quarrel etc. were treated as manslaughter cases. In short the finality of the capital punishment had forced the administrators of justice to try to avoid murder charges and in that way to fail in their duty as by law provided. Now, a law which forces a breach of duty on the part of its administrator tends to lead to disobedience of the law!

There are other grounds for the abolition of the capital punishment. It rules out all the opportunity for the reform of the convict. Hanged men cannot reform. If, Saul, the bloody persecutor of Christians had been hanged, he would never have become Paul, the leading apostle.

Nor is execution dangerous to the body only. It is even more dangerous to the mind of the convict. It involves extreme mental torture. It is the worst form of cold-blooded murder.

Even Al Capone never gave his victims several months notice of the termination of their lives. Nor did he even confine his murder victims under locks and keys surrounded by armed guards and watch them sweat it out in a whirl of worries!

Any present rulers of Uganda who takes the trouble to review the history of Uganda would be disposed to regard extreme sentences as warnings to be avoided and not as examples to be followed.

In 1985, Obote's government, in a fit of servility and animosity passed a law prohibiting the granting of bail to persons charged with the offences of terrorism. The law had hardly been passed when the fortune of the government changed. It fell. The new government now arrested several leaders of the fallen government and charged them under the law prohibiting the granting of bail. By an oversight the former

Minister for Power Mr. Akena P'ojok was charged under the law which permits bail and the court released him on bail. When the government learnt about this, it rearrested him, withdrew the charges pending against him and filed new charges based on the same facts. This time, however he was charged under the law prohibiting the granting of bail. Meanwhile, many former leaders including Vice-President Paulo Muwanga, Minister Andrew Kayiira, Minister Chris Rwakasisi, Deputy Minister Ben Etonyu and Minister Ben Rwanyarale etc. were arrested and charged with offences carrying capital punishment.

Whether by virtue of natural law of cause and effect, or by some providential decree our leaders who have been insensitive to harsh laws have thus suffered severely under the laws they have tolerated. Some of our people being who they are seldom hesitate for valuable consideration to commit perjury in order to justify the actions taken by the government against fallen leaders. From such singular examples of the vicissitude of fortune we would have by now learnt the need for moderation in laws.

Yet, because many of our people are pathologically alarmists, they have been frightened by the talks about the dangers to which human lives would be exposed if capital punishment was abolished. It proves a waste of time explaining to some of them that the dangers they feared did not materialize in countries which have abolished death sentences such as, for instance, Switzerland, West Germany, Italy, Portugal, the Netherlands, Denmark, Venezuala and Brazil, Canada, etc. Since they must always be afraid of something they dismiss your explanation with the answer, "Uganda is different; Germany is different too,". Because of such attitude, it has been seriously suggested that Uganda follow the example set forth by countries like England and Wales, which have abolished capital punishment in most of the cases where it used to apply and restricted it to treason and piracy cases only. The proponents of such restriction had argued that perils lie thick on both sides; the side of abolition, on the one hand, and the side of retention, on the other hand. To keep far from one set of perils was to draw near to another set. The best course was therefore to weigh the perils against each other and to observe carefully the way the scale leaned. Having so weighed and watched the scale, they could abolish capital punishment in most of the cases and retained it in a minimal number of cases only.

It is admitted that in so far as the abolition of death sentence in most cases was concerned, it was a step forward. Half a loaf, as they say, is better than none.

But, in so far as the retention of some cases punishable by death is concerned then the action taken was merely half a cure which is no cure at all. For a cure of sickness to take place, the demand of nature has to be met. There is no haggling. There should be no haggling. Let us therefore begin to reason afresh. Capital punishment is either good or bad. If it is good, then let it be retained for all murder cases. Why retain it only in some and not in others? If it is bad then it must go in all cases. There is thus no need to haggle about it by diminishing the cases to which it should apply. It is laughable to argue that because it has been abolished in some cases in which it was never necessary, therefore it should be retained in a few cases in which it is equally not necessary! The fact that some people have resorted to that kind of logic is proof that the subject is so charged with emotion that many are bound not to reason at all about it and that some are bound to reason very badly about it and to end up persecuting those who deflate their arguments.

Let us now sum up in one sentence paragraphs;

Since the government cannot give life, it should not take life.

A convict may be a bad man but his life may contribute to the cause of all good men.

The murder of a man and the execution of the murderer are not very different, they are the taking of the human life.

Nor is there an infinity between the life of a murderer and that of his victim.

The taking of the human life under any circumstances and for whatever reason

is thus indefensible; any attempt to defend it only makes the case worse. No State should thus be deaf to the entreaties of reformers who ask neither for pardon, nor for mercy but for the imposition of life imprisonment instead of death.

As things now stand, the existence of capital punishment in a statute book is increasingly becoming a testimony of the detestable malignity and unbearable arrogance of the rulers.

CHAPTER 9

AGAINST CAPITAL PUNISHMENT IN NIGERIA

Eluen Emeka Izeze *

There is a certain irrationality attached to absolute measures or actions. Oftentimes, they are very subjective and even repressive. They could also be illegal depending on who is at the receiving or giving end. All these contradictions manifest themselves so glaringly in the principle of capital punishment.

The principle ensures that anyone who betrays his country, say in times of war or who plots the overthrow of a government, would on conviction face death. Then, there is the provision that anyone who takes another person's life, would on conviction also face death. In recent times, we

* Eluen Emeka Izeze is the editor of Nigerian Guardian

have had new additions to offences punishable by death, offences such as drug trafficking, economic sabotage, like tampering with oil pipeline or National Electric Power Authority (NEPA) installations or selling petroleum products outside the country illegally. The fact that the later group of offences attracting the death penalty, has since been amended, in no way diminishes our contention here. In actual fact, it reinforces it, for it shows that not enough homework was done before the laws were promulgated, so that when sent on trial in the market place of public opinion, they were found not to stand any chance. They are thus a very good example of the type of irrationality attached to such absolute actions as the capital punishment.

I must admit that there are some very strong reasons on which proponents of the capital punishment base their argument. For instance, you are asked, would you still oppose the death sentence, if you have seen someone murdered? And if that victim is in one way or the other related to you, would you still see the irrationality of prosecuting the Mosaic Law of a tooth for a tooth, and an eye for an eye? Actually, before the death sentence for hard drug traffickers was amended, you were asked: if you have been a drug victim, or if you were related to someone who had been, either as a son, daughter, father, mother, brother or sister, and so you had a first-hand experience of how it sucks the life out of the body and leaves the sufferer wandering like a zombie, would you still oppose its punishment with death?

Proponents would maintain that backed up with scientific findings, a person with a propensity to kill people would keep at his obnoxious pastime if he is not stopped - by killing him, of course. Also, there is the argument that a murderer and an armed robber or even a coup plotter, could become an evil influence on others if he is allowed to go scot-free. For in a way, it would amount to giving others the licence to kill. And, of course, there is the well-known argument that in pressing for an amendment of the provisions for capital punishment you must take cognizance of the level of development of a nation - the stability and psyche of its people. The conclusion here would be that Nigeria and Nigerians have not reached a stage where they should dispense with such legal provisions as the death penalty.

Legitimate as these contentions may be, they remain badly flawed. For one thing, the principle of the Mosaic Law has since been replaced by latter-day injunctions in the world's major religions. Though not exactly in the same words and context, it now sounds like the biblical advice, if anyone slaps you on the right cheek, turn the left also to him. And for another, the effectiveness of capital punishment is clearly suspect. Armed robbery has not diminished since we started executing robbers, for instance. Instead, robbers have become more sophisticated, daring and highly brutal. Then there is the moral question that since you cannot create a life, you have no right taking one.

Beyond these moralistic perspectives to the capital punishment issue, is the frightening prospect, which it holds for our judicial system. To start with, there is no debate whatsoever, among our dispensers of justice, over whether the capital punishment is both desirable and effective as a punishment for a criminal offence. That is perhaps because, the law does not allow for such time-wasting polemics. Unlike other provisions in law which give the maximum as well as minimum terms for which a person can be sentenced, that on capital punishment allows the judge just one narrow room: when anyone facing trial for murder or violent robbery, is convicted, the only punishment allowed by the law is death. The judge is thus reduced to a robot and not the learned gentleman that he is. He cannot question the provision because he has no liberty to say anything else than pronounce the death sentence.

Of course, for an offence that involves the taking of a person's life and whose punishment also involve death, the least that could be expected is to have a little opportunity for debate on the issue. The Nigerian legal system does not allow this.

Yet, the same law which punishes murder with death, also legitimizes or turns a blind eye to other types of killing. There are people whose only job is killing other people, like the hangman or executioner or it is imposed on them by circumstances like in the military, when the country is in a state of war. The law says that the hangman and the executioner are committing legal murder and so cannot be punished. The same law also allows murder if one can prove that he was acting in self-defense, or that he was extremely provoked into taking the action. This is what is known as manslaughter in law. Of course, there is a contradiction here in that the same law calls the spade a spade in one breath, and in another says that it is a hoe.

This is worrying enough, but consider that as in anything handled by humans, there must be a margin of error. In the case of illegal murder which is punishable with legal murder, it is almost certain that some people would have been sent to their death for offences they did not commit.

Moralists would tell you that when you kill a person, you lift the burden of the guilt from him. It is perhaps for this reason that many countries, especially the liberal democracies of the West, regard the death sentence as a very ineffective punishment even for murder. To them a long prison sentence, actually a life term is the worst form of punishment you can mete out to any person since it deprives him of his freedom forever. Everyday for the rest of his life, he has the tortuous opportunity of ruminating over his crime. No punishment is greater than this. But aside from the vindictive urge to hurt someone who has hurt you or someone close to you, when a murderer is jailed for life, he has the opportunity to repent from his evil deed which is what the prisons are supposed to do. And let me add that this has nothing to do with the level of a country's development. It is purely a matter of crime, punishment, and reformation.

By opting for the death sentence, the Nigerian legal system passes a vote of no confidence on the reforming abilities of our prisons. And this by implication denies the prisons of any chance of being turned into reformatory homes. The capital punishment also turns all of us into vindictive brutes. But above all, it shows that those who made the law have little faith in the past, present and future generations of Nigerian jurists to truly adjudicate in a serious offence such as murder, so that they have to be told what to do: release the accused or send him to his death. No human, I dare say, ought to be given such a task. But then it shows the appalling extent of the law on capital punishment in this country.

PART FOUR

WAR CRIMES AND CRIMES AGAINST HUMANITY

CHAPTER 10

INTRODUCTION

Yossi Schwartz *

1. While the title of my talk suggests that I support capital punishment I do so only in the case of Nazi war criminals. I further support capital punishment for such class of war crimes and crimes against humanity, as: colonialism, genocide, apartheid and slavery.

2. It is true that these crimes have been committed through-out the history of the human race. Few examples are: the extermination of the native population by the colonialists, in South America, North America, Africa, Indo-China etc.; the extermination of Bulgarians, Greeks, and Armenians by the Ottoman Empire etc.

* Yossi Schwartz is a Toronto lawyer

3. Yet the crimes of the Nazis were unique in their systematic and methodological performance. When the prisoners of Auschwitz, Majdanek, Treblinka were liberated the worst nightmare was discovered: false shower rooms where the victims were gassed to death; piles of human hair used for mattresses, ground human bones used for soap; boxes of golden teeth to be melted for the gold, etc.

4. By the end of the war, about six million Jews were murdered, four million in the death camps. Many thousands of Gypsies were also killed. The Polish people lost six million people (22%) of the population, 877,000, civilians, half of them Jews. Yugoslavia out of 15 million, lost 1,685,000 including 1,274,000 civilians ; 425,000 out of the 6 million Greeks were killed, 400,000 of which were civilians. The Soviet Union lost 20 million, mostly civilians.

5. Many have posed the question, how do you explain these inhuman deeds of the same people who produced great musicians, philosophers, writers?

6. The answer is complicated and has to do with the decline of capitalism, at the same time even those who do not see the decline of the capitalist system would agree that racism was an important element of this inhuman behavior.

Racism was deliberately planted in the mind of millions of Germans long before the Nazis took power. Huston Stewart Chamberlin, Ludwig Woltman and Eugen Dureng who preached white superiority, were very respected in Kaiser Germany. The rulers of Germany practiced genocide on the people of Namibia who opposed the German occupation, long before they exterminated Europeans.

The Nazis elaborated on Nietzsche's teaching about the superman, and spread¬ their faulty ideology claiming that the human race is divided into the superman, and the subhuman, and that social progress can be achieved only when the subhuman were removed.

7. After the war very important resolutions were adopted by the U.N., in order to prevent such deeds in the future.

a) On November 3, 1947 the General Assembly adopted the resolution about crimes against peace: the planning, preparing and waging aggressive wars. This includes the propaganda of war.

b) Crimes Against Peace and Humanity. The Statutes of Nuremberg and Tokyo included in this category, crimes of war and crimes against humanity. The International Law Commission in 1953 defined such acts as: any act of aggression; a threat to peace, preparation to employ armed force unlawfully, the organization of armed bands for incursions into the territory of another state, annexation, genocide, intervention in affairs of another country by political and economic means.

c) The 1949 Geneva Conventions protect victims of war. War crimes are defined as: The use of methods of warfare banned by international law, destruction of human settlements, brutal treatment of prisoners of war, plundering, enslavement.

d) In December 1948 the Convention on the Prevention and Punishment of the Crime of Genocide was signed. According to this conventionally "killing members of the group with intent to destroy, in whole or in part, a national, racial, ethnic or religious group is genocide".

e) According to the 1968 Convention on the Non-Applicability of Statutory Limitation to War Crimes and Crimes Against Humanity, such limitation are not applied to these crimes and states are required to cooperate in order to prosecute such criminals.

8. Someone could expect that at least the Nazi

criminals would be brought to justice, and hope that war crimes and crimes against humanity would be stopped, but as we all know this is not the case.

As we know thousands upon thousands of Nazi criminals escaped to North America, South America, and Australia with the active help of the American, British and Canadian Governments and their secret services, as well as with the help of the Vatican.

The name of Klaus Barbie, the butcher of Lyon, is still fresh in memory, but he was not the only one. In 1980 ABC television showed a documentary film by Michael O'Connor and Tim O'Brian. They maintained that there were Nazi criminals living in the U.S.A. who were responsible for the death of two million people, many of them claiming to be "displaced persons", escaping from "communism", and the American authorities turned a blind eye to their crimes. In his movie Eli Wiesel, not a great friend of the Soviet Union said: "We can never succeed in punishing all the war criminals. There are too many of them, and they have highly placed protectors. It is painful for me, as a citizen and a human being, to realize that these people live freely in America violating the principles of democracy and justice".

The Deschenes' inquiry into the Nazi war criminals revealed not only that Nazis escaped to Canada, but that for 43 years the federal government obstructed any attempt to bring them to justice. Even today after the inquiry and after the Criminal Code was amended to allow the federal government to prosecute alleged war criminals nothing has been done.

But even this inquiry failed to point out the actual numbers of Nazi war criminals in Canada. It found 20 Nazi war criminals and 218 suspected war criminals. How can it be when a whole Ukranian S.S. Wofen found refuge in Canada ?

9. Some people believe that these old Nazis should not be prosecuted because they committed their crimes in the far past, and they have been reformed. They might be anti-communist, these people argue, but they do not commit any wrongful act. The best I can say about these people is that they are not informed, and that they are used to protect the continuation of international crimes against humanity.

10. Why have these criminals not been extradited to Eastern Europe where the crimes occurred not tried in the West?

Some lawyers and politicians argue that they

should not be extradited because by Western standards the legal system in the socialist countries does not provide for justice, and the Soviet evidence cannot be trusted. Others argue that there are no extradition treaties between the West and the socialist countries.

This argument strikes at the heart of international law itself. The U.N. (and the U.N. Charter) is not a framework of cooperation between the capitalist and socialist countries but a framework for cooperation between states of different social political and legal systems in order to prevent wars and crimes against humanity.

Secondly, if indeed the governments of the West were worried about the fairness of the socialist legal system they could have tried them in the West, which they have failed to do.

Thirdly, Demjanjuk's trial, in Jerusalem proves that those who cry that Soviet evidence is fabricated are wrong at best, and some even lie at worst. All the attempts to discredit the Soviet evidence have failed miserably.

There are particular extradition treaties with Yugoslavia for example, and yet the previous Prime Minister of Croatia, a regime that was set up by Nazi Germany in Yugoslavia, and which collaborated with the Nazis found political refuge in the U.S., and was not extradited. Furthermore, the West ignore the international Postdam and Yalta agreements which include extradition.

11. The reasons are very different. These arguments are no more than a smokescreen which is used to hide the fact that many of these criminals continued and continue in their criminal activities in support of western interests.

There are many other ways in which old Nazis are used by Washington and its allies:

i) After the war in the countries where the left led the resistance to the fascists, but the West occupied, like Greece, Italy, West Germany, Philippines, the same Nazis and those who collaborated with them were put back in power. Take West Germany for example. Erhard Dabringhaus, who was Barbie's U.S. Intelligence Control Officer, in his book Klaus Barbie (p. 131) wrote: "In December 1945, I passed through Schwarzenback on my way to visit my wife in Belgium. I stopped to see how the mayor was getting along in his job. I was surprised to find that the former concentration camp inmate, a social Democrat, had been replaced by a former SS officer who had been cleared of war crimes and returned from an internment camp".

The BND-West Germany Security service has many Gestapo and SD officers on its payroll, for example, Stern, the liberal West German magazine reported that SS Oberfureer and Gestapo inspector Kirchbaum are in the employment of the BND. Other known Nazis are Gestapo Chief of Kiel F. Fanzinger, chief of Budapest H. Sommer. The SS are given pensions.

ii) While for some years the Nazis in West Germany worked in a semi-clandestine manner, with the new wave of ultra-conservatism, Reagan-Thatcher etc., the old and the neo-Nazi organizations have been legitimized. Today close to 30 such organizations operate in West Germany. The Nazi national anthem: "Deutschland, Deutschland Uber Alles", is a legitimate song. Contrary to the attempt to white-wash his action, Reagan's visit to the Nazi graveyard was not a mistake, but part of the same policy.

iii) The Old Nazis who escaped to Latin America, Argentina, Chile, Paraguay, Brazil, where incredible atrocities were committed against the people, helped and trained the butchers in their own methods. In Chile there is a mini-Nazi state. According to reports more than 2,000 Nazis live there in this secretive colony. Many Nazis found employment in the Pinochet Government. One example is Walter Rauff who is responsible for the death of 250,000 prisoners in the Ukraine. After the Coup d'etat organized by the CIA, Pinochet appointed him as chief adviser for the board investigating communist activities.

Klaus Barbie escaped to Bolivia. There under his leadership the storm troopers were trained in secret camps at Santa Cruez de la Sierra later to take part in the military coup conducted by General Garcia Meza in July 1980.

The President of Paraguay, Alfredo Stroessner have hosted among others Josef Mengele, the white dead angel of Oswiecism responsible for the death of 200,000 prisoners. Among others are former gestapo chief Heinrich Muller Pavelic, the leader of Nazi Croatia, who is responsible for the death of 800,000 Yugoslavs.

In Brazil Alfred Boettcher as an SS officer served in Holland, and whom the Hague Tribunal sentenced in absentia, became a director of the atomic board, and a coordinator of a nuclear treaty with South Africa.

Thus the old Nazis have not disappeared but they function in the service of the West to prepare war against socialism and to enslave the people of the third world.

And how can the West try these criminals for their crimes, when the same type of crimes have been committed by the West since the end of the War. Take for example the question of Genocide:

A) US

The U.S. committed large scale war crimes against the people of Vietnam, whose crime in the eyes of the American ruling circles was that they wanted to be independent from American domination and exploitation. The Americans used Napalm, which is illegal according to international law. 100,000 tons were thrown on Vietnam according to the U.S. Air Force. In South Vietnam more than one million civilians perished in concentration camps. Children and women were murdered. Le Monde Diplomatique reporter wrote in March 1967: "There were 2 children to each of the 25 cots in the room. Two children had both legs amputated to the knees. One of the medical personnel told me that Americans had shot them like rabbits. I could not take my eyes away from the blood-soaked bandage. I read the card on the hospital cots: Vo Van Mung, seven years old, Nguyen Van-Nong, eleven years, Van-Minh, thirteen years, Nguyan Van Hot ten years. Their only crime was that they were tending buffaloes, which in the opinion of the Americans, meant contact with the Viet Cong". The Americans used chemical weapons. The New York Times of September 10, 1966 reported: "This year operation ranch hand, using an average of six C-123 spray planes, has squirted 1,324,430 gallons of non-toxic herbicide."

In those regions where this herbicide was spread 56% of the population developed intestinal diseases and 70% bronchitis. The U.S. claimed that these chemicals were not lethal, but these chemicals claimed the lives of at least 80 American soldiers who were exposed to them. United Press International of March 1967, reported that civilians are dying of exposure to these chemicals. All in all, over 15 million people in Vietnam were either killed, wounded or maimed.

B) Israel

During the invasion of Lebanon, over 30,000 Lebanese and Palestinians, mainly women and children were killed, and some 70,000 were wounded. Fourteen Palestinian refugee camps were destroyed, and the main cities suffered devastation. Schools, hospitals, daycares, orphanages were bombed. Canadian ambassador, Theodore Arcand said about the destruction of

Beirut: "The destruction would make Berlin of 1944 look like a tea party".

The massacre of Sabra and Shatila as they became known and the man who conducted this massacre, Ariel Sharon is still a minister in the government of Israel.

Israel put thousands of people in concentration camp - Ansar. The Prime Minister of Israel during the 1982 war, Begin addressing the Kneset, echoing Nazi propaganda, referred to the Palestinians as "Two-legged animals". For many the war of 1982 was the first time they have begun to doubt about the nature of Zionism, but the Zionist movement has practiced genocide against the Palestinians for many years. The Massacre of Dir Yasin, in 1948, of Kufar Quasim in 1956 are some of the more known examples.

C) The crimes of Apartheid are quite known, but there is no doubt that if U.S., France, West Germany, Britain and Israel would not support this regime the struggle of the People of South Africa and Namibia for national liberation would be much easier. In this context, we should remember that the U.S. and South Africa intelligence services are aiding the terror of the MNR, the contras of Mozambique.

D) El Salvador, Guatemala, Chile under Pinochet, Paraguay, Argentina under the Generals, are all known for their genocide of the people, and are all U.S. client states.

E) Kampuchea is another horrible example. The Clique of Pol Pot exterminated about 3 million people. The attempts of the West to accuse socialism of this crime, because of the Maoist ideology of Pol Pot, is ridiculous in light of the fact that after this clique was overthrown by the Vietnamese, the West made a political and military alliance with the same murderers.

F) The support of the contras in Nicaragua whose activities in the killing of civilians, farmers, workers, teachers, doctors and nuns and to destroy the crops and machinery is another crime against the peace. The contras are not freedom fighters as Reagan claims but are war criminals.

Why support capital punishment for these criminals? Some people would argue that since such crimes are either part of the human nature, or part of the social condition we live in, capital punishment cannot have a general deterrence effect, and since they oppose retribution, they cannot see why it is necessary to impose such punishment at all.

These horrible crimes are not the result of human nature, but of decaying imperialism which in its effort to survive against the general course of history brings about destruction.

We have to view the demand for capital punishment for such criminals as part of the struggle to emancipate the human race from the conditions of exploitation of human beings by other human beings. Racism which justified these horrors is not normal, but it is an ideology which was created to justify enslavement. The demand for capital punishment for certain criminals who put themselves outside of humanity would make it much more difficult to commit such crimes again. Would Oliver North be such a hero if the people of the U.S. were aware that he belongs to the same camp of the Nazis. Would Reagan be a President under such circumstances? Those who commit such barbaric crimes against humanity know that they have a place to run to when they fall, if not to the U.S. at least to a country controlled by the West. Would they be able to escape were the American people aware that their government is sheltering war criminals, and criminals against humanity?

Some Liberals argue that by supporting capital punishment for war criminals we legitimize this punishment and because of it the government would be in a better position to impose it on all people, including the left.

They are wrong. Governments are not bounded by formal logic, but by relationship of power between the ruling circles and the people they rule. The history of capital punishment in the U.S. since the second war proves it easily. Poor people, people of colour, and the left wing etc are the people executed. Those who ordered the crimes in Vietnam and the known Nazis were not even brought to trial.

In other words, if the progressive movement will be strong enough to demand capital punishment for war criminals they may get it as a concession.

Why kill these criminals and not jail them for life? In the abstract nothing is wrong with this approach, but under the existing conditions, they will not sit long in the prisons in the West. After the war, thousands of war criminals were sentenced to long periods, many to life, and yet within 2-4 years these criminals were not only free but held important positions in the administrations of the West. History should not be allowed to repeat itself, at least not with our acquiescence.

CHAPTER 11

THE DEATH PENALTY IN TEE CONTEXT OF COMMISSION OF CRIMES AGAINST HUMANITY IN SOUTH AFRICA*

Munyonzwe Hamalengwa **

The death penalty in South Africa unlike elsewhere, could not be divorced from the general context of the commission of crimes against humanity perpetrated by the apartheid regime in South Africa. Article 1 of the International Convention on the Suppression and Punishment

* This is part of a larger work I am doing on war crimes in Canadian law.

** Munyonzwe Hamalengwa practices law in Toronto, Ontario, Canada of the Crime of Apartheid (ICSPCA) stipulates that:

(1) The States Parties to the present Convention declare that apartheid is a crime against humanity and that inhuman acts resulting from the policies of apartheid and similar policies and practices of racial segregation and discrimination, as defined in article II of the Convention, are crimes violating the principles of international law, in particular the purposes and principles of the Charter of United Nations, and constituting a serious threat to international peace and security.

(2) the States Parties to the present Convention declare those criminal organizations, institutions and individuals committing the crime of apartheid.

Thus apartheid is recognized as a crime against humanity by treaty law. As is common knowledge, treaties are one of the most important sources of international law, commanding adherence not only by states parties to a particular treaty, but by the international community generally. Apartheid was a crime violating not only international law but was also a serious threat to international peace and security. The crime of apartheid as a crime against humanity was not limited to its practices in South

Africa and Namibia, it extended to similar practices elsewhere as article 11 of ICSPCA makes clear:

For the purposes of the present Convention, the term "the crime of apartheid," which shall include similar policies and practices of racial segregation and discrimination as practiced in Southern Africa, shall apply to the following inhuman acts committed for the purpose of establishing and maintaining domination by one racial group of persons over any other racial group of persons and systematically oppressing them:

(a) Denial to a member or members of a racial group or groups of the right of life and liberty of person:

(i) By murder of members of a racial group or groups;

(ii) By the infliction upon the members of a racial group or groups of serious bodily or mental harm by the infringement of their freedom or dignity, or by subjecting them to torture or to cruel, inhuman or degrading treatment or punishment;

(iii) By arbitrary arrest and illegal imprisonment of the members of a racial group or groups;

(b) Deliberate imposition on a racial group or groups of living conditions calculated to cause its or their physical destruction in whole or in part;

(c) Any legislative measures and other measures calculated to prevent a racial group or groups from participation in the political, social, economic and cultural life of the country and the deliberate creation of conditions preventing the full development of such group or groups, in particular by denying to members of a racial group or groups basic human rights and freedoms, including the right to work, the right to form organized trade unions, the right to education, the right to leave and to return to their country, the right to a nationality, the right to freedom of opinion and expression, and the right to freedom of peaceful assembly and association;

(d) Any measures, including legislative measures designed to divide the population along racial lines by the creation of separate reserves and ghettos for the members of a racial group or groups, the prohibition of mixed marriages among members of various

racial groups, the expropriation of landed property belonging to a racial group or groups or to members thereof;

(e) Exploitation of the labour of the members of a racial group or groups, in particular by submitting them to forced labour;

(f) Persecution of organizations and persons, by depriving them of fundamental rights and freedoms, because they oppose apartheid.

The Apartheid Convention is broader in compass than the Nuremberg Principles. The principle of the illegality of racial discrimination, like that practiced in South Africa had increasingly been elevated in international law if not already recognized as part of jus cogens -- peremptory norm of international law which cannot be derogated from or set aside by treaty or acquiescence. Non-discrimination as a case of jus cogens, apartheid as practiced in South Africa constituted a specific and particular case of violation of jus cogens.2 Racial Discrimination was also outlawed by treaty law, as recognized in the International Convention Agrainst Racial Discrimination.3 Racial discrimination was thus a violation of international law. I.C.S.P.C.A. defines discrimination as practiced under apartheid as an international crime. Considering the numerous U.N. resolutions against apartheid practices in South Africa; numerous treaties similar to I.C.S.P.C.A.; various national legislations; various pronouncements in international circles; press releases, policy statements etc., apartheid was a violation of customary international law, conventional international law as well as general principles of law recognized by the community of nations.

Apart from being an international crime on the basis of being a crime against humanity in regard to its treatment of the majority population in South Africa as defined above, apartheid according to Brahme4 was also a crime against peace. This was because of:

(a) its continued colonial and illegal occupation of Namibia, which in itself was also a violation of the principle of the right to self-¬determination of peoples,5 and, (b) its aggression and de-stabilization of neighbouring states. It was very possible and indeed inevitable that in the course of its occupation of Namibia and its aggression against neighbouring states, apartheid also commited war crimes as defined in the Nuremberg Principles. If this was the case, then apartheid had committed and continued to commit all the major international crimes, namely, crimes against peace; war crimes and crimes against humanity for which the international community had universal jurisdiction to prosecute the perpetrators.

It is thus necessary to review in brief the precise manner in which apartheid commited these international crimes, particularly the crime against humanity.

"Violation of human rights on a substantial scale has characterized the situation in South Africa for many years. Recently, there has been a further, marked escalation of political imprisonment and detention without trial, torture and political killings. The judicial death penalty continues to be used at a high rate."6 It is not necessary to go far into the history of South Africa in order to demonstrate the criminality and violence of apartheid (the laws in South Africa resembled to a large extent the laws of Nazi Germany), suffice to review the immediate period of the 1980s, with sporadic references to the period between 1948 and the 1980s.

Apartheid was not an arbitrary system of governance. It was based on laws governing all aspects of life. Of interest to us are the "security laws" that justify the arrest, detention, torture and sometimes killings of Africans. The most comprehensive law to date that has set the legal framework of repression was the Internal Security Act of 1982.7 This Act was a consolidation of all previously existing security laws, most of which it also repealed. The earlier security laws included8:

(a) The Suppression of Communism Act No. 44 of (1950);

(b) The Bantu Administration Act No. 38 of (1927);

(c) The Public Safety Act No. 3 of (1953);

(d) The Criminal Procedure Act No. 56 of (1955);

(e) The Riotous Assembly Act. No. 17 of (1956);

(f) The Unlawful Organizations Act No. 34 of (1960);

(g) The General Amendment Act No. 37 of (1963);

(h) The Terrorism Act No. 83 of (1967);

(i) The Affected Organizations Act No. 31 of (1974).

The publication of the International Defense and Aid Fund entitled Apartheid:

The Facts9 had captured neatly the utilization and compass of these security laws at the hands of the South African police and army:

The widest powers derive from the so-called 'security' laws. These are aimed at people or organizations whose activities and aims the regime describes as 'furthering the aims of communism', 'terrorism', 'endangering the security of the State or the maintenance of order', 'endangering the public peace' or 'threatening essential services'. The definition of these terms is so loose and the power conferred by the laws so wide, that the regime is able to use the law to act against any form of effective opposition to the apartheid system. The limits to its capacity to use these powers are not contained in the laws, but are set only by political and practical considerations.

Under the 'security' laws, there are powers to detain people without trial; to ban people, organizations and meetings; to break up meetings: and to imprison people. By the restrictions they place on meetings, the laws licence attacks against protesters and demonstrators, which on many occasions have included the police killing people. The laws have also created conditions under which the torture of detainees has become routine.

The application of the Internal Security Act brought ominous results.[10] Section 28 of the Internal Security Act for example empowered the Minister of Law and Order to order the preventive detention of any person he considered engaged in, or likely to be engaged in, "activities which endanger or are calculated to endanger the security of the State or the maintenance of law and order." Section 29 permited police to hold detainees for interrogation indefinitely, in isolation and without access to relatives or lawyers. Section 30 empowered a State Attorney-General to issue an order denying the court its usual authority to release a charged person on bail if he "considers it necessary interests of the security of the state or the maintenance of law and order." Section 31 empowered a state Attorney-General to authorize incommunicado detention without charge of potential state witnesses until the end of the trial at which they were expected to testify. If they refused to testify, they could be sentenced to up to five years imprisonment for contempt of court. If they refuted in court a statement made while in security police detention on the grounds that it was made under duress, they could be charged with perjury.

In 1984 for example the above Internal Security Act sections were used to detain the following numbers of people:[11]

Section 28 (Preventive Detention)
28

Section 29 (Detention for interrogation)
280

Section 31 (Detention of potential witnesses)
13

Section 50 (Short term preventive detention), or
no 72

Section 50 of the Criminal Procedure Act or no legislation at all, for period of less than 48 hours.
152

It was also the sometimes end result of these indefinite and incommunicado detentions without family or lawyers' visits that incriminated apartheid as a crime against humanity. According to Amnesty International, many detainees had been tortured or severely ill-treated while detained incommunicado.[12]

Many studies have in fact also confirmed that opportunities for torture exist when detainees are held incommunicado anywhere in the world.13 It is not surprising that torture and ill-treatment are now outlawed by the treat law. Not only did incommunicado detentions offer opportunities for torture in South Africa, they also led to extra judicial killings by security police of those tortured. At greater risk of torture and death in prison were political detainees, though even mere criminals had been known to die in prison.

Indications of torture were not only revealed in numerous deaths in prison (to which I will return shortly) but also in numerous cases of detainees requiring hospitalization during or after detention due to injuries or serious mental disturbance. Dr. Wendy Orr, a district surgeon responsible for medically examining detainees and prisoners in the Port Elizabeth area, for example submitted evidence on 25th September, 1985 to the Supreme Court of widespread and regular torture and ill-treatment of detainees. Her evidence was supported by sworn statements from over 40 people, including detainees.[14] The figure for the whole of South Africa would be staggering. Tortured detainees had no recourse to law as existing laws and regulations granted immunity in advance to all law enforcement officials for any actions committed "in good faith" in the exercise of their powers.

The inquests that were conducted after the deaths in prison of Steve Biko, the leader of the Black Consciousness Movement, and Neil Aggett, a white trade unionist revealed the extent of torture in South African prisons.[15]

The gravity and widespread use of torture in South African prisons had also been revealed more clearly by a nation-wide empirical study conducted by three professors at the Institute of

Criminology of the University of Cape Town.16 One hundred and forty-four former "security legislation" detainees were interviewed. The period covered was between 1974 and 1983. Most of those detained were involved in all kinds of political work: student organizations, trade unions, community and political organizations.

Using the operational definition of torture of the United Nations Declaration on Torture, the results came as follows and I quote the whole tabulation:

Only 17% of cases claimed no form of physical torture. The most frequent form of torture (75%) was beating, which included punching, hitting, locking, slapping as well as beating and whipping with a variety of implements and other forms of assault. The next three most frequently reported forms of physical abuse were forced standing (50%), maintaining abnormal body positions, which includes crouching, standing on toes with arms upstretched, holding chairs or other objects above the head, and holding a position as if sitting in an imaginary chair (34%), and forced gymnasium-type exercises (28%). In addition, 25% reported having been subjected to electric shock, 18% to strangulation either by hand or by means of a cloth or towel, and 14% to suspension in various forms.

Other forms of physical torture were reported by 27% of cases. Hand analysis of these other descriptions revealed the following most frequent forms of abuse: manacles, including handcuffs, legs constantly chained and chains placed around neck (15%); pulling out or burning hair or beard (5%); genital abuse (3%), and falanga, which involves beating the soles of the feet with some implement (3%). A further rage of abuses were reported by one or more cases and included: being wrapped in canvas, kept barefoot, burning match sticks placed under nails, sand in shoes while doing exercises, being thrown into the air and allowed to fall, given salted water to drink, hands cut with knife, placed in boot of car, nose twisted, fingernails crushed by brick, petrol poured over body and set alight, breasts squeezed, held out of moving car, tied to a tree, and scrubbed on face and body with a hard brush. Even this substantial list does not entirely exhaust the range of abuses reported.[17]

In addition to physical torture, psychological torture was also part of the system.

The findings on this aspect of torture were reported as follows:

No cases reported an entire lack of psychological abuse. Over half of the cases reported having been subjected to the following forms: false accusations

(83%);solitary confinement (79%); verbal abuse (71%); threats of violence to self (64%); contradictory styles of interrogation (57%); and being given misleading information (51%).18

These figures show that almost no one was safe from torture in South African prisons. Torture was so pervasive that the system itself can be called "torturous" i.e. it was based on torture.

Gordon Winter, an ex-intelligence officer in South Africa also described from experience some of the horrible torture methods and causes of numerous deaths in South African prisons in his book Inside BOSS, South Africa's Secret Police.[19]

Torture resulted in many deaths in South African prisons as already stated. As of the period from 1963 to 1984, for example, sixty individuals had been recorded as having died in prison. I think this was perhaps the greatest number of deaths in prison anywhere in the world. The majority of the deaths occurred in 1969 (6); 1976 (13), and 1977 (14). There may have been many deaths that were not reported.

The torture and deaths of political prisoners in South Africa was only part of the story. There were many deaths caused directly by apartheid in South Africa. There were firstly official "judicial murders" whereby political prisoners were forced to confess under torture to crimes they did not commit. These "confessions" were then used to convict the victims which convictions in turn attracted the death penalty. Secondly the nature of apartheid induced the subject population to commit all sorts of crimes which directly lead to imprisonment.20 Some of these ended up dying mysteriously in prison. Thirdly, there were many arrests due to infractions of the pass laws. Pass laws were the cornerstone of apartheid. According to Amnesty International's publication, South Africa: Imprisonment Under the Pass Laws,21 238,000 Africans were arrested in 1984 alone for pass law and other infractions. A sizeable percentage of those arrested either for committing certain crimes or for pass law infractions never saw the light of the day again. According to the report, Torture is Part of the System22 there were on average two hundred (200) deaths in South African prisons every year. Again my supposition is that this was probably the highest number of deaths in prison anywhere in the world.

Again, many may not have been reported.

Further as already stated, there were those who commited horrendous crimes, some of which were induced by the psychology of poverty and political frustration under apartheid, which crimes were punishable by the death penalty. South Africa had one of the highest execution rates under the death penalty in the world. For example there were 130 people hanged in South Africa in 1980; 96 in 1981; 100 in 1982; 90 in 1983; and 115 in 1984.23 In 1985, there were 137 executions, 121 in 1986 and 164 in 1987.24 This totals to 627 executions between 1983 and 1987 in South Africa. These were only the reported cases. Add these to the over 200 people who die mysteriously in South African prisons per year, in addition add political detainees who died as a result of torture, then you have a very critical situation. Consider also the unreported cases.

The death penalty was also as much a political weapon to deter political opposition as it was a legal instrument. Over the last several years, the number of people on the death row for committing "political" crimes had increased. As opposed to common criminals, these political convicts were categorized as having committed "unrest-related" crimes. A good number was constituted by those alleged to have committed "terrorist" acts. By the end of 1987, the number of unrest-related death row prisoners had risen to an estimated 44. By the end of 1987, five had been executed.25

The number of political death row inmates increased as time went on because of the introduction of the doctrine of "common purpose" by the government in the 1980's. This doctrine held that if a person were associated with those who had committed a crime, that person was also liable. The famous Sharpeville six were convicted and sentenced to hang on the basis of this doctrine.

The doctrine of common purpose certainly deepened South Africa's commission of crimes against humanity. Jo-Ann Bekker26 in her appeal, stated "Those who dispassionately endorse the death penalty should spend a few afternoons outside Pretoria Central Maximum Security Section when the bereaved pay their last visits to the doomed."

The death penalty was abolished when Apartheid was abolished, perhaps suggesting to some extent that capital punishment is a function of the nature of the dominant political culture.

NOTES

1. The International Convention on the Suppression and Punishment of the Crime of Apartheid (United Nations General Assembly Resolution 3068(XXVIM, 30 November 1973, entered into force on 18 July 1976. As of December 1986, there were 86 ratifications) defines apartheid as a crime against humanity. I call those who commit the crime of apartheid, hence crime against humanity as apartheid criminals.

2. "Declaration of the Seminar on the Legal Status of the Apartheid Regime and Other Legal Aspects of the Struggle Against Apartheid" Introduction to Apartheid: South Africa and International Law (New York: LTN Center Against Apartheid, 1985) p. 8.

3. International Convention on the Elimination of All Forms of Racial Discrimination (United Nations, Treaty Series vol. 660, p. 195). Entered into force on 4 January 1969.

4. G. Brahme, "Some Remarks on Responsibility for the Crime of Apartheid Under International Law" in Apartheid, supra note 2.

5. See Declaration on the Granting of Independence to Colonial Countries (United

Nations General Assembly Resolution 1514(XV) of 14 December 1960).

6. Amnesty International, South Africa: Briefing (London, 1986) at p. 17.

7. For a good study of repression in South Africa using the Internal Security Act, 1982, see I.E. Sagay, State Terrorism in South Africa (New York: UN Center Against Apartheid, 1984). See also Nicholas Haysom, "Human Rights Index" in (May 1985) I South African Journal of Human Rights 80, hereinafter referred to as S.A.J.H.R.

8. Sagay ibid at p. 3.

9. In cooperation with the UN Center Against Apartheid (New York and London, 1983).

10. See Amnesty International supra note 6.

11. S.A.J.H.R. supra note 7 at p. 81.

12. Supra note 6.

13. Nigel Rodley, The Treatment of Prisoners Under International Law

(Oxford: Oxford University Press, 1987).

14. Reported in Amnesty International surpa note 6 at p. 8.

15. See Torture is Part of the System: State Violence in South Africa and Namibia (London: African National Congress, 1984) and Catholic Institute of International Relations (C.I.I.R.) et al, Torture in South Africa (London, 1982).

16. D. H. Foster, D. Sandler and D. M. Davis, "Detention, Torture and the Criminal Justice Process in South Africa" in (May, 1987) International Journal of the Sociology of Law 105. See also their forthcoming book, Detention and Torture in South Africa (London: James Currey, 1987).

17. Ibid at pp. 111-113.

18. Ibid at p. 113.

19. Gordon Winter, Inside Boss: South Africa's Secret Police.

(Harmondsworth: Penguin, 1981).

20. This should be a subject for another paper, "South Africa's big crime rate ... the highest in the 'Western' world [is] linked directly to the socio-¬economic conditions created by apartheid" Jo-Ann Bekker in Weekly Mail 5 to 11 February 1988.

21. (London 1986).

22. Supra, note 15.

23. Amnesty International supra note 6 at p. 16.

24. Human Rights Commission, Human Rights Update (July-Sept. 1988) Vol. 1, No. 4, p. 52.

25. Jo-Ann Bekker, supra, note 20.

26. Ibid.

PART FIVE

THE DEATH PENALTY IN INTERNATIONAL LAW

- DR. MUNYONZWE HAMALENGWA

CHAPTER 12

CONCLUSION: THE DEATH PENALTY IN INTERNATIONAL LAW

Dr. Munyonzwe Hamalengwa *

International law as evidenced by the present international human rights instruments does not outlaw the death penalty. It recognizes that many nations do retain this form of punishment. Taking that reality into consideration, international law tries to proscribe arbitrary killings that are not provided for by law.

On first reading one may get the impression that international law does indeed sanction the death penalty. The first guarantee in the U.N. "Safeguard, Guaranteeing Protection of the Rights of Those Facing the Death Penalty"1 stipulates "in countries which have not abolished the death penalty, capital punishment may be imposed only for the most serious crimes..." one wishes that the United Nations would come out with a convention that bans the death penalty outright along the lines of the Torture Convention. This convention outlaws any form of torture per se.

Arbitrariness in the death penalty is banned by many human rights instruments, the major format almost being the same, e.g. article 4 of the American Convention;2 article 4 of the African Charter on Human and People's Rights; article 2 of the European Convention; article 3 of the Universal Declaration of Human Rights etc. If the death penalty is not arbitrarily imposed, from the point of view of international human rights law, it seems to be allowable. As already stated this should not be surprising given the number of retentionist countries.[3] There are about 120 countries that retain the death penalty.

Western Europe seems to be the leading region where the death penalty is fast disappearing. Only four states retain the death penalty.[4] The death penalty is most prevalent in the Middle East and North Africa, indicating the strong religious influence on the issue. Most African countries also retain the death penalty. Canada's attempt to reintroduce capital punishment was defeated in June 1987. In the United States, close to 40 states authorize the death penalty.5 In the 1990's New York State reintroduced the death penalty.

Amnesty International is one of the most important non-governmental organizations opposed to the death penalty. Amnesty International has declared that the death penalty is a violation of the right to life and is the most cruel, inhuman and degrading of all forms of punishment.6 Amnesty International's relentless campaign is getting through to many governments. It is possible that in the near future the U.N. will draw up a convention for the purpose of outlawing one of the most barbaric forms of punishment - the death penalty.

In the meantime, the U.N. has prolungated Safeguards guaranteeing protection of the Rights of those facing the Death Penalty. I reproduce the Safeguards herein below:[7]

ABOUT THE AUTHOR

Dr. Munyonzwe Hamalengwa

"He is a prolific writer and has done considerable work in the area of systemic racism, through his writing and his legal advocacy", so stated The Honorable Sidney B. Linden Commissioner for the Ipperwash Inquiry, May 7, 2004, in reference to Dr. Munyonzwe Hamalengwa.

Born in Zambia, a landlocked Country in South Central Africa, he is the second of four siblings.

Munyonzwe Hamalengwa - in Tonga, his mother's tongue, translates into English as 'Sweet Trouble' , spent his childhood in the eastern part of the agrarian town of Monze, that lies 2.5 hrs from Lusaka the Capital.

His matchless individuality is informed by a wealthy of experiences brought about from the early days when he played with his friends, on red sandy yards of eastern Monze, creating ingenuous toys as well as providing care to his younger siblings while his mother and father planted the nearby farm-land to provide the family with nutritious basic staples. He cherishes his peasant upbringing, calling himself The Village Author.

The teenage stubborn years that followed, full of teen rivalry and rebellion were replaced by years of youthful idealism at the University of Zambia in Lusaka. In 1976 Munyonzwe was detained with other student leaders in solitary confinement in Mumbwa, following demonstrations against the Zambian government's handling of issues related to Angola's Independence and issues of freedom of speech and expression. Seven months later he was released and threatened with banishment to the countryside. He then fled to neighboring Tanzania where he stayed for a year clandestinely studying at the University of Dar Es Salaam because he was not permitted to enrol and study for political reasons. From there he came to Canada in 1977 on a World University Service scholarship.

In Toronto, he studied at York University (1977-79) and later went to the Norman Paterson School of International Affairs at Carleton University (1979-80), Antioch School of Law (now District of Columbia School of Law) in Washington DC(1982-83) and then Osgoode Hall Law School (1986-89). He obtained an LLM in 2001 and a PhD in Law in 2013. While in law school, he served on the Editorial Board of the Osgoode Hall Law Journal. He articled for Ruby and Edwardh, Barristers and solicitors (1989-1990). Dr. Hamalengwa has trained at the following institutions or organizations: The International Institute of Human Rights in Strasbourg, France; International Centre for University Teaching of Human Rights, Strasbourg,; The Hague Academy of International Law; The United Nations in the Modern World in Geneva; The International Labour Organization in Geneva, and The Canadian Human Rights Foundation, Charlottetown, Prince Edward Island.

Dr. Hamalengwa has taught at Carleton University, Seneca College, York University, Nelson Mandela Academy of Applied Legal Studies, Osgoode Hall Law School and School of Law at The Zambian Open University. The courses he has taught include: Legal Process; Criminal Law, International Law; Jurisprudence; Public Law; Police Law; Law and Journalism; Immigration Law; Human Rights Law; The political Economy of Africa; Introduction to the Study of Politics; Introduction to International Relations; State and Revolution in Africa; Urban Economies; African Politics; Sports and Entertainment Law and Scriptural Foundations of the Law. He has held the positions of Co-ordinator for Africa and the Middle East in Washington, DC and Director of African Studies at York University.

Dr. Hamalengwa paracticed Administrative Law, Human Rights Law , Immigration Law, Criminal Law, Constitutional law, and Family law all at both trial and appeal levels and International Law of Human Rights . His zeal for law and justice are influenced by terrible circumstances he endured in his shaping years. His vigorous representation had no subordination to any other interests - ideological, career, personal - but the legitimate interests of the client.

Dr. Hamalengwa has defended all types of cases including murder, arson, drugs, fraud and others. He has also brought novel constitutional challenges that were not popular in Canada at the time including racial profiling in the immigration and criminal law context. His first constitutional case on racial profiling was brought in 1993 (Ritchie et al v.Her Majesty) in Superior Court of Justice. He then did immigration cases on racial profiling some of which went all the way to the Supreme Court of Canada. Dr. Hamalengwa specialized as well in human rights advocacy before the Human a Rights Tribunal of Ontario and in Immigration and Deportation Law before the Federal Court and Federal Court of Appeal. In criminal courts, he specialized in trial advocacy defending a number of significant murder cases. He developed the strategy of Class Action Law Suits against systemic racial profiling and filed class action law suits against both the Federal and Provincial governments and police boards and police services.

Dr. Hamalengwa has also battled his own cases in courts and the Law Society of Upper Canada on racial profiling and to advance the principle of the equal application and benefit of the law without discrimination on any specified or analogous grounds.

Before leaving Canada for Zambia in 2016, Dr. Hamalengwa was an active member of the Toronto community, founding or co-founding many organizations like Forum For African Students in Toronto (FAST)(1980); African Human Rights

Research Association (1983 in Strasbourg, France); York Student Movement Against Apartheid; Development And Underdevelopment Series; Nelson Mandela Law Society (1986); Lawyers Against Apartheid (1989); African Canadian Legal Clinic and others.

He has served as an Adjudicator on the Liquor Licence Board Of Ontario between 1991 and 1994 and the Board of Inquiry under the Human Rights Code between 1995 and 1998.

His passion for politics and activism made him run for Mayor of Toronto in 1997.

His many travels, conferences and written words reflect his advocacy for human rights issues in Canada and at a broader level in the International Law of human Rights fora. He writes and argues with much fervor and outspoken candidness heated themes about social justice, racial profiling, government corruption, appointment of minority and female judges to all courts including the Supreme Court of Canada and other social issues. He is a specialist in the area of diversity and human resources in the judicial and legal sector.

During the many intervening years, Dr. Hamalengwa has written a legal/ criminal

/immigration/political column, which appeared weekly or regularly in Pride newspaper (Toronto, ON., Canada) ; African Affairs (Montreal, QC, Canada), Contrast Newspaper (Toronto, On., Canada), Share newspaper and Diversity News(Toronto, ON., Canada).

His articles and letters have also appeared in various magazines and newspapers such as For the Defence , Law Times , Lawyers Weekly, Law Union News, Canadian Lawyer, Nairobi Law Monthly, The Platform and newspapers such as Globe and Mail , Toronto Star , National Post , The Zambia Daily Mail, The Post (Zambia), The Mast (Zambia), The African Executive, Pambazuka and many online forums like the Zambian Eye, and others.

He has published so far ten major books and others are still in progress.

He worked in Washington, DC for a human rights organization and has traveled to Australia, Brazil, Kenya, Namibia, Japan, China, Europe, Hong Kong, Nigeria, Cuba, South Africa, Tanzania, Grand Cayman Islands, Jamaica, Zimbabwe, Egypt and other parts of the world on human rights causes and the reform of criminal law or to study law and tourism.

Dr. Hamalengwa picks his heroes carefully: for many years he worshipped heroes like Nelson Mandela, Muhammad Ali, Thurgood Marshall, Paul Robeson, Mahatma Gandhi, Johnnie Cochran and other legal giants and social justice advocates.

His passion and admiration for Nelson Mandela led him to form the Nelson Mandela Law Society in 1986 at Osgoode Hall Law School, named after his hero. He also championed the idea of bestowing an award of recognition to Nelson Mandela resulting in the award of the Honorary Doctorate of Laws to Nelson Mandela by York University, Toronto, Canada on 16 June 1989 (this was the first Canadian University to do so) and later the formation of Nelson Mandela Academy of Applied Legal Studies in 1996, an institution that reflects his passion for legal education and legal advocacy. This school trained paralegals for self-employment, a much needed service in the visible minority community in Toronto in order to take legal education to people at the grass-roots level for self employment and empowerment. Education is a never ending investment in oneself.

Dr. Hamalengwa also marked his presence in the Toronto Community by sponsoring many African events among a few are the African Canadian Achievement Awards where for many years he sponsored the law award which recognizes the contributions of lawyers, judges and organizations to the better administration of justice in the community and MissAfriCanada Pageant 2004 which aimed at training young women especially for self awareness, confidence in self and self assertiveness. Dr. Hamalengwa has received many awards for his service to the community and for his efforts in the education sector.

Dr. Munyonzwe Hamalengwa is in 2017, serving as the Dean of the School of Law at Zambian Open University, Lusaka, Zambia.

OTHER BOOKS BY THIS AUTHOR

Hamalengwa M. (2017). The Book On Judges. Diamond Books. Toronto, Canada

Hamalengwa M. (Ed). (2017). Political Halley's Comet: The Death Penalty In Global Comparative Perspective. Diamond Books. Toronto, Canada

Hamalengwa M. (2016). African-Canadians Under Legal, Judicial, Political and Media Attack. Africa In Canada Press. Toronto, Canada.

Hamalengwa M. (Ed) (2016). The Case Against Tribalism in Zambia. Africa In Canada Press. Toronto, Canada.

Hamalengwa M. (2015). Getting Away with Impunity: International Criminal Law and The Prosecution Of Apartheid Criminals. Africa in Canada Press. Toronto, Canada.

Hamalengwa M. (2012). The Politics of Judicial Diversity and Transformation: Canada; USA; UK, Australia; South Africa; Israel; Colonial and post-colonial world and international tribunals. Africa in Canada Press. Toronto, Canada.

Hamalengwa, M (2002) How Are We Gonna Win This One: Doing Time WITH Clay C. Ruby, Criminal Lawyer Extraordinaire. Africa in Canada Press, Toronto.

Hamalengwa M. (1992). Class Struggles In Zambia, 1889-1989 & The Fall of Kenneth Kaunda 1990-1991. University Press of America. New York, USA.

Hamalengwa, M (1991) Thoughts Are Free: Prison Experience and Reflections on Law and Politics in General. Africa in Canada Press, Toronto

Hamalengwa M, Flinterman C and Dankwa EVO (eds). (1988). The International Law Of Human Rights in Africa. Martinus Nijhoff Publishers. Dordrecht. Holland.

LIST OF CHAPTERS IN BOOKS

Hamalengwa M. (2015). Foreword. Public Intellectualism. In Mwenda K. (2015). Public Intellectualism through Metaphors and Musings. Africa in Canada Press. Toronto. Canada.

Hamalengwa M. (1992). The Legal System of Zambia: Law, Politics And Development in Historical Perspective. In E Bondzi-Simpson (ed). The law and Economic Development in The Third World. Praeger. New York, USA. First Chapter.

Hamalengwa M. (1991). The Legal System of Zambia. In W Krawiet. (ed). Legal Theories. Verlag Duncker, Germany. First Chapter

Hamalengwa M. (1985). Primitive Accumulation and the Reproduction Of Rural Population In Africa. In J Havet. The Village and Shantytown, Retention and Migration Of Rural Populations Of Africa. University of Ottawa Publications. Ottawa, Canada. First Chapter.

Hamalengwa M. (1984). The Contradictions of Post-Colonial Social Transformation: Mozambique, Angola and Zimbabwe. In D Wilson. Africa: A Continent in Crisis. Ontario Institute in

Studies in Education Press. Toronto, Canada.

Hamalengwa M. (1984). Class and Nation: A Contribution to The Debate on the Politics of Liberation in South Africa. In D Wilson. Africa: a continent in crisis. Ontario Institute in Studies in Education Press. Toronto, Canada.

JOURNAL ARTICLES

Hamalengwa M. (2016) Memorandum on Class Action Law Suits Based on Racial Profiling in Ontario, Canada in ZAOU L. J, forthcoming.

Hamalengwa M. (2016). Don't Talk about Diversification. Just Do It. Zambia's bulletin and record. June 2016.

Hamalengwa M. (2015). The Case for The Establishment of an International Tribunal Against Apartheid in African Executive, Nairobi, Kenya, June 2015.

Hamalengwa M. (1992). The Death Penalty in the Context of the Crime of Apartheid. Social Justice. 18: 95-105.

Hamalengwa M. (1986). Human Rights and Development in Geneva-Africa, September 1986

Hamalengwa M and cobbah J. 1986). The Human Rights Literature of Africa. Human Rights Quarterly. February

Hamalengwa M. (1985). The Political Economy of Human Rights in Africa. Journal of African Marxists. 7.

Hamalengwa M. (1983). The political economy of human rights in Africa: historical and contemporary perspectives. Philosophy and social action. IX (3) 15-26.

CONFERENCE PROCEEDINGS

Hamalengwa M. (2003). The role of the judiciary in racial profiling: the case of Canada. In Proceedings of the 18th International Conference of the International Society for the Reform of the Criminal Law, Convergence of Criminal Justice and Building Bridges. The Hague, Netherlands, 23-28 August, 2003.

Hamalengwa M. (2003). Problems and prospects in the prosecution and defence of international terrorists. In Proceedings of the 18th international Conference of the International Society for the Reform of the Criminal Law, Convergence of Criminal Justice and Building Bridges. The Hague, Netherlands, 23-28 August, 2003.

Hamalengwa M. (2003). Revolution and counter - revolution: problems of litigating race in criminal and immigration cases in Canada, an exploratory analysis of judicial resistance to allegations of racial profiling. In Proceedings of the 2nd Annual Human Rights Symposium, Focus on Racial Discrimination. Toronto, Canada, 22-23 May 2003.

Hamalengwa M. (2000). Constitutional challenges to the differential treatment of Canadian and non-

Canadian citizens. In Proceedings of the International Conference of the International Society for the Reform of the Criminal Law, Human Rights and Administration of Criminal Justice. Johannesburg, South Africa, 3-7 December, 2000.

Hamalengwa M. (1994). Problems with the proceeds of crime legislation under Canada's criminal law. In Proceedings of the International Conference of the International Society for the Reform of the Criminal Law, Proceeds of Crime. Hong Kong, China, December 1994.

Hamalengwa M. (1994). African-Canadians under legal, judicial, political and media attack. In Proceedings of the Ad Hoc Group of Africans Canadians Conference on African-Canadians Under Legal, Judicial, Political and Legal Attack. Toronto, Canada. 24 September, 1994.

Hamalengwa M. (1989). A contribution to the debate on civilian control of police powers in Toronto 1980 to 1989. In Proceedings of the International Conference of the International Society for the Reform of the Criminal Law. Sydney, Australia, March 1989.

Hamalengwa M. (1987). The application of the amended Canadian Criminal Code to Apartheid

Criminals in Canada. In Proceedings of the Conference, Political Halle 's Comet: Law, Politics and the Death Penalty in Global Comparative Perspective organized by the Nelson Mandela Law Society of Osgoode Hall Law School, Toronto, Canada. 20-21 October, 1987.

BOOK REVIEWS

Hamalengwa M. (2015). Police state in our times. Review of Spence G's Police State: How America's Cops Get Away With Murder. St. Martin's Press, New York, USA, 2015. African Executive, Nairobi, Kenya, September 2015.

Hamalengwa M. (2000). Justice delayed: Cassius Clay versus the USA. Review of Bingham H and Wallace M. Muhammad Ali's Greatest Fight: Cassius Clay V. The United States of America. Evans and Company, New York, USA. Law Times. Toronto, Canada. September 2000.

Hamalengwa M. (1990). Young offenders new law in Canada. Review of Platt P. (1989). Young offenders law in Canada. Butterworths. Toronto, Canada. Criminal Law Quarterly. 32:394.

Hamalengwa M. (1990). Native survival in Australia. Review of Martin P. (ed). (1988). Raparapa: stories from the fitzroy river drovers. Magabala Books, Broome, Australia. Canadian Native Law Reporter. 4:1-2.

Hamalengwa M. (1990). A new kid on the block. Review of Watt D and Fuerst M. (1990). 1990 Tremeesr's Criminal Code. Criminal Lawyers ' Association Newsletter. 1:36-37.

Hamalengwa M. (1989). The dialectics of las and politics. Review of Mandel M. (1989). The charter of rights and the legalization of politics in Canada. Wall and Thompson, Toronto, Canada. Obiter dicta. 3 April 1989.

Hamalengwa M. (1989). Order without law: review of books on South Africa. Obiter dicta. 27 February 1989.

Hamalengwa M. (1989). Feminism: The New Frontier. Review of Adamson N, Briskin L and Mcphail M. (1988). Feminist Organizing for Changes: the contemporary women's movement in Canada. Oxford, Toronto, Canada and Day S and Persky S. (1988). The Supreme Court of Canada decision on abortion. New Star Books, Vancouver, Canada. Obiter dicta. 13 February 1989.

Hamalengwa M. (1983). The CIA in South East Asia. Review of McGehee R. (1983). Deadly deceits: my 25 years in the CIA. Sheridan, New York, USA. Crime and Social Justice. No. 20, 1983.

Hamalengwa M. (1982). The struggle continues. Review of Petras J. (1981). Class, state and power in the third world. Allanheld and Osman, Montclair, USA. Human Rights Internet Reporter. 7 (5), 1982.

RESEARCH REPORTS

Hamalengwa M. (2016). A proposal for the Establishment of the graduate studies programme in the School of Law at Zambian Open University. Submitted to the Dean of the School of Law, Zambian Open University. Lusaka, Zambia, May 2016.

Hamalengwa M. and Mwewa C. (2014). Critical notes on the legal system of Zambia. A submission made to the Legal and Justice Sector Reform Commission of Zambia. Lusaka, Zambia. September 2014.

Hamalengwa M. and Mwewa C. (2012). A proposal towards the establishment of the Michael Mundale School of Business Establishment and Legal studies. Toronto, Canada, 2012.

Hamalengwa M. (2010). The politics of war crimes legislation in Canada. York Research Series. Toronto. Canada. February 2010.

Hamalengwa M. (2000). Practising law in the public interest. Submission made to Supreme Court of Canada Justice Peter Cory's Commission entitled, A Framework for Regulating Paralegal

Practice in Ontario. Toronto, Canada, February 2000.

Hamalengwa M. (1998). Reducing derivative costs to Ontario's Criminal Justice Process and other related issues. Submission to the Criminal Justice Review Committee of Ontario. Toronto, Canada. April 1998.

Hamalengwa M. (1996). Professional underdevelopment and systematic discrimination: prospects for professional development for minority lawyers in Canada". Submission to the Canadian Bar Association's Task Force on Racial Equality in the Legal Profession, chaired by Professor Joanne St. Lewis. Toronto, Canada, 16 December 1996.

Hamalengwa M. (1993). Has the Canadian Charter of Rights and Freedoms demobilized Canada's democracy? A thesis submitted to Professors Ian Green, George Szablowski and Reg Whitaker. Toronto, Canada.

Hamalengwa M. (1992). The law and politics of abortion in Canada. A report submitted on behalf of the coalition for pro-choice politics. Toronto, Canada.

Hamalengwa M. (1990). War crimes and Canadian immigration law and policy. Submission

Presented to Marlys Edwardh, Barrister and Solicitor. Toronto, Canada.

Hamalengwa M. (1990). Information, freedom and censorship: the case of Canada. Report on the freedom of information in Canada submitted to "Article 19" Group. London, England.

Hamalengwa M. (1990). Does Canada's new amendments to its Criminal Code apply to Apartheid Criminals. Submission made to the Commission of Inquiry into Apartheid on Parliament Hill. Ottawa, Canada, 25 May 1990.

Hamalengwa M. (1989). Judicial power and discretion in criminal law: how judges protect and defend their inherent power under the Canadian Charter of Rights and Freedoms. Submitted to Clayton Ruby for "The Charter and Sentencing Commission". Ottawa, Canada.

Hamalengwa M. (1989). Retroactive legislation and political offence exception to extradition and deportation. Consultative Research Report submitted to Marlys Edwardh, Barrister and Solicitor. Toronto, Canada.

Hamalengwa M. (1989). What constitutes an act that is contrary to the purposes and principles of the United Nations. Consultative Research Report on the Acts Contrary to the Purposes and

Principles of the United Nations. Ruby and Edwardh, Barristers and Solicitors. Toronto, Canada.

Hamalengwa M. (1989). Political offences and extradition in international law. Consultative Report submitted to Marlys Edwardh, Barrister and Solicitor, on Extradition in International Law. Toronto, Canada.

Hamalengwa M. (1986). Report on race and ethnic relations at York University. Being a member of the Presidential Committee on Race and Ethnic Relations at York University, Chair Professor Cumming P. Toronto, Canada. 1986.

Hamalengwa M. (1984). The politics of international education with respect to foreign students at York University. A Report Commissioned by the Canadian Union of Educational Workers, Local 3. Toronto, Canada. 1984. Pp.140

FEEDBACK

Now that you have read the book ...

Was it interesting?

Did you enjoy what you wanted to read?
Was there any room for improvement?

Let us know at:

http://www.hamalengwa.ca/feedback

Your feedback is highly appreciated.

Thank you!

- DR. MUNYONZWE HAMALENGWA

MY AUTOBIOGRAPHY

THOUGHTS ARE FREE

PRISON EXPERIENCE AND REFLECTIONS ON LAW AND POLITICS IN GENERAL

THE INTERNATIONAL LAW OF
HUMAN RIGHTS
IN AFRICA
BASIC DOCUMENTS AND
ANNOTATED BIBLIOGRAPHY
DR. MUNYONZWE HAMALENGWA
PhD (Law).

POLITICAL HALLEY'S COMET

THE DEATH PENALTY IN GLOBAL COMPARATIVE PERSPECTIVES

CASE STUDIES OF
Canada, India, Apartheid South Africa,
Nigeria, Jamaica, Grenada, Uganda
Nazi War Crimes and International Law

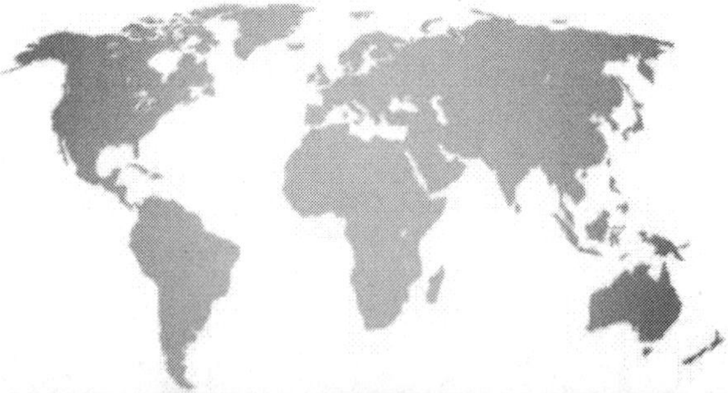

DR. MUNYONZWE HAMALENGWA
PhD (Law).

THE POLITICS

OF JUDICIAL DIVERSITY AND TRANSFORMATION

DR. MUNYONZWE HAMALENGWA
PhD (Law).

GETTING AWAY WITH IMPUNITY

INTERNATIONAL CRIMINAL LAW AND SOUTH AFRICAN APARTHEID CRIMINALS

DR. MUNYONZWE HAMALENGWA

PhD (Law).

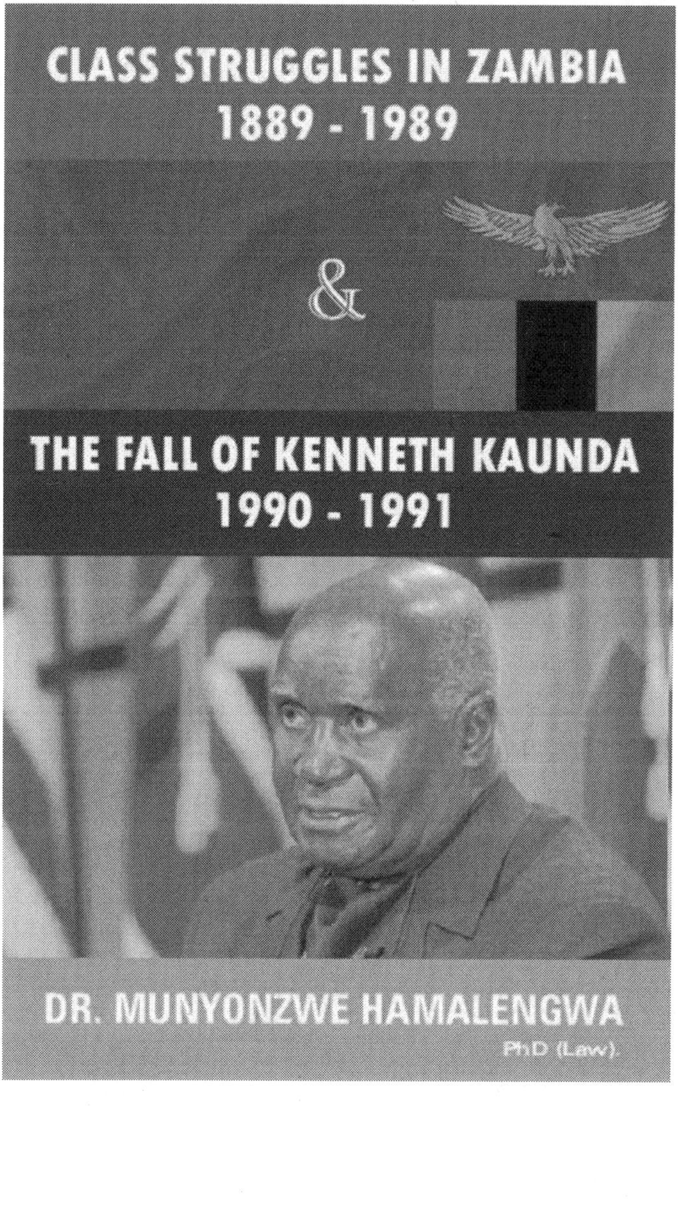
CLASS STRUGGLES IN ZAMBIA
1889 - 1989
&
THE FALL OF KENNETH KAUNDA
1990 - 1991
DR. MUNYONZWE HAMALENGWA
PhD (Law).

TRIBAL POLITICS A TIME BOMB IN ZAMBIA

THE CASE AGAINST TRIBALISM IN ZAMBIA

COMPILED BY

DR. MUNYONZWE HAMALENGWA

PhD (Law).

FROM THE DIARY OF AN ARTICLING STUDENT

HOW

ARE WE GONNA WIN THIS ONE

?

VOLUME 1

DOING TIME FOR **CLAYTON C. RUBY**
CRIMINAL LAWYER EXTRAORDINAIRE

DR. MUNYONZWE HAMALENGWA
PhD (Law).

AFRICAN CANADIANS UNDER LEGAL, JUDICIAL, POLITICAL, POLICE, AND MEDIA ATTACK

STRATEGIES FOR SURVIVAL

DR. MUNYONZWE HAMALENGWA
PhD (Law).

NOTES

NOTES

NOTES

NOTES

Made in the USA
Monee, IL
08 November 2026

68063219R10294